This collection of personal testimonies experiences provides a unique and polyc... experience. Woollacott's and Lorimer's volu... in both its grammar (first person) and topic... objective). Yet both are essential aspects of h... for those who peer most deeply into the mysteries of the material world. It will prove a thought-provoking resource.

Tom McLeish, PhD, FRS
Professor of Natural Philosophy in the Department of Physics, University of York

The reader may discover that reading the first essay of this compendium feels much like sitting on an airplane next to the most fascinating person that you ever have met, sharing in a life-changing profound spiritual awakening of love, unity or clarity. The resonance of the traveler's account feels moving and exciting, perhaps because you always have so wondered or sensed this depth of reality. Quite by surprise, you then discover that the fellow traveler is a scientist! Hereby upending a long-held outdated view that science for its rigor, is a method that somehow cannot look into ultimate questions of spirituality. Well, perhaps that was just one scientist? But then you board your connecting flight, to find yourself in an equally deep engagement with the next fellow traveler, again a leading scientist, who shares that so too their landmark work was driven by spiritual awareness. So then you might wonder, how really is landmark, field-making science achieved?

Lisa Miller, PhD
NYT Bestselling Author of The Spiritual Child and #1 National Bestseller The Awakened Brain, Professor and Founder of the Spirituality Mind Body Institute at Columbia University, Teachers College

What a wonderful way to make Spiritual Awakenings more accessible and real to everyone. This collection allows us to access them through the personal stories of the experiencers who reveal how the events and insights came about and how they fit into their lives.

Elisabet Sahtouris, PhD
Evolutionary biologist and author of *EarthDance: Living Systems in Evolution*

This book will confirm the intuition that on this planet we are living in a Sacred Order, that there is no essential separation between the transcendent and the immanent orders of reality, and that the creative and sustaining power of the universe is Love.

Anne Baring, PhD (hons)
Author of The Dream of the Cosmos: A Quest for the Soul

Spiritual Awakenings

Scientists and Academics Describe Their Experiences

Volume III
Postmaterialist Sciences Series

Edited by
Marjorie Woollacott, PhD
David Lorimer

Press

AAPS Headquarters, Tucson, AZ.
AAPS Press and Information on AAPS,
P.O. Box 156,
Battle Ground, WA 98604

L.C. Cat. No.: 1-11397895951

ISBN-13: 978-1-7354491-4-2 print edition
ISBN-13: 978-1-7354491-5-9 e-book editions

This book was typeset in Baskerville.

The cover image represents the nautilus, one of the earth's oldest ocean creatures, and a symbol of growth, expansion, and renewal. Its spiral is in the form of the Golden Ratio, based on the Fibonacci series. This ratio is found throughout the universe, from the shape of our galaxy to the arrangement of seeds in the sunflower. Thus the nautilus is a perfect metaphor for spiritual evolution. (Illustration ©Daniel Holeman, used with permission. Cover design by Rupert Soskin.)

To send correspondence: aapsglobal@gmail.com

All matter originates and exists only by virtue of a force...
We must assume behind this force the existence of a
conscious and intelligent Mind.
This Mind is the matrix of all matter.

Max Planck

Table of Contents

Academy for the Advancement of Postmaterialist Sciences

The Academy for the Advancement of Postmaterialist Sciences (www.AAPSglobal.com) is a non-profit membership and education organization whose mission is to promote open-minded, rigorous and evidence-based enquiry into postmaterialist consciousness research. Our vision is to inspire scientists to investigate mind and consciousness as core elements of reality.

To achieve this paradigm changing mission, AAPS embraces the following values:

Support rigorous applications of the scientific method

Nurture curiosity and creativity in research

Encourage open-minded exploratory and confirmatory investigations

Model integrity and honesty in communication and education

Value experimental and empirical data over dogma

Create safe settings for sharing theories, evidence, and experiences

Promote evidence-based innovation and positive societal change

Expand awareness of the interconnectedness of all things

Share postmaterialist evidence and understanding with the public

With these values in mind, AAPS is publishing an Advances in Postmaterialist Sciences book series to educate scientists, students, and science-minded readers about postmaterialist consciousness research and its applications. Our intent is that each volume combines rigor and creativity, expresses first person (inner experiences) as well as third person (external observations), and facilitates the betterment of humanity and the planet. Some volumes will address specific topics or themes, others will be wide ranging and diverse collections of research topics. Collectively they will help define and advance the evolution of postmaterialist theory, research and applications.

Foreword

Tasting the Bread

Dr Peter Fenwick, MD, FRCPsych

Dr Peter Fenwick is Emeritus Consultant Neuropsychiatrist, Maudsley Hospital and Emeritus Senior Lecturer at the Institute of Psychiatry. His other appointments included Consultant Neurophysiologist at St. Thomas's, Westminster and Broadmoor Hospitals. For ten years he was a Trustee of the Prince of Wales Foundation for Integrated Health. He is Emeritus President of the Scientific and Medical Network and former Chair of the Board of the Study Society. He is the author, with his wife Elizabeth, of many books on consciousness and death, most recently **The Art of Dying** *and his autobiography* **Shining Light on Transcendence**.

Until the 17th century science was irrelevant to our understanding of the world. But then, slowly, we came to think of the world as physical matter. Miracles no longer happened; everything in our understanding of the world could be created by the brain. Even with the flowering of physical experimentation and design there seemed to be no need to progress away from the view that the brain 'did it all.' Indeed, by the end of the 19th Century there was a strong feeling that current physics could explain everything. It was all dead matter. The mind was just a simple brain function and the concept of consciousness was never discussed.

A whole generation of us scientists was misled by this certainty. The advent of quantum mechanics in the early 20th Century, with its important principle that the observer was part of the experiment – no observer, no experiment - had not yet filtered through, leaving a gap in our understanding of reality. When I went up to Cambridge in the 1950s, my supervisor, Nobel Laureate Sir Andrew Huxley, pointed out to us that little was known about consciousness, and levels of alertness were what we should be considering. This was much simpler as it could be easily measured by changes in physiology. We came across no broader thinking in the science faculty.

My psychiatric training did not help, as William Sargent was one of my teachers, and his book, *Battle for the Mind*, was a purely physicalist interpretation of mind and its functioning. We were taught to give much less weight to the work of Jung.

And then, during a vacation in Kenya soon after I had qualified, I read a recently published book by Colin Wilson called *The Outsider*. This suggested that there was a transcendent realm of consciousness to which the great artists, musicians etc had access and it also made me aware of R.M. Bucke's 1901 book *Cosmic Consciousness* and the *Bhagavad Gita*. This transfixed me and started me on a search to find more about awakening and cosmic consciousness. Bucke defined four main characteristics. First, it arises with an intense, sudden experience in an immersion of flame or rose-coloured cloud, with a perception of inner light. Secondly, it is accompanied by a state of moral exaltation, joyousness and ecstasy. Third is intellectual enlightenment or illumination and fourth, cosmic consciousness, accompanied by a sense of immortality and eternal life and a loss of fear of death.

Bucke pointed out that this could be studied with no more difficulty than other natural phenomena. He also observed that this state of consciousness was common to the Buddha, Lao Tzu, Socrates and Jesus and several others and concluded that a new race was in the act of being born and in the near future would occupy and possess the earth.

Back in London, in 1966 I joined the School of Economic Science, where I learned about Ouspensky and his model of the universe, in which transcendence was centre stage. From there I moved to the Study Society and was introduced to meditation, which took me into a part of myself that I had not really visited before. I became conscious of an inner core of love and light which was central to me. At times this would expand to fill my moment of perception.

Around this time I came across this poem, Vacillation, by W.B. Yeats:

My fiftieth year had come and gone,
I sat, a solitary man,
In a crowded London shop,
An open book and empty cup

On the marble table-top.
While on the shop and street I gazed
My body of a sudden blazed;
And twenty minutes more or less
It seemed, so great my happiness,
That I was blessed and could bless.

Echoes here of the flaming self in Bucke's book.

It was on a retreat that I first had a cosmic experience. I was using Bright Path meditation when I became aware of a strong light surrounding me which occurred after a period of meditating for two hours a day. The light showed the outside world as transcendent and it was with me for almost a week. I was very aware of the much greater reality. It slowly became evident that love is the basis of the universe. When I examined the light in detail, it was much more in my left visual field, suggesting that there was a major right brain hemisphere component to it.

In my own personal life I went on to have many openings into this transcendent world. Weekends spent with Mother Meera were often such occasions. She had the capacity to open me so that I could see the transcendent within. I remember going for walks in the woods where I was one with the universe and everything happened automatically. The sheer beauty of the physical world around me was extraordinary. When I went to sleep at night there were lights at play within me, all pointing to the experiencing of a very wide transcendent realm.

Of course, when we left and returned to England this gap was closed but never so completely that I lost it altogether. On one retreat with the Brahma Kumaris I was meditating and the internal light started to shine. By the second session it was there constantly and touched everything that I experienced. Fortunately, it was a silent retreat so I didn't have to maintain social contact. In between the sessions I could walk outside in this glorious world, transformed by the light. Everything was as it was meant to be. Broken fences or fallen trees were just as they should be. Each new meditation session was a delight, because I could focus without distraction on the joy of the internal light. The difficulty, which increased as the days wore on, was my apprehension about whether I would be able to drive home in such a state, but in the final few sessions I was slowly able to diminish the intensity of the experience until I felt I could drive safely.

It was in the early 1980s that I was asked to be chair of the newly expanded SMN and met David Lorimer. The two of us together, with the help of many others, took the organisation forward. It was always designed to be non-hierarchical so that we were all equal. Its meetings provided a safe and open forum where it was possible for members to discuss their experiences without being denigrated by the predominant scientific view as mere quirks of brain function.

We now live in a world where consciousness is discussed widely and more and more people are getting closer to the wide experiences of the transcendent in which they are embedded. This collection of articles shows the path taken by each of the authors. Each one is necessarily different and each gets one closer to the transcendence within and without.

But bear in mind this story told to me by Metropolitan Anthony.

One cold winters' day a young half-starved Russian boy was walking in the snow on his way to school. He passed by a bread shop; the door was open and there flowed out wonderful warmth with the delicious smell of newly baked bread. He stood transfixed by the warmth, and savoured the delicious smells. But eventually he had to walk on. After a few paces he was beyond the shop and again in the cold. He was no fuller after the experience because the bread was someone else's meal – not his.

So remember that these experiences are someone else's not yours. Some day you may enter your own bread shop and who knows what loaf you will be given!

Background and Overview

This volume forms part of the AAPS book series *Advances in Postmaterialist Sciences*, created with the intent to educate scientists, students, and science-minded readers about postmaterialist consciousness research and its implications and applications. We are delighted that it is also being co-sponsored by the Scientific and Medical Network's Galileo Commission, with its mission to expand the scope of science beyond the limitations of the currently predominant materialist world view. Our intent is that each volume of the AAPS book series combines rigor and creativity, expresses first person (inner experiences) as well as third person (external observations), and facilitates the evolution of humanity and improved conditions on the planet. The first volume, *Is Consciousness Primary?*, shared both the contributing authors' first-person experiences that transformed their understanding of the primacy of consciousness and the research that supports that perspective. The second volume, *Expanding Science*, offered perspectives on what the unfolding of the postmaterialist paradigm might be like.

With the current volume we take this exploration further, by going to both scientists and other academics, typically with PhDs or other Doctoral degrees, and letting them share the experience of their own spiritual journey. This includes a description of their spiritually transforming experience(s), the subsequent transformation including both an inner change (world view, values and beliefs) and outer changes (how this experience manifested in their day-to-day life). Finally, authors discuss the challenges to their credibility in academia and the scientific field, if they shared these experiences publicly, obliging them to live a 'divided life' between the personal and the professional. This fear of losing credibility with professional colleagues was the reason that three authors chose to submit their essays anonymously, supporting the concept of epistemological policing of thinking out of the 'power knowledge' (Foucault) box as elaborated in *The Flip* by Jeffrey Kripal (2019). The Galileo Report already demonstrated that the standard model that the brain produces consciousness is not an established fact but rather a philosophical assumption whereby, as Kripal puts it 'our conclusions are a function of our exclusions.' As far back as the 1890s, FCS Schiller, William James and Henri Bergson were advancing another possible theoretical approach: that the brain might serve as a 'transmitter' or filter for consciousness. More recently, this approach has been further elaborated in the three volumes initiated by the Esalen Institute and the Division of Perceptual Studies at the University of Virginia, especially *Beyond Physicalism: Toward Reconciliation of Science and Spirituality* (Kelly et al., 2015).

A further point on 'the divided life' is the separation between private and public, personal and professional. It is our experience that many more people are happy to broach topics around spiritual experience in private settings but would not consider doing so professionally. One of our hopes for this volume is that by reading these accounts, more scientists and academics will realize how common they are (a fact already established by research following up the original work by Sir Alister Hardy in the 1960s). The irony is that the same people who are reluctant to speak to their colleagues would find that their colleagues are in a similar situation, so that if more people 'came out', spiritually speaking, this might contribute to a welcome change of culture toward greater openness in this respect.

In these essays you will note that we use the term "spiritual awakening" as typically characterized by two elements: 1) the spiritually transforming experience (STE) itself (the triggering experience(s)) and 2) the process of transformation, including both inner and outer changes. Inner transformation was characterized by a change in an individual's "world view", that is, their understanding of the nature of reality. This includes the narratives we each create about the nature of the world and the subsequent interpretation of these experiences. A 'crucial experience' carries far greater weight than any 'crucial experiment' in bringing about fundamental change.

These essays describing the contributors' STE and subsequent transformation in world view were varied and very nuanced, leading us to contemplate the subtle nature underlying these processes, and how they may be quite distinct for each individual. We realize that the essays share experiences along a continuum related to the content and intensity of the original experience as well as the timeframe of transformation, especially where this was more gradual and did not involve a single dramatic experience. Despite the nuanced nature of individual spiritual awakenings, a number of themes emerged with respect to both the nature of the STE and the subsequent transformation, so we have grouped the essays into categories based on these themes.

Thematic categories include: 1) mystical awakenings triggered as a result of spiritual practices; 2) STEs occurring during or awakening from sleep; 3) STEs occurring spontaneously during other daily activities, often without a specific triggering event; 4) STEs occurring as synchronistic transmissions through the word; 5) dramatic STEs facilitated through the use of psychedelic substances; 6) STEs triggered by near-death experience (NDEs); and 7) STEs triggered by psychic phenomena, such as telepathic connections, precognition, after-death communication or awareness of remote events.

A leitmotif that runs through essays in all of the categories is a quieting of the mind, specifically a reduction in the ongoing mental narrative. This quieting of the ongoing mental narrative appears to be an important element within the STE. Interestingly, research by a number of labs has examined changes in the state of the mind-brain complex during some of these categories of experience, including deep states of meditation, psychedelic experiences and NDEs (Woollacott & Shumway-Cook, 2020). For example, the research of Judson Brewer and his colleagues used brain imaging to track these changes during meditation in a part of the brain called the Default-mode (DMN) or mind-wandering network, often considered a source of our egoic identity (Brewer et al., 2011). They demonstrated that there was both a reduction in mind-wandering during meditation in advanced meditators vs. control participants, and that this was associated with a decrease in the activity of the DMN.

This reduction in brain activity, specifically in the DMN, has been reported in many types of spiritually transforming experiences such as when using psilocybin and other types of drugs. This research has led to the proposal that quieting the mind (reducing activity in the DMN) reduces the filtering process of the brain, allowing the experience of expanded awareness not normally available when the DMN is active (Woollacott & Shumway-Cook, 2020). You will see our comments on this throughout the introductions to the various sections of the book, as we believe the stilling of the narrative mode of thinking is an important adjunct and possibly a causative agent in these experiences.

Within and across these categories the transformation process ranged along a continuum from an immediate change in world view occurring at the time of the STE, to a gradual shift in world view over time, or a combination. With this awareness in mind, we propose to use a metaphor for the experiences shared in this volume. As the experiences frequently consisted of an initial awakening to a new understanding of the nature of reality that shifted the individual's world view, we may liken it to a seed that has been planted, as you see in the accompanying figure. In some individuals, their previous narrative framework or world view is immediately superseded by a more expansive one, being likened to the seed germinating immediately and, like a new seedling, rising above the surface, to be seen in changes in attitudes and behaviors. In others there may be smaller shifts in world view with continuing experiences and insights, or a longer germination period, depending on the ability of the individual to incorporate the experience into an expanded world view.

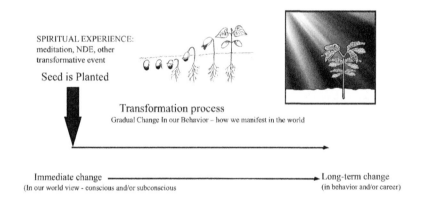

The difficulty in applying a conceptual framework to nuanced spiritual experiences is that the very framework used to organize experiences can blind and bind us – a characteristic of predominantly left hemisphere orientation that does not recognize its own limits, as explained in detail by Iain McGilchrist (2019). In addition, the range of meanings associated with many words used to describe STEs makes understanding their import challenging. For example, one of our contributors, who had his own concerns about the word "spiritual", challenged our request to contribute an essay in this way:

> As I reflect, I find the very idea of a 'spiritual awakening' disturbs me. The word 'spiritual' points tacitly toward a transcendence of this worldly realm; for me that which is sacred is immanent on Earth. And the metaphor of 'awakening' harks back to the conceit of Enlightenment: my experience is that the dark is as full of meaning as the light. Further, my experience is not of one turning point but an unfolding process over decades. I can, however, trace some moments of grace, of subject-to-subject encounters, that lead me tentatively to experience the world as sentient.

This challenge to the wording of our invitation helped us see that, though our own definition of the word 'spiritual' includes the sacred as both immanent - within the world - and transcendent - beyond the world - these nuances need to be made explicit. And we also agree with the contributor that awakening includes the understanding of the sacredness of both darkness and light within our lives. And as you will see in the essays, the unfolding process continues throughout the lifetime, with many contributors saying that they are still in the process of understanding their original experiences.

As you read through the essays on spiritual awakening, we invite you to think about your own life, and whether you have also experienced spiritually transformative experiences and any resulting insights that gave you a new way of seeing the world, perhaps shifting the trajectory of your life. We hope that the cumulative effect of reading these essays will encourage you to 'come out' and share your own unfolding journey so that it becomes easier for scientists and academics to lead lives integrating the personal and the professional rather than continuing with a divided life, as noted above. In this way we can hasten the expansion of our culturally dominant world view beyond the limits imposed by scientific materialism. If you are a scientist and/or academic we also encourage you to submit your own experience of the evolution of awakening and transformation to the section of our AAPS website, TASTE, The Archive of Scientists' Transcendental Experiences.
(link: https://www.aapsglobal.com/taste/)

After the essays we have included an epilogue, with further contemplation about the nature of the transformation process and the meaning of these experiences both in the authors' lives and their interactions with others. It is significant that individuals often found it difficult to share the experience and subsequent change in worldview with friends, family and colleagues. Many reported keeping their experiences private except for a few close friends, others feared ridicule or dismissiveness by academic colleagues. Most reported that the STE prompted a shift in careers or finding new approaches to their scientific or academic career that would allow them to incorporate new understandings into their teaching, research, or healthcare.

Note: We have retained the authors' own writing styles in British and American English.

Marjorie Woollacott, PhD
David Lorimer, MA

References

Brewer, J. A., Worhunsky, P. D., Gray, J. R., Tang, Y. Y., Weber, J., & Kober, H. (2011). Meditation experience is associated with differences in default mode network activity and connectivity. *Proceedings of the National Academy of Sciences USA*, 108(50), 20254–20259.

Kelly, E. F., Crabtree, A., & Marshall, P. (2015). *Beyond physicalism: Toward reconciliation of science and spirituality*. Roman and Littlefield.

Kripal, J. (2019). *The flip: Epiphanies of mind and the future of knowledge*. Bellevue Literary Press.

McGilchrist, I. (2019). *The master and his emissary: The divided brain and the making of the western world*. Yale University Press.

Woollacott, M., & Shumway-Cook, A. (2020). The mystical experience and its neural correlates. *Journal of Near-death Studies*, 38, 3-25.

PART ONE

STEs Through Spiritual Practices

This first category of essays encompasses STEs that include awakenings that have occurred through a variety of spiritual practices, including meditation, mantra repetition and other practices that often awakened a tangible spiritual energy within the body. In some individuals the awakening occurred as a dramatic stilling of the mind the first time they were introduced to a practice, including being in the presence of or receiving initiation by a master of meditation. For example, in her essay one woman describes her first meeting with a spiritual teacher. "Once seated before the master, I was suddenly transported into another state of being by a powerful and irresistible force. I felt totally exposed; totally seen; totally known; totally accepted; totally loved."

In others the awakening came as a result of intense effort over a long period of complete devotion to study and meditation. For example, in one of the essays in this section, the meditator had an awakening that came as a result of intense effort over a half-year retreat, in which he devoted himself completely to study and meditation. He said, "Then, in a sudden and unexpected rush, the seeking of the past six months and the concentration of the past three days finally burned a hole through the 'ego-I.'"

For another person this quieting of the verbal narrative happened as a result of intense mantra repetition, over a period of seven days. He said, "This was the seventh day since I had started [mantra repetition]. I continued my mantra deliberately as I walked out of my office, then out of the building, across the street, and onto the grassy meadow. And then the universe opened up to me. I seemed to be one with the cosmos, the grass, the trees, the sky."

Just as in many of the following categories of awakenings, the current experiences often occurred as the normal verbal egoic narrative associated with the stories of who we are and how we relate to the world, were suddenly stilled. As was discussed in the preface, researchers examining changes in brain activity during deep states of meditation found that among advanced meditation practitioners there was reduced activity in the DMN and a concomitant decrease in self-referential or ego-related narrative, enabling an experience of expanded awareness.

You may recall moments in your own life, when a meditative practice, even walking contemplatively in nature, may have moved your mind toward silence and expansion.

Chapter One

Awake Presence

Athena D. Potari, DPhil

Dr. Potari is Fellow at the Center for Hellenic Studies at Harvard University (2022/23). She received her PhD from the University of Oxford, specializing in Political Philosophy, and holds an MA in Political Theory summa cum laude from the London School of Economics and Political Science (LSE). In 2020, she was the youngest female scholar to receive the prestigious Academy of Athens Award of Philosophy. She is the founder of Atheonoa - a forum devoted to the study of Ancient Greek Philosophy as a non-dual wisdom tradition which combines scientific reasoning with the experiential realization of Logos and Being as Eudaimonia. She is the author of **A Call *for a* Renaissance *of the Spirit in the* Humanities** *published by the Galileo Commission.*

There is that one moment in my spiritual journey thus far which I can call "the" moment of awakening; although, as an Indian sage notes, the spontaneous is preceded by a long process of ripening. Leading up to this awakening was a deep existential realization that nothing external could ever give me the deep, lasting happiness and feeling of oneness for which I longed. I was on the path of self-exploration already for 7 years. I had been studying spiritual teachings and practicing meditation diligently for endless hours. I had tasted powerful and deeply transformative spiritual experiences and expanded states of consciousness, however their effect would only last for days, at best weeks, and then again, a feeling of an existential lack would again appear inside, as if there was still something 'missing'.

The days leading up to the awakening on that summer evening in Athens, however, I had come to experience that this seeking itself was an illusion. For a few weeks, I felt completely fed up with the futility of impermanence and the ever-changing conditions of life, the ups and downs, the fragility of happiness when that depends upon those. That night, alas I gave up! I wanted nothing else anymore, my desires all appeared as illusory efforts: I wanted to taste the truth of my existence, access that unwavering wholeness that all spiritual teachers since antiquity describe, I wanted to "know God" right here, right now. I found no other desire to search anymore, and even live if I were to continue this hamster wheel at the whims of impermanence. That night, I felt that decision deep in my soul: it's all or nothing! Even if that meant leaving my body, I didn't care! I had come to the end of seeking.

That evening we had gathered with my sangha (i.e., group of fellow spiritual practitioners) in our meditation hall in Athens. The collective energy was vibrant and blossoming. During the practice, I let myself 'sink' into my decision. During meditation, one may experience deep states of absorption where sometimes it feels like the body is drifting away. That experience can be frightening, and thus there is often resistance to letting go; but that evening I did not care anymore. I allowed myself to let go completely into a deep absorption state which felt like I was literally dying. Everything stopped; my entire body numbed; I could not move. My thoughts stopped; I fell into an abyss that felt like death and life at the same time. Truly, no words can describe it!

An invisible fire was swallowing me up. I gracefully let go into that swallowing until I was not there; or rather, there was "I" yet not "me". After a while (I do not know how long since there was no sense of time) an abyssal sobbing crying begun - a lamenting cry coming out of me, so powerful, as if emerging from the depths of time and soul. It was seismic, like the cry of something dying. My mind had dropped, there was no understanding nor the desire to understand. My teacher was close to me at that point. After a while, I cannot recall duration, it was like I cracked open from the center of my heart and everything opened up. Everything was, is ONE! I was not anymore, and I AM everything! There was no I; living consciousness revealed itself as ALL. All IS IT, and I am That!

The walls, the chairs, the ceiling, my fellow practitioners, the sky, the earth, everything that we believe as alive and not alive, animate and inanimate, the entire scenery we call "life" and "the world" revealed itself as one and alive vibrating consciousness "waving at itself". Waking up to itself! Dropping the veil of the "cosmic cinema" ~ "the drama" that covers the divinity and oneness of Being. Matter is consciousness; space is consciousness; everything is One spirit playing the role of "you" and "I", of "it" and "them", "here" and "there" in a vast dimensionless eternity which our mind divides into time. Veiling itself through the forgetting that there is only that one being, pure consciousness, alive emptiness-wholeness, apparently dividing into many, appearing as mind and matter, space and time.

What I "saw" ~ realized in an indescribable living way, is that the entire world, or rather Being is one, alive, vibrating self-knowing consciousness. That 'experience' was not an experience per se, but rather being beyond experiencing, a seeing that cannot be described in words, as it does not belong within the realm of the mind or knowing, since it is that prior to mind from which mind and understanding emerge and draw their essence. Now I understand why Ancient Greek philosophers had called it "agnoston" (i.e., beyond intellectual knowledge) and "allipton" (beyond concepts); hence "arrheton" (beyond words, ineffable). What for so many years I was reading and - vainly - tried to grasp with the mind, was alive! It was here and now, beyond mind, grasping, understanding or words.

The cry soon turned into laughter - the most liberating laughter ever! After "dying" came a "rebirth". A laughter of freedom, ecstatic, exalted, right from the center of my heart. There was no reason for that, but what appeared as utterly comical was the deep sensation that all the searching, all the striving, the sorrows I had taken so seriously in my life, the story of "the character" I had mistaken myself to be and whose role I had been playing in the cosmic cinema, was all a play. Nothing had every truly existed, and I was searching with so much angst for what is already here and now, the most self-apparent mystery, right in front of our eyes each moment, the very essence of everything.

I felt expanded, free, no boundaries. I am vastness itself, a free-flowing spaciousness, all so light and flowing, pure freedom. I remember that moment when I briefly exchanged some words with my fellow practitioners and I was literally experiencing that it was I – logos – that spoke through each of us. One Self playing the role of all of us, speaking to itself through itself by assuming different forms or roles. Like in a puppet theater, there appear to be different characters on the screen, but it is the same artist playing all roles by wearing different puppet gloves!

From that moment everything was new and fresh! I no longer existed and yet it was the first time I felt truly alive. A new Life began! All questions dropped – no intellectual explanation can ever give the taste of truth. Of course, the intellect can lead us to the gate of truth, but then one must jump. Intellectual exploration is only a bridge; hence one must cross and leap beyond it. Once you cross, you don't need it anymore! Truth is beyond understanding and mind. The dropping of all seeking for answers was such a profound ontological relief. But at the same time, it entailed profound implications for my life, and especially my career as an academic.

On a relational level, experiencing the oneness of being entailed a curious paradox: I am already, ontologically, in the most intimate relationship with everyone – since our being is one and the same. At the same time, it seems odd seeking to form a relationship with "another", since, essentially, there is no other! What is the point of forming 'special' relationships, such as intimate relationships, when I am already whole in myself? Of course, in time I realized that one can of course form relationships that no longer aim at filling an inner sense of lacking happiness, but in a new light, as a way of celebrating and sharing happiness.

Realizing the unity of our being overflowed my heart with so much love for everyone. For the first month, I would greet people, for example in the street or in shops, with so much warmth and care, feeling connected to them even though in 'practical' life they were total strangers. That, as one may expect, was often received as strange since not everyone was experiencing the same feeling of oneness and love! I had to work through my spontaneity of being so open and loving, since our society operates on the established belief that we ought – or it is "appropriate" - to be loving and open only with those 'few' 'close to us', and not all beings around us. Societies have us discriminate our offering of love, compassion and kindness according to how well we 'know' another on a level of personality; in reality, should we all recognize the unity of our being, that distinction is a fallacy based on a misinterpretation of our true nature.

This awakening also entailed profound implications for my professional life. Realizing that the philosophical knowledge ~ in the ancient Hellenic sense of gnosis ~ which I was seeking and seeking to serve through my specialization, is not a product of mind, but rather, as Plato indeed had defined, "a merging with the ocean of oneness", I found it hard to continue on my career path as before. I saw the way Philosophy is approached at various institutions as detached from the way the very thinkers whom we supposedly study define it: most of the Hellenic tradition approaches philosophy - qua gnosis - as a path of self-liberation and awakening. Despite Hellenic Philosophy's own definition of its nature and goals, according to the primary text sources handed down to us, the way numerous modern institutions approach the study of Ancient Philosophy does not endorse awakening as the goal of our education; nor are the practices towards "attaining the goal of philosophy" taught and explored at university level.

A lot of what was practiced at university felt like merely as mind games, projections on the screen of "the cave". Most academic studies of philosophy approach it solely on an intellectual – rational – historical level, exploring different arguments and interpretations, while leaving out entirely the lived aspect, which is its most essential part: the aspect of cultivating virtues, emotional intelligence and compassion on a personal level; knowing ourself through self-exploration and the practices of meditation; practicing the inner work necessary for transforming the knower in order to lead her to the realization of the 'unity of being' which amounts both to self-liberation and to true gnosis beyond both intellectual and sensory phenomena. And, ultimately, "merging with the One", as Pythagoras stated.

Following this awakening, it became increasingly hard to continue to approach my area of study and research in a purely mind-oriented way; it felt futile given the very nature of Philosophy, and indeed my ontological experience. I wanted to share with everyone around me that Philosophy can be approached experientially, and what the Ancient thinkers present is indeed possible to attain, should we approach it not only in a "museum way" – where we study those texts from afar as something dead, but as a living path of self-exploration and awakening.1 Argumentation and rational exploration are important, but only so long as they are complementary to the lived practices which lead us to an experiential and self-transformative contact with the essence of what we study.

---

[11] A year and a half after this awakening experience, I wrote an article named "*The Light of Hellenism*", where I explore those aspects of ancient philosophy in greater detail. The article was initially published in the Journal "Tarka" (issued by *Embodied Philosophy*), and then re-published by Paradigm Explorer.

It was quite very hard to discuss these matters with my fellow peers at the time. Whenever I tried, I experienced a resistance to this idea, and indeed sometimes hostility. I often refer to this experience as "epistemological discrimination". In an era where we all acknowledge the importance of endorsing diversity and difference - for instance in matters of gender, race and sexual preferences - there are still residual barriers to showing the same spirit of openness to alternative ontological worldviews and epistemological possibilities.

For that reason, the focus of my career took a big shift, which initially was quite hard for me, given how devoted I was to the idea of seeking tenure and a long-term career as a Professor at a University. However, in this new light, that prospect felt restrictive and no longer true to the way I now experienced life and knowledge and wished to explore it with others. Therefore, while I continued some of my work in academic institutions, I decided to approach the teaching and research of philosophy beyond academia too. I created a school in Athens where Philosophy is open to all and can be learned, taught, and practiced in a more lived and experiential way; accompanied with practices of self-knowledge, meditation, cultivation of virtues (in the ancient sense), and a lived, self-explorative approach for realizing the nature of our being.

I hope that in the near future, as more and more academics share their stories of spiritual exploration and personal spiritual experiences, our academic institutions will become more open in the possibility of exploring alternative ontologies and epistemologies as possible starting points for approaching and practicing knowledge.

Chapter Two

I'm Home: Awakening to a Deeper Connection With My Heart, My Mind, and the World

Marjorie Woollacott, PhD

*Dr. Marjorie Woollacott has been a Professor and Chair in the Dept. of Human Physiology and a member of the Institute of Neuroscience, at the University of Oregon. In addition to teaching courses on neuroscience and rehabilitation, she taught courses on complementary and alternative medicine and meditation. Dr. Woollacott has received over $7.2 million in research funding from the National Institutes of Health and other research agencies for her research in child development, aging, rehabilitation medicine and meditation. She has published more than 200 scientific articles and written or co-edited eight books, the most recent being **Infinite Awareness: The Awakening of a Scientific Mind**. She has recently (2017) accepted the position of Research Director for the International Association of Near-Death Studies (IANDS) and is the President of the Academy for the Advancement of Postmaterialist Sciences. Website:* https://marjoriewoollacott.com

In 1976, I had an experience in meditation that opened me to the awareness of a dimension of reality I had never before experienced. I was invited by my sister to a meditation retreat by an Indian meditation master, and though I was skeptical, I was curious and decided to attend. In the first session of the retreat, it was announced that during the meditation period the meditation master would walk around the room and initiate everyone there. The host described this as a spiritual awakening, and that it would occur through the master's touch. As a young neuroscientist I was skeptical. But I was already there, so I made the decision to put my skepticism aside for the duration of the retreat. And, in fact, I was curious to see what might unfold (Woollacott, 2015).

When he reached me, I felt the swami's thumb and fingers on the bridge of my nose, right between my eyes. I was deeply attentive - I had closed my eyes, but my other senses were fully aware. So when I became aware of what seemed like a current of electricity enter from the master's fingers into my body, I had a sense of utter certainty about what had happened. It isn't that I understood precisely what had occurred. To this day, I can't explain it. But it felt as if a mini-lightning bolt leapt from his fingers to a point between my eyes and then down into the center of my chest. I could feel the precise point where it stopped. It was my heart, not my physical heart but more like my true heart than my physical heart had ever been. I felt this astonishing energy radiate outward from my heart and filling my whole being. It felt like nectar - like pure love pouring through me. Words came to mind, and they were unrelated to scientific analysis: I'm home, I'm home! My heart is my home.

What was most surprising to me was what happened after the retreat was over. When I returned home, without any effort I made a complete shift in my habits, beginning the morning after the retreat. I spontaneously awakened at 5 am, and got up to meditate, and this new habit has continued to this day. I meditated knowing that just below the surface of my awareness simmered a quiet ecstasy. I had tapped it once. I knew it was there waiting for me.

As a result of this meditation experience, I experienced a shift in my worldview and I began to question my materialist perspective. I now had a professional dilemma: I had to consider if the world I live in is truly Newtonian, as I originally believed, or if it is actually consciousness-based. I began to explore the nature of consciousness through my own meditation practice, and through research into the characteristics of conscious experience. I asked: what is consciousness? Is it tied to neural activity? Or could consciousness somehow exist without neurons?

Though I was meditating every morning, in my early years as a meditator I considered myself first and foremost a scientist. The scientific part of me had no interest in finding research support for phenomena that are considered mystical or paranormal. Such experiences are not within the scope of Newtonian science, and this precise, cause-and-effect materialist view of consciousness was still the perspective I held.

This led to a fragmented life. It seemed like there was an almost impossible chasm between my life as a scientist and my life as a meditator. I would reveal one type of experience to my friends who meditated and to my students in the yoga and meditation classes I taught. And then I would bring up the other, very different experiences of mine with my colleagues in neuroscience—those I worked with in various areas of rehabilitation. I was so afraid of losing my credibility with my scientific colleagues if they found out about my life as a mediator.

After 25 years of leading two lives, I felt a bit schizophrenic. It was a problem I decided to resolve by publicly integrating the two halves of my experience. I first began to try to bridge this chasm between the two sides of myself by doing scientific research on meditation. I asked, "Does looking at meditation from the third- person scientific perspective inform us about the origins of Consciousness?" I wanted to understand if meditation changes our mental abilities—and, if so, how it does this. What could be the physiological basis of such changes? And in fact, our research did reveal that meditation significantly improves our mental abilities. Our lab and many others have shown that meditation improves mental focus and emotional regulation, for example, and that our attentional networks get stronger. This research shows that meditators, in fact, are like high-powered athletes of the attentional arena—their attentional systems become both strong and flexible.

After an extensive period of research and reflection, I wrote my first book on this topic: *Infinite Awareness: The Awakening of a Scientific Mind* (Woollacott, 2015). In writing it I was seeking another level of integrity: in addition to summarizing current research on the nature of consciousness, I wanted to speak frankly and openly about my own experiences of expanded awareness as a meditator. I wanted to explore what these experiences have to say about the nature of consciousness and the nature of the human mind. From my continued exploration of meditation, I have learned that to understand the true nature of consciousness, the third-person or scientific perspective is not enough. We also need to include the deep mystical experiences that come from meditation and other spiritual practices. Since that time I have expanded my research to include the exploration of mystical phenomena such as spiritual awakenings, near-death experiences and end-of-life experiences. And I have offered my time to organizations such as the Academy for the Advancement of Postmaterialist Sciences (AAPS), as co-founder and current president, the International Association of Near-Death Studies (IANDS), as Research Director, and the Galileo Commission. It is one way I have found of sharing my joy and insights related to this new understanding of the world with others.

Note: this essay is adapted from Marjorie Woollacott's book: *Infinite Awareness: The Awakening of a Scientific Mind,* Rowman and Littlefield, 2015.

Chapter Three

My Most Important Spiritual Experience

Amit Goswami, PhD

*Amit Goswami PhD is a theoretical quantum physicist and retired full professor from the University of Oregon's Department of Physics. He is the author of **The Self-Aware Universe**, in which he pioneered the idea of "science within consciousness" and elucidated the famous observer effect in quantum physics. Amit was featured in the film What the Bleep Do We Know!?, and is the author of nine other books based on his research in quantum physics and consciousness. Amit started the quantum activism movement, establishing a transformative education institution, Quantum Activism Vishwalayam, based on quantum science and primacy of consciousness. Amit is a spiritual practitioner and calls himself a quantum activist in search of Wholeness.*

There is a story about a tourist visiting New York. He is looking for the way to the Carnegie Hall. He sees a passer-by who seemed reliable; so he asks, "What is the way to the Carnegie Hall?" The passer-by is a musical maestro. He replies, "Practice, practice, practice." Indeed, if you want to perform in Carnegie Hall, the maestro's advice is good. But what good is it for the tourist?

What happened to me is similar. I was looking for not one but two Carnegie halls. One was the answer to the question, "How do I integrate quantum physics with living my life?" The second was, "How do I learn to love my wife?' People who I thought were reliable all would answer, "Meditate, meditate, meditate." But meditation from what I knew about it, was the way to God, spiritual enlightenment. Do I have to be enlightened to find answers to my questions?

A long time ago, I read in somebody's book that the Bible says, "Whoso knoweth love, knoweth God." The reverse could be true: whoso knoweth God, knoweth love.

In the West, God means an almighty individual usually pictured as a white male with a long beard; as the king of kings, God stands as a model for the mortal king's majesty and authority. Writers for women's lib are scornful about this depiction; but would it be any different if God was a white female? More pretty to look at to be sure, but that's about it. In fact, it could be a problem for men. The great Indian poet Kalidasa was a devotee of the female goddess Saraswati and he wrote a salutation to her. But you know what? The salutation glorifies the twin peaks of the goddess more than anything else. That is not particularly spiritual, is it?

I am being facetious. In the East, where I grew up, there is no scope for making this confusing picture of God. In the Eastern tradition, what they glorify is a Oneness or Wholeness; reality is nothing but, they say. The world of multiple objects is illusion for which the Sanskrit word is maya. The gods, spelled with a small "g" like Saraswati, were archetypes whose exploration helps to get you to the unity; that is their only importance.

But of course, I rejected the concept of Oneness as God long ago, because that, too, to me, made no scientific sense. How are we one, when every part of the being I know dwells in separateness from you even when you are my intimate one!

But when you are desperate you grasp at straws. Could I find Eastern guidance to God or Oneness in America? No worries. Since the sixties, Eastern spirituality has been gaining popularity in America. I have mentioned the Hare Krishnas elsewhere, but the Beatles had popularized Maharishi Mahesh Yogi and his TM movement; the philosopher Alan Watts and Zen master Suzuki Roshi had popularized Zen Buddhism; Swami Muktananda had brought the idea of Shaktipat, kundalini energy. Jiddu Krishnamurti was another popular name on the spiritual scene and there was Bhagwan Shri Rajneesh who later became Osho. Other Hindu teachings go back even further: Vivekananda and his Vedanta societies; Paramahansa Yogananda established a group too, the divine life society; and so on.

But wherever I went, one advice was common, "Meditate, meditate, meditate." So one day I thought why not? I decided to go back to my family practice, a mantra recitation called japa. This time something happened. This was fall, 1976.

As I said, japa is a simple repetition of a one syllable mantra in your mind. After you do it for a while, the mantra is internalized. What that means is that the mantra goes on inside you somehow even when you are attending to other chores. So it was supposed to be going on while I taught or when I read a scientific paper. Once in a while, I'd check this out, and it was true. Whenever I checked, the mantra was right there. After I did this for seven whole days, as I said, something happened. It was so special, I wrote down, the experience:

On a sunny November morning, I was sitting quietly in my chair in my office doing japa. This was the seventh day since I had started, and I still had a lot of energy left. After about an hour of japa, I got an urge to take a walk outside. I continued my mantra deliberately as I walked out of my office, then out of the building, across the street, and onto the grassy meadow. And then the universe opened up to me.

> "... when meadow, grove and stream
> The earth, and every common sight,
> To me did seem
> Appareled in celestial light,
> The glory and freshness of a dream."
> [W. Wordsworth in Hutchinson and de Selincourt (1967)]

I seemed to be one with the cosmos, the grass, the trees, the sky. Sensations were present, in fact, intensified beyond belief. But these sensations paled into insignificance compared to the feeling of love that followed, a love that engulfed everything in my consciousness--until I lost comprehension of the process. This was ananda, bliss.

There was a moment or two for which I have no description, no thoughts, not even feeling. Afterwards, it was just bliss. It was still bliss as I walked back to my office. It was bliss when I talked to our cantankerous secretary, but she was beautiful in the bliss, and I loved her. It was bliss when I taught my large freshman class; the noise in the back rows, even the back-row kid who threw a paper airplane was bliss. It was bliss when I came home and my wife hugged me and I knew I loved her. It was bliss when we made love later.

It was all bliss.

The feeling of all bliss did not stay long. By the end of the second day, it started fading. When I woke the next morning, it was all gone.

A comparison with the literature told me that what I had experienced was called ananda Samadhi, Samadhi with bliss as an aftereffect. The Sanskrit word Samadhi stands for a convergence of the two poles of experience, subject and object. In our ordinary ego experience, the split of subject and object is huge and quite distinct. In my experience, in that split second, there was hardly a distinction.

So who am I then? The more stable ego-I, or this very special oneness-I that took seven days of meditation to precipitate? How can the brain produce both experiences? Also, the aftermath of the experience—bliss—came to me as a capacity to love anyone. I was curious. Can one have this capacity to love not just temporarily but permanently? So many questions and no answers? Is this how it's going to be, my journey of integration? I could not help thinking.

Quantum physics began my journey; it also led me eventually to creative exploration of consciousness. When that culminated in a creative aha moment, the insight lead to a quantum science of consciousness and experiences that I have ever since been engaged in.

Did this change my career? I had a tenured position and I never gave it up, but I never went back to a mundane way of doing physics either. I kept on publishing first some papers, then a book, then more papers and more books. I fully retired in 2003. Soon after, I established the Center for Quantum Activism, an activist movement to spread the quantum worldview.

In 2018, my friends and I established a fully affiliated Masters and PhD program in quantum science of health, prosperity, and happiness where we teach our students not only concepts but also how to live them.

And I still continue my journey in wholeness.

Chapter Four

Scientist, Poet and Mystic – Complementary Ways of Knowing and Being

Marilyn Monk, PhD

Marilyn Monk, BScHons, MScHons, PhD, is Professor Emerita at University College London Institute of Child Health. She has been a research scientist for 60 years, university lecturer, head of UCL Molecular Embryology Unit, and has published over 200 scholarly papers. She is known for her work on DNA replication and repair, amoeboid cell signalling, regulation of differential gene expression in development, discovery and establishment of epigenetics, discovery of deprogramming to stem cells and, technically, the miniaturization of molecular analyses to the sensitivity of the single cell. Her pioneering work on preimplantation diagnosis of genetic disease earned her an invitation from the Nobel Secretariat to speak at Karlskoga. Marilyn Monk is also an Alexander Technique teacher and Psychosynthesis Counsellor.

In the beginning....

People are always asking young children, "What do you want to be when you grow up?"

I can remember my childhood answers quite clearly. I grew up in the country in Australia. At night, I would lie on the ground and gaze at the stars stretching across the vast and mysterious dark sky; stars so dense that they formed an iridescent cloud – the Milky Way. I wondered, "Does it go on forever? Are there other beings out there like us?" I was transported away in overwhelming awe and wonder.

I was going to be an astronaut ...

In the daytime, I was fascinated by the mystery of life forms close at hand. My attention was absorbed by armies of marching ants, the hovering dragonflies, the lizards who could shed their tails if caught, the huge hairy spiders that came to rest on my bedroom ceiling – a sign that it was going to rain. I loved to herd the chooks around the back garden and watch their chicks peck their way out of their eggs on the kitchen floor. I loved the snakes as they crawled across my feet while I was collecting blackberries or mushrooms. I loved the huge dairy horses snuffling around my head as I sat near the fence offering them a blade of grass. Later, when I had my first pony, I would ride through the huge temperate forests of the mountain ranges where we lived. I would meet these strange, funny creatures along the way: duck-billed platypuses, wombats, kangaroos, koalas and the lyre birds mimicking the sounds of the forest. I wondered how all these wonderful creatures had come into being. Where did they come from? Was it true that each came from a sort of seed – a single tiny egg cell?

I was going to be a biologist (maybe an embryologist) ...

Then there was the influence of my parents – ballet dancing, piano lessons, painting in oils. And of course, the gatherings of the clans - the endless birthday parties of other kids – social engagements that I never liked (and still don't today). I had learned that I could trust animals not to hurt me - but other human beings were a different matter. My night terrors were about dangerous humans – never animals. I shied away from social gatherings and instead immersed myself in nature and in art, which suited my fearful and reclusive character.

I was going to be an artist (perhaps a poet) ...

As it happened, I went on to become a scientist (mainly because I could get 100 per cent in maths exams). But remembering those childhood polarities today – the stargazer, the budding biologist, the reclusive artist – I realise that the most important awakening in my life arose from my involvement with a spiritual master in India. I first went to the ashram in Pune in 1976 – not because I was seeking spirituality but because a friend was living there and Bombay was a convenient stopover flying home to Australia to visit parents. However, it was normal for new arrivals at the ashram to attend a darshan (meeting) with the master. This proved to be such a momentous experience. Once seated before the master, I was suddenly transported into another state of being by a powerful and irresistible force. I felt totally exposed; totally seen; totally known; totally accepted; totally loved. And another two overwhelming unforgettable experiences happened due to the experience - as if infectious - of connection with the master. Difficult to describe but I call them 'whoosh and wow' transitions into another plane of being – of vibrant, dancing, sparkling energy.

The accompanying feelings of ecstasy, exhilaration and amazement were life-changing.

But how to reconcile these new spiritual experiences with my identity as a serious orthodox scientist wedded to rational, logical facts and evidence – objective truth reproducible by anyone, anywhere. My spiritual emergence caused major problems in my scientific life. I was ridiculed by my colleagues; publicly denounced, 'made fun of' – no longer to be taken seriously. My male colleagues were particularly vociferous in their condemnation – perhaps also because they felt that my scientific discoveries were making them 'wrong'. But my discoveries, including several paradigm shifts, were simply the result of my natural curiosity and wonder. Both in life and in the lab, I was always attracted to things that did not fit with the accepted dogma. Today, it is difficult for me to keep up with the science. But strange things continue to happen, and I have had other mysterious experiences – correct premonitions of impending danger, friends and loved ones visiting me in dreams (and in other powerful experiences) when they die, and constant telephone telepathy.

In addition to the awakening experiences in India there was also a discourse given by the spiritual master on aspects of science, art, and mysticism, seen as complementary ways of knowing and being. This discourse had a huge impact on me as it revealed, and healed, the conflict between the scientist, poet and mystic within myself. At the time, these three parts of me were so separate that they hardly knew each other. By 'mystic', I mean one who attains a sense of knowing by dissolving into the whole. By 'scientist', I mean one who actively seeks knowledge through fragmentation of the whole and examination of the parts. They are, in some ways, complementary opposites – the scientist is concentration and effort; the mystic is zooming out into the whole. And then there is the poet, who encapsulates my love of nature and my love of beauty. Of course, the three parts talk to each other. They influence and inspire each other. In my science, I experienced so much serendipity. Sometimes I even made inexplicable mistakes that revealed new insights. And I also needed to learn to be appropriate – not to take my scientist into a love affair; not to take my mystic into the lab.

I spoke about my childhood desire to be a biologist and my particular fascination – where do live beings come from? One day in my laboratory many years later, I was looking down a microscope at a four-cell embryo. Suddenly, my childhood wonder came flooding back. I was suspended in a state of awe looking at the magical symmetry of this tiny embryo and the glow of the cells as they reflected the light. I could almost sense the whole mysterious potential of this simple life form to develop and grow into a new being. I realized in that moment that I was involved in the very research that absorbed me as a child. I also realized in that moment that one could never absolutely define the magic of the awe and wonder of existence and I was happy that this was so.

Chapter Five

A Spiritual Awakening and Turning-Point in 1965

Nicholas Hagger

*Nicholas Hagger has lectured at universities in Iraq, Libya and Japan, where he was a Professor of English Literature. He is the author of nearly 60 books that include a substantial literary output and innovatory works within history, philosophy, literature and international politics and statecraft. As a man of letters he has written over 2,000 poems, two poetic epics, five verse plays, 1,200 short stories, two travelogues and three masques. He has pioneered a cross-disciplinary Universalism, a philosophy of the oneness of the universe and humankind, in seven disciplines. In 2016 he was awarded the Gusi Peace Prize for Literature, and in 2019 the BRICS silver medal for **Vision for Future**. His full body of work can be seen at www.nicholashagger.co.uk.*

My spiritual development was a lengthy process during which I experienced full illumination in London in 1971, as I describe in *My Double Life 1: This Dark Wood* and *My Double Life 2: A Rainbow over the Hills* (both O Books 2015). My awakening and turning-point took place nearly six years earlier in 1965 in Japan, where I was a Professor of English Literature. That was when I underwent a centre-shift without fully understanding what was happening, and began living in a deeper part of myself with unitive vision that eventually came to be permanently aware of the order, unity and harmony within the universe.

I had always known I had to get myself to Japan to uncover the wisdom of the East. In 1964 I was taken to meditate in the Zen Koganji temple, and glimpsed the first glimmer of dawn as light reflected in its polished floor. In January and August 1965 I made two visits to the Zen Ryoanji Stone Garden in Kyoto, and both times, looking at stones and rocks that could be mountains, clouds, earth, sea and sand, I experienced the oneness of the universe. On 11 September 1965 I began an intense five weeks when I saw many images behind my closed eyes, a sequence of visions: scrivenings in foreign languages in yellow and blue, a puddle and an orb of fire within it, corn stalks with many ears of corn, a descent into a well.

I had more visions on 13 September: a series of gold heads, diamonds in green and mauve. When I got off to sleep I dreamt of an earthquake and rushed down stairs to a courtyard of fallen masonry. When I awoke I thought I had dreamt of a centre-shift I was undergoing, from my rational, social ego to my deeper spiritual self. I thought I had opened to my imagination, and that the images were bubbling up from the spring of my Muse.

On 5 October I met the 1920s Japanese poet Junzaburo Nishiwaki (known as Japan's T.S. Eliot) near one of my universities in a small café with sawdust on the floor, and over *saké* (rice-wine) I asked him to sum up the wisdom of the East. Talking of Confucius's use of *yin* and *yang* and the *Tao*, he said, "The Absolute is where there is no difference" and wrote out on a business reply card that was poking out of a copy of *Encounter* I had with me: "$+A + -A = 0$". And I immediately saw that a oneness, a unity, reconciles all opposites: day and night, life and death, the finite and the infinite, time and eternity.

On 11 October I went to the bathroom and was flooded with golden light behind my closed eyes. The pattern was of rings, a golden net. On 17 October I fell asleep in the afternoon and woke at 4.30 pm and went to my study and seemed to be "a floor below my thoughts". My centre-shift was nearly complete. The next morning, Monday 18 October 1965, I stayed at home and something extraordinary happened. I recorded in my diary, which is in *Awakening to the Light* (Element, 1994): "All morning I have been filled with a round white light: I cannot see it, except occasionally when I glimpse it and am dazzled, but I know it is there. It is like a white sun. This is, I suppose, what Christians refer to as the soul – the centre of the self. And the mystical experience is given meaning by the relation between the centre and the sun, so that everything is one." That experience of the Light ended my First Mystic Life.

Nearly six years later, after a long Dark Night of the Soul, I began my Second Mystic Life on 3 September 1971 with a number of intense images and visions, far more intense and profound than I had had until then. On Friday 10 September 1971, a day that has meant as much to me as Monday 23 November 1654 meant to Pascal, in the lining of whose doublet that date and the word "FIRE" were found sewn after his death in 1662, I had an overwhelming and momentous experience of illumination for an hour and a half, of a white light flowing upwards, a tree of white fire. Visions wobbled up like bubbles from a spring, and I saw a white flower, like a chrysanthemum or dahlia – my first glimpse of the Golden Flower – and many patterns and old paintings of gods and saints. A small circle of white light went deep up into the heavens behind my closed eyes and changed to a celestial curtain blowing in the wind, like the *aurora borealis*. And: "A centre of light shining down as if from a great height.... A sun breaking through cloud.... A fountain of white light." This experience was followed by more visions and "raptures" in the coming months, many of which can be found in my poems. I have recorded 112 experiences of the Light in my works.

My awakening in Japan proved to be a turning-point in my life. It took over 'The Silence' in mid-poem, and as I grappled to understand what was happening to me and cope with the many images and visions, I knew I had to pursue a writing career and set out the oneness of the universe in several disciplines. I knew I had to prioritise becoming cross-disciplinary like a Renaissance man over being a one-discipline Professor, and although I was offered a Chair for life in the Tokyo university where the polymath poet and critic Sir William Empson taught in the 1930s I left Japan and applied myself to the cross-disciplinary research that would result in my writing nearly 60 books.

Initially I cast around for references to the Fire or Light in Tokyo bookshops and spent 25 years getting together the research for *The Fire and the Stones* (Element, 1991), which appeared towards the end of my Mystic Way. I could have done with that work in 1965 when I was hunting for similar experiences in books. I did not grasp until recently that my Universalism – my philosophy of the fundamental unity of the universe and all humankind, and of all history, philosophy, literature and international politics, which should arguably be a new university subject in its own right – came out of that awakening in 1965, as did all my books. Many of my works refer to the Eastern formulaic thinking of "+A + -A = 0", and I have just completed a draft of *The Algorithm of Creation* (O Books, 2023), which traces the course of the creation and expansion of the universe to its end in terms of that Eastern wisdom.

My mystical experience of the Fire or Light after a centre-shift transformed my way of looking at the universe as I instinctively saw its oneness and harmony. My thinking turned to the lot of humankind and I set out a political Universalism that will benefit all humanity: a partly-federal democratic World State (*World*

State, O Books, 2018). Over the decades I had turned 180 degrees from nationalism (thinking in terms of self-contained nation-states) to supranationalism (thinking in terms of the unity behind all nation-states and history's civilisations).

I did not know it at the time, but the Mystic Way would take me three decades to complete. It begins with awakening and continues with purgation and a First Mystic Life and centre-shift to the first illumination, then a long Dark Night of the Soul which further purges, then a Second Mystic Life and full illumination, then a further long period of darkness (the Dark Night of the Spirit in which new powers flow in, infused knowledge), and then two more Mystic Lives separated by yet a further long period of darkness. At its end is permanent unitive living in which the universe is perceived instinctively as a unity, as there has now been a permanent centre-shift to living through the spirit.

Spiritual awakening is a key sequence of events in a long process that in my experience can take the best part of 30 years. The new self then instinctively lives in permanent knowledge of the underlying harmony of the universe and humankind, and this is what I have reflected in my works for a further 30 years.

Chapter Six

A Day in April

Hardin Tibbs, MSc

Hardin Tibbs is a UK-based strategic analyst, futures thinker, adviser and innovator with over 30 years' experience of future-oriented strategic thinking. His consulting work has spanned product design and innovation, industrial ecology, environmental sustainability, strategy development and futures thinking. His futures work is focused on gaining insight into issues on the horizon that will drive an enduring shift in strategic agendas. Hardin helped to develop the executive education scenarios programme at the Saïd Business School, Oxford University. He has taught futures and strategy related topics at the Cambridge University Judge Business School and the Møller Institute; the University of Bath School of Management; and Ashridge Business School, among others. More details about his work can be seen at www.hardintibbs.com

One day in April 1978 I had an experience that felt like a kind of inner earthquake and which initiated an extended process of personal transformation.

This spiritual awakening was the culmination of a personal search triggered some years earlier. During a holiday in North Wales I had been shown how to dowse – an experience that, according to my scientific worldview at the time, ought not to be happening.

My immediate thought was, "If this is true, what else might be true? What if God exists?" I decided I had better find out. And so my search began.

I soon discovered Watkins esoteric bookshop in Charing Cross and began reading voraciously. I studied for two years under a Sri Lankan Buddhist monk who was living in London. And I practised biofeedback-based meditation under physicist and researcher Maxwell Cade, who with Geoff Blundell had invented the MindMirror, a portable real-time electroencephalograph display.

All this led me to Subud, described by Lawrence Blair in *Rhythms of Vision*, and by John Bennett in his autobiography *Witness*. Subud is an experiential spiritual practice that came from Indonesia in the late 1950s. John Bennett was one of the earliest westerners to experience it, having previously been a proponent of Gurdjieff's spiritual method. Blair's description prompted me to track down a Subud group in London and I applied to join. I then experienced my own version of what he had described in his book.

The spiritual process at the heart of the Subud experience arises from and operates in a spiritual domain which Western cultures have all but forgotten. The basic Subud experience is described using the Indonesian word "latihan" which means training. Although at times it resembles physical exercise, this training is of the "inner self" and relates to its growth and connection with the outer self. The power behind the latihan is referred to as the "great life force" or the power of God.

That day in April I was asked to stand quietly with my eyes closed, and to "receive" the latihan for the first time. At first nothing seemed to happen, but then I began to move spontaneously: small movements at first and then I started to walk. The feeling was as if you relaxed your arm, say, and allowed someone else to move it. You can stop it at any time by tensing your muscles, but if you allow the movement to happen in the latihan gradually your whole body begins to move and you might walk, run, jump, or dance in a stream of "training" activity flowing from the inner self.

The most remarkable aspect of my first latihan was the impact on how I felt inwardly. I felt as if I had experienced a kind of inner earthquake. I could clearly feel I had an inner self, distinct from my ordinary sense of self. I had always identified myself with my intellect, but now I could see that the essence of my being was not my thinking brain, but was centred in my chest and would survive beyond my death. This had a profound effect on me which took some time to absorb.

A month or two later, during a regular twice-weekly half-hour latihan session, I heard in my "mind's ear" these words: "Your wife is having an affair". At the next opportunity I told her about this. She said, "It's true. What of it?" I was stunned on several levels. After some months thinking it over, she decided she wanted to continue the affair and we ended up divorcing.

The latihan can confront one's preconceptions with uncompromising honesty, but it always leaves the choice of action open. The question of how to act on information presented in the latihan becomes a personal challenge that forms part of the learning process, particularly if it highlights or involves facing up to previously unseen inner emotional or psychological obstacles.

Another, more positive latihan experience happened a few weeks later. I was made to lie on the floor and close my eyes. The latihan then used my experiences with biofeedback mediation and took me rapidly to a deep meditative level and then into visual blackness, where I was no longer aware of the room or my body. I suddenly found myself high above what looked like a desert landscape, looking down as if from 35,000 feet in an aircraft. Between my vantage point and the desert surface was a layer of fluffy white clouds, scudding rapidly across the landscape. Then I gradually began to descend. When I reached the cloud layer I was rotated so that my view was now facing upwards. As I went through the clouds I realised, "Oh, these are my thoughts". Then suddenly, like a jump cut, I was one with the landscape, facing upwards.

Then I became aware of two things. One was that the topology of the landscape, which also resembled a complex set of musical chords sustained on some vast cathedral organ, represented my essential self, encoding my unique identity somewhat like the serrated edge of a key. I also became aware that time had stopped. As I looked upwards to where I had started high above, I could see the panorama of time stretched out from the past to the future. I realised that I could reach far up and contact any point in time, past or future. Directly overhead was "the present" where I had started. Instantly after I had taken all this in, I was suddenly back in the room, lying on the floor with time running normally again.

This experience, followed by some later prompts, caused me to develop an interest in the future. This led, about ten years later, to being offered a job with a futures research consultancy in California. My new professional direction was accompanied from the outset by a deep insight into the nature of time. One practical result of this was that I was always suspicious of any overly mechanistic approach to forecasting based on a "colliding billiard balls" view of causation, and more open to unconventional approaches such as remote viewing.

My experience of the Subud latihan was not a single inward event leading to specific personal changes downstream, but a continuing process of spiritual development accompanied by various larger and smaller experiences which cumulatively transformed my entire state of being. All this had a huge impact on my life and it certainly revolutionised my intellectual perspective. Now I knew with certainty that there is a "spiritual realm" existing behind or beyond the familiar physical aspect of reality. I could also see that this spiritual side of reality is not homogeneous or simplistic but that it has as much functional complexity as science has disclosed in the outer world. In effect my sense of reality had suddenly expanded. It became obvious to me that the conventional scientific idea that everything is purely physical and that all phenomena arise from material causes is completely inadequate and superficial. Reality is imbued with a conscious awareness that is the power behind the world. The latihan appears to be an initiative or gift from this level to counterbalance the pressure of materialism associated with advanced technology.

Chapter Seven

A Few Stops on a Path With Heart

Bo Ahrenfelt, MD

Bo Ahrenfelt, BA, MD. Former psychiatrist at St. Sigfrid's mental hospital in Växjö and visiting consultant in private institution in Hovmantorp, Sweden. Radio producer at the Swedish national network within his fields of competence. Founder of Institutet för Liv och Arbete (Inst for Life and Work), which he led for twenty-five years, a network of professionals working with change and development on individual, group and system level in the private and public sectors. Author of **Conflict Management Handbook** *(1993),* **Territories and Leadership** *(2012) and* **Change as Being State** *(3rd edition 2013). Currently partner of SustainChange AB, www.sustainchange.se, with a focus on human sustainability. Writing a new book on adult personal development and how adults cope with change and development in life and work.*

I am twelve years old, enjoying my corn pipe in the entrance hall of the town library of Umeå, Northern Sweden. As usual, I have picked a book by chance. It is about Zen Buddhism. One sentence hit me hard – the thought of death intensifies life. I was fascinated and a seed was planted, growing into a lifelong interest in consciousness. It was the first experience I can remember from my spiritual path. I have had many since. One was when my first son was a month old. I asked him in Swedish, English, French and German to tell me where he came from. One drowsy summer afternoon a couple of days later, I suddenly realized he had answered me in pictures. In the moment I felt a distinct, warm, streaming feeling between my eyebrows. Awake and surprised, the message was gone. But the experience was so strong that I believed he had had an earlier life before birth. A friend, Bishop Emeritus, has a joke that the Swedish Church accepts life after death, but not life before birth. Materialism takes another position – consciousness exists by chance and has no meaning. In both cases, denial is an effective way of handling a complex reality, but not very creative.

My grandmother's relatives lived on a small family farm in northern Sweden. During one of my visits as a child, one of the sisters burst out "My brother is early today!". I went out to meet him but didn't see him anywhere. Shortly after, he walked into the kitchen. They often communicated by thought alone. As long as I can remember reality has had two complementary facets. One materialistic and one mind-spiritual.

At twenty-six I started to meditate. After a few months, I had an out-of-the-body experience, where to my surprise I walked along a creek in the forest without my dog. Soon afterwards, I saw my body beneath me meditating, while I was on the ceiling. Immediately awake and scared, I wondered what would have happened if I didn't get back into my body. Today, a meditator for forty years, I have yet to experience it again.

Once, I asked Claudio Naranjo (1932-2019), a pioneer in transpersonal psychotherapies, what the purpose of psychotherapy is? "To restore the capacity to love", he said. Another statement which hit me deeply as a young man. Both the Buddhist sentence and this statement are still valid for me. People who work in hospices have told me that what bothers the dying most is to restore relationships with people they love before they pass away. As a young psychotherapist I learned that the best way to help ourselves, others and the planet, is to find our personal path with heart and be curious and honest.

A transformative phase in my life started when I focused my meditation on "Who am I?" I remembered situations when people had hurt me and when I had hurt others. It was painful to experience the pain I had inflicted upon others. This dialectical process was followed by deeper relaxation. Eventually, I felt a very pleasant wordless calling or longing. One morning my world became totally still. I don't know how long the experience continued. An absolute stillness and natural primordial state to rest in. Emptiness filled with warm acceptance. Afterwards, I realized that the absolute stillness was extraordinary and something I never had experienced before. A stunning insight that enabled me to realize that, "All is One". I can't name a trigger. I just had my usual morning meditation, completely relaxed with an empty and clear awareness. When the clock rang, I continued as if nothing had happened. But it had.

I came back to the conditioned ego after finding a treasure beneath the floor of my house. The whole experience came from somewhere within, but cannot be explained in our daily language. The search as personal development was over and something grew within. It was like the Hero's Journey, described by Campbell in his classic book "*The Hero with a Thousand Faces*". From many different cultures and ages, it has been a human experience that finding the personal primordial treasure has nothing to do with the outer world: to perform, to know, to look or to create a tool. The treasure of life is already within us. All we need to do is to wait for ourselves, which is not easy. Here, psychotherapists and meditation teachers have an interesting meeting place.

When I returned home in a meditative state, it was as if a personal, yet non-personal and primordial state of being or egolessness existed at the same time. Meister Eckhart (1260-1328) calls the process to meet God as Isness, which is a good word for the consciousness I found twenty years ago. It just is. Nothing was inclusive or exclusive. Intensive and focused, yet limitless. More of a whole body-mind than a sensory experience without emotional and cognitive content. "All-is-One" came after the experience. The first, second and third person didn't exist. It was something else, yet familiar.

I sometimes get glimmers of that state. It has been and still is an interesting challenge to accept, comprehend and integrate these few minutes, which I believe occurred clockwise or in space-time. I need to accept a not-knowing-state-yet-experienced Isness. Since then my path with heart has transformed into a heart with path. I often think of it as "good choices" and "wholeness", in my every-day life. A "Beginner's mind" is helpful to stay open.

The experience changed everything seen as a view from within and will probably continue to do so for the rest of my life. Isness is a state of being. My interest has moved from brain-mind to consciousness. Personal development is not only an emotional and cognitive process as in psychotherapy, although all sorts of feelings and thoughts exist and the mind is still very interesting for me. In a state of being we cannot see our own face. However, we can experience, use, enjoy and explore the whole in stillness from within. It is a treasure and a gift.

Chapter Eight

Openings and Promptings

Edward F. Kelly, PhD

Edward F. Kelly is a Professor in the Division of Perceptual Studies (DOPS) at UVA. He received his Ph.D. in psycholinguistics/cognitive science from Harvard in 1971, and spent the next 15-plus years working mainly in experimental parapsychology, followed by a similar stint with a large neuroscience group at UNC-Chapel Hill where he carried out EEG and fMRI studies of human cortical adaptation to natural tactile stimuli. He returned full-time to psychical research in 2002, serving as lead author of **Irreducible Mind** *(2007),* **Beyond Physicalism** *(2015), and* **Consciousness Unbound** *(2021), all produced under the auspices of Esalen Institute's Center for Theory and Research. He is now returning to his central research interest – functional neuroimaging studies of psi and altered states in exceptional subjects.*

Let me start by saying that I feel more than a little diffident in talking about these experiences of mine, which seem pretty pale in comparison with many of the others reported in this volume. Like William James I have only a "mystical germ"—the sense that "thither lies truth"—and nothing resembling a full-fledged mystical experience of my own. Nevertheless, the events I'm about to describe represent for me instances of genuine contact with James's "More" or Myers's "Subliminal Self," and they certainly influenced my personal and intellectual trajectory in major ways.

The first occurred when I was on my way home from France on a student ship in late Spring of 1963, following a year of wandering around in Europe and North Africa after graduating from college with no clear sense of what to do next. One evening I smoked hashish with some new-found friends on board, and finding myself a little disoriented and uncomfortable went back to my cabin and flopped down on the bunk in semi-darkness with my eyes closed. After a few moments I imagined myself being up in the air, flying about, and realized I could probably go anywhere I chose.

I suddenly found myself transported to a great height above the Nazi meeting hall in Nuremburg, of which I had recently seen a picture. I could barely recognize it from that altitude, and decided to try to go down toward it to have a better look. At once I found myself standing on the ground in that horrifying place, seeing the sights, hearing the sounds, and even smelling the sweat of overheated SS troopers in their leather uniforms. I had written my undergraduate honors thesis on creativity, and was aware of the role often played in it by unusual forms of imagination, but I had never before experienced anything remotely this intense, even in my most vivid dreams. Somewhere inside me, I realized, exist imaginative capacities that I'd never before encountered but that could be accessed when conditions were right. In retrospect, I had made contact with the Imaginal realm.

The second occurred late in graduate school, around 1969. I was working on my dissertation, which involved development of a computer program intended to improve automated content analysis by supporting recognition of the main senses of high-high-frequency English words in context. During that process I had become deeply disillusioned with the emerging "computational theory of the mind" (CTM), because it had become evident to me that no computer-based "intelligence," lacking consciousness, could genuinely grasp linguistic meanings, or distinguish systematically between metaphorical truth and literal falsehood.

At about the same time I had developed an interest in psychical research and experimental parapsychology, resulting from the sudden and totally unexpected appearance of mediumistic abilities in my only sibling, an older sister. I looked into the subject a bit on behalf of my mother, who was clearly worried, and quickly discovered its importance to William James, which surprised me. A thousand or so pages of my sister's automatic writing contained only marginal evidence of psi, but other aspects of her mediumship directly echoed observations made by James himself almost a century earlier. Her controls, for example, included typical characters such as an oriental wise man, an American Indian, and a couple of Christian saints. Their communications, moreover, seemed mostly to exemplify the "curiously optimistic blend of philosophy and water" that James had suspected of all coming from the same source.

A couple of other things, however, really grabbed my attention. For example, when "Wu Sung" came on board her face would undergo an extraordinary transformation, with her eyes seeming to stretch out and take on an oriental cast. I didn't think anybody could do that voluntarily. It also struck me as physiologically odd and puzzling that after a half hour or so of just sitting and talking quietly she would rush to the kitchen and slug down a large volume of orange juice or similar, as though dehydrated from intense exercise of some sort.

My interest had been piqued, and while continuing to work on my dissertation I began to read more widely on psychical research and experimental parapsychology. It was approaching time to take a job decision, but what to do? I had already received an offer for a lucrative position in San Francisco related to my dissertation, but had also begun corresponding with J. B. Rhine in Durham about possibly going there to do psychical research. In the midst of all this internal turmoil, our department was visited by Daniel Broadbent, one of the pioneers of the cognitive revolution, who gave a talk based on his book *Decision and Stress.* The central point of the talk was that even statistically sophisticated persons routinely fail to adjust their opinions as rapidly as they could, and should, in response to new evidence.

That night I had an unusually vivid dream in which I was again attending a lecture by Daniel Broadbent, but this time it was taking place out in a field somewhere, and I was standing at the back of the audience, at the edge of a stream that ran behind me alongside a tall bank on the far side. At some point in the talk I looked over my shoulder and saw that the bank was eroding, and that emerging from it were the spines of two imposing leather-bound volumes inscribed with the title "The Blake" in big gold letters. I rushed across the stream and clambered up the bank with the intention of retrieving those volumes, and woke up with my job decision made. I had recently been reading about the mystical poet and artist William Blake, you see, and clearly understood that this "Big Dream" was counseling me to head to Durham to engage with the really important stuff. Thus was made the most significant career decision of my life.

Another significant event that had occurred late in graduate school was that I attended, almost by chance, what turned out to be an enormously impressive talk on Advaita Vedanta by Swami Ranganathananda, a high-ranking member of the Ramakrishna Vedanta Society. I resonated both intellectually and emotionally to the core ideas of Vedanta and have continued to do so ever since. That talk also inspired me to make my way over to the Society's Boston branch, where its director Swami Sarvagatananda introduced me to the Yoga Sutras and some basic practices for meditation. I began twice-daily meditations at once, and continued this after moving to North Carolina in September 1971. I was living in an old farmhouse west of Chapel Hill, and had set aside a room specifically for that purpose. Two striking things happened that confirmed the potential significance of meditation as a tool for cognitive-psychological investigations of normally hidden potentials of the mind. In the first, I was just sitting there observing my breath and repeating an accompanying mantra, when I suddenly realized with crystal clarity that my consciousness had assumed the same relationship to the dimensions of the room that it normally bears to those of my body. In effect, "I" had become the size of the room. The instant I recognized this startling change, of course, it vanished.

In the second, I found myself standing on the back porch of the house I had grown up in, in Amawalk New York, on a large rural property associated with the reservoir system of NY City where my Dad was employed as a civil engineer. As I stood on the porch, looking toward the trout stream that issued from the bottom of the reservoir, I "saw" in a single vivid glance everything from the dam, far to my left, to our barn and the woods beyond, far to my right, and everything in between, all at once. What was startling about this is that I knew it was not physically possible to take in that much scenery without moving my eyes at least once.

Similarly, lots of other experiences I'd had in or near that spot were also simultaneously present in a way impossible to describe. Something within me, again, had been able to integrate large amounts of information into a single hyper-complex cognitive unit in a way I would not normally have been able to do. The bottom line? Serious scientific exploration of meditation and mystical experiences has barely begun, in my opinion, and is urgently needed!

These are the kinds of experiences that caused me to become an academic researcher exploring the fundamental nature of consciousness and to step away from the prevailing neuroscientific paradigm in experimental psychology. Following my work with J. B. Rhine, an appointment at Duke, and work at other Institutes in the area, I moved to the University of North Carolina and from there, in 2002, to the University of Virginia, where, as a research professor, I could devote myself full time to investigating the paranormal topics that most interested me.

Chapter Nine

The Awakening of Energy Flow Through an Eastern Body-Mind Practice

Anonymous, PhD

The author, who wishes to remain anonymous, was born in China and received a Doctoral degree in Neuroscience from a university in China. He is currently a professor at a University in the United States and has published extensively in the area of neuroscience and mind-body research. He has also received grant funding for this research from both NIH and private foundations.

When I was young my grandfather, who was a spiritual adept in China, began training me in intensive physical and mental practices. As a child, there were times when I was not a very good student as I wanted to play rather than make the full effort he asked for. Despite my ambivalent approach, the intensive training changed my body. The physical exercises were designed to train not only the muscles, but the control of the subtle energy or chi. For example, when training to find the energy point of the meridians in the body, a subtle energy channel would open and I could move further. I wasn't aware of it at an intellectual level, but I felt it and it worked. As my proficiency improved, I started to enjoy the training and there was no need to force me to do it.

I was 14 when I had my first spiritually transformative experience. I was training but had not had any experiences and was very frustrated. My teacher said, "You are making too much effort. Let's stop." So we stopped and I went to my room. That evening I did my dynamic practice and then sat down to meditate between 8 – 9 pm, and had my first transformative experience. To understand this experience, I need to provide some context. In China we divide the day into 2- hour units of time, and every 2 hours, our body's energy channels will switch in their dominance. For example, 7-9 pm is one time unit and at 9 pm there would be a switch to the dominance of different channels. This switch indicates a shift in the part of the body responding to the energy and the feeling of the energy changes. At 9 pm I suddenly felt the switch. I wondered, "What happened here?" And then realized, "Oh this is a switch in energy flow because of time." During the 7-9 period corresponding to the earth element, I felt the color of the energy as yellow. At 9 pm the energy shifted and became deep blue, as the water element became dominant. I both felt and saw this in a sensory fusion. Once I finally had the experience, I understood the underlying concept. It is similar to hiking and actually experiencing the topography shown on a map, as opposed to just looking at the graphic representations of the topography on a flat paper map.

My experience that night allowed me to finally grasp experientially what I had learned intellectually. It ignited an awakening, and I knew that the gift of training with my teacher had finally taken hold. Now I could feel the movement of energy as a strong flow rising up and moving through my body, modulated by the time of day and the spatial directions – east, west, south or north. The shifts in energy were accompanied by a feeling of expansion of my brain/mind, body and environment. The feeling of movement of energy within me also was linked to seeing unusual lights or sparks, usually bright and pure light, both inside and then outside, as the energy would follow certain paths.

Following this energetic awakening, I began to experience intuitive "messages" related to people I was interacting with. For example, I met a neighbor who was quite overweight. Usually obesity is associated with hypertension, but the "message" I received was clearly that this person had low blood pressure. I asked my neighbor, "Do you have low blood pressure?" He confirmed he did and I knew these intuitive messages were accurate. These intuitive messages regarding the health of others were a continuing part of my life that accompanied my continued practice of certain techniques.

After my initial energetic awaking, at about the age of 15, I found I was able to regulate the energy dynamics of my body using breathing patterns. I began to sense the energy characteristics in other people and in the natural environments. I learned that all natural environments have different energy characteristics that are related to the five elements. In addition, the human energy system has a frequency that can resonate with a certain environment, thus specific environments can help a person with a certain disease balance themselves. For example, water resonates with the kidney. I found I could send energy out to others. For example, one of my family members had a disease. I found I could use my hands to send out healing power. There is a caveat that is important to include concerning this feeling of energy and healing: I found that these experiences faded when I surpassed this stage but could be regained through certain techniques. However, my experience was that if one is attached to certain sensations or experiences, one will fail to progress in one's spiritual growth. Nevertheless, this awakening was associated with an intuitive understanding of the energetics of health and disease, and planted a seed for my future career.

At this time, I also began to have out-of-body experiences and vivid lucid dreams that contained revelations. These experiences began a new stage in my awakening process, with an unfolding of new skills and potentials. New information was suddenly revealed to me through images and messages. For example, I could suddenly write poems predicting events in the lives of others and thus help them in their own life journeys. Another time I received the message "the path is the goal," and suddenly understood that when we practice, our intention is focused on achieving the goal. But in focusing on the goal, we lose sight of the present moment experience. I realized that paying attention to the experience of the present moment IS the goal itself.

The process of spiritual awakening that began in my teens had a lasting impact on my career path. My dad, who was a professor, wanted me to study a pure science like physics or chemistry. However, when the seed of spiritual awakening was planted, I had a huge interest in human interaction and physiology, and wanted a career in medicine or psychology. To please my father I studied physical chemistry, but despite ranking top of my class, I was unhappy. Despite my Dad's disapproval, I began to study medicine, but quickly realized that medical school was focused on western medicine. Given my interest was in the psychological aspects of human disease, I continued my career in psychology and physiology in order to understand the relationship between the brain and behavior. Then I earned a PhD in neuroscience and I became an institute director in China. I eventually came to the US to be a researcher and professor.

The awakening process continues to transform different aspects of my life. Over time I have developed a deep connection with others and the environment. I feel my body connecting with many things in an invisible but deep and subtle way, that is, at the energy level. This formless connection feels direct and sensitive and beyond my thinking and judgmental mind. I call it intuition or an inner call. At the energy level, there is no separation, there is no you and me, you are in me and I'm in you. When I feel connected with a flower, I feel the desire for growth and power within the flower. These experiences have deepened my sense of kindness and compassion. When you have real feeling for a flower, then you are part of it; and then there is no differentiation between the two of you anymore. It is an experience of nonduality. However, in our current culture, we experience feeling separate from each other and have forgotten this "oneness;" this creates most of the problems we experience in our society. One way I like to express this is that human beings like human "doing" in modern society, and they forget the deep will, the deep inspiration, from within. For those who have not had a transformative experience, it is impossible to understand what the experience of deep connection really means. This is the real value of spiritually transformative experiences: they are the philosopher's stone that turns the base-metal of our feeling of separateness and isolation into the gold of connection with others and with this entire universe.

Chapter Ten

Swimming in the Blissful Ocean of Myself

Anonymous, PhD

The author, who wishes to remain anonymous, has an early background in art history and architecture, and then received his PhD in religious studies from a major university on the west coast of the United States. He is currently a faculty member in religious studies at a university in the eastern United States. His research is in South Asian studies.

This year is the 26th anniversary of the most profound event of my life, and its reverberations continue to ripple through my awareness at every moment. It happened on New Year's Day, 1996. The year before was characterized by a sense of personal chaos and turmoil; the wheels had come off the cart of my life. I recognized that I had to take a deep hold internally and provide my own agency to transcend the turmoil of what had been taking place. It was during this time of self-effort and initiative to steer myself through the wreckage around me that an awakening happened, just weeks shy of my 31st birthday. The experience was mystical, spiritual, and illuminative - a complete $180°$ shift.

There were precursors, murmurings, almost like tremors before a volcanic eruption. For example, during this time I began reading Indian philosophical texts and was experiencing low levels of bliss, and a sense of my consciousness floating upward above my head. I found that the more absorbed I was in the content of my reading, the more intense the experience of expanded consciousness became, and a sense of recognition that there is something greater.

I shared these experiences with my closest friend from high school who had grown up in an Indian meditation tradition. She said, "I wish you could meet my Guru. What you are reading is the philosophical foundation of my tradition." The next day she said, "You are not going to believe this, but She is coming to California!" I went to hear this monk, this meditation master talk on

Thanksgiving Day. During the talk, I felt overwhelmed by fatigue, as if a great weight were pushing me down into sleep; this was followed by a profound experience when my friend took me up to meet the teacher in what is called darshan. She introduced me to the teacher and as I looked into the Guru's eyes, I felt like I was looking into an infinite void – there was nothing there, absolutely nothing, and it shook me. It was terrifying. Over the next few weeks, I felt the presence of this teacher as a voice in my head – "Are you just going to keep going as if everything is the same? How long are you going to play this game of your daily routine, your life, your friends - this play that you have been involved in? You know it is not real anymore. It is not what you thought it was."

On New Year's Eve, I found myself with no plans, and I decided to enter the new year alone—to face my hardships and step forward without any distractions. I had recently been gifted a small crystal statue of Ganesh, the elephant-headed Hindu god of beginnings, believed to be the remover of obstacles and guardian of important thresholds. And so I thought, why not, and at midnight I prayed to Ganesh for the removal of any obstacles as I crossed the threshold into the new year. After which I settled down to meditate, even though I had never done so in my life... I lasted about a minute before I was derailed by my agitated mind. I thought, "I can't meditate. This is impossible! How do people do this?" Still, I had entered the new year bravely, alone, facing my fears, and it felt good.

I wanted to embrace the first day of the New Year, to mark it somehow. I remembered my friend's Guru was giving a New Year's talk three hours' drive away. I sent my friend a message and drove down to meet her. As Indian music was playing, I was ushered in and given a seat on the floor. While waiting for the program to begin, I suddenly felt a wave of pressure hit me from behind, shifting the entire atmosphere of the room. I turned to see a yellow-robed monk coming in—the teacher had entered the room and it felt like the sun was walking down the aisle. I was awestruck. She took her seat and as she talked, I felt she was speaking straight to me. Everything she said seemed to be addressing what I had gone through in that past year and what I was looking forward to. In my mind, I kept saying "Yes, yes!"

When they announced darshan, I felt great excitement that I could go up there. I wanted to tell her, "Yes!! I am on board with everything you are saying!" I wanted to be as close to her as I could, for as long as I could. I sat to her right and just watched her. I felt like a little child, bathing in the presence of the sun. In that moment a deep prayer arose, "Please, let me look into your eyes again." At that moment, she turned and looked right into me. Light was flooding out of her eyes and I couldn't hold her gaze. It was as if my head was pushed down to the ground. When the feather wand she used for offering blessings touched the back of my head it was like a tiny lightning bolt went through me. I saw this internal luminosity go from the crown of my head to the very center of my heart where I felt a tiny palpable pop, like a seed bursting open. I thought, "What was that?" As I sat up, that burst began to expand from the center of my heart outward in all directions like a well overflowing, and it was exquisite.

I experienced an expanding feeling of blissful freedom, contentment, clarity, and familiarity. It was the recognition, "I am home. I have never NOT been here." As I stood up and started for the back of the hall, I had the feeling, "Oh my God, I am going to fill this entire room! I've got to get out." I headed for the exit, and as I pushed through the door my consciousness expanded out over the entire desert and mountains, the whole vista. I felt like a floating point of perception in this expanded field of consciousness—swimming in the blissful ocean of myself.

The next day I returned to my apartment and sat to meditate with the same Ganesh statue: I closed my eyes and plunged deeply inward into a meditation that lasted for four hours! When I came out of meditation I was humming, my heart was like an internal sun, a nuclear furnace. It felt like the sun radiating - giving off this enormous power of luminosity in all directions intoxicating me as it flowed out through my being. While euphoric, I was simultaneously infused with a deep calm and clarity, and I knew this was my natural state. These meditations continued with powerful experiences for months.

After the awakening, all my senses were heightened. I had an increased sensitivity, especially to nature—a sense of aliveness: I recall how I marveled as I looked at the world again after this initiation because of how acute everything was: everything was sharper, there was a greater luminosity, it seemed everywhere I looked was exploding with vibrate color. There was an increase in the feeling of love for my family and others. It was like a veil had been lifted off. After the awakening love was more deeply revealed, and within that, the notion of unconditional love had matured well beyond my previous understanding.

Only afterward did I learn that I had had a classic experience of initiation called Shaktipat. Understanding the experience and integrating it into my life has become a lifelong process. Initially it was so powerful that I felt the need to remove myself from regular society. I voraciously consumed spiritual literature and deeply committed to the practices of the tradition. It was like a monastic period. By June, I had sold everything and moved to the meditation ashram of the teacher. There I learned to become more grounded and to integrate this internal experience with the active engagement of my external environment. It was a full two years before I reentered society, and my daily meditation practice has kept me tethered, if not anchored, to this vast calm internal awareness as I navigate my mundane activities and external responsibilities.

The spiritual awakening resulted in transformations in many aspects of my life. The experience has completely reoriented my manner of being in the world, my way of engaging with the world. It compelled me to redirect my academic interest toward Indian philosophy and theology, and I went on to complete a PhD in religious studies with a specialization in South Asian religions and Sanskrit. Specific to my university teaching and research, I am very aware that my awakening deeply shifted my own worldview; it opened me up to the truth values of the many philosophical, religious, and spiritual traditions of the world. I see part of my role as a teacher is to introduce students to the manifold ways of conceiving of reality and one's relationship to that reality—that these traditions are gateways to a deeper understanding of self through direct experience. They are aids to experientially engaging the most fundamental of human questions— who am I and what is all this?

Chapter Eleven

A Flash of Recognition

Anonymous, PhD

The author, who wishes to remain anonymous, received his PhD in South Asian Studies at a major East Coast university. His training is in the history of Indian religions and intellectual history. He is currently an assistant professor at a university in the West.

The main awakening event of my life was rooted in relationship. As a seven-year-old boy, I had the good fortune to find myself in the presence of the teacher in a tradition that fans back across multiple lineages that all emphasize the centrality of the guru-disciple relationship, most prominently Vedānta, Bhakti, and Classical Tantra. Upon being introduced to the teacher, she turned to me and gazed intently into my eyes; a powerful moment of recognition flashed between us.

Years later, at the age of nineteen, I experienced a series of tragic events that culminated in something like a dark night of the soul. In the wake of that ordeal, I began attending the local meditation center of the same teacher I had encountered as a child. Sitting formally in meditation for the first time, I noticed waves of luminosity dance in my inner vision, and as I watched the light my mind became tranquil. Encouraged by this and other initial experiences, I began attending retreats at the main ashram of the lineage of that teacher and offering selfless service. Through the practice of selfless service, I noticed the development of a new sense of inner confidence and self-respect and discovered what has become a lifelong inquiry: the power and potential of discipleship. In the course of participating in a few meditation retreats and workshops, I began to experience surges of love and ecstasy, an abiding wonder at the simple fact of existence, and an ardent longing for inner freedom.

During the summer of my twenty-third year, these and other momentums culminated in a spontaneous inner initiation on the birthday of that teacher whom I now recognized as my Guru. At the conclusion of a collective practice of textual recitation, the lights in the hall dimmed and we sang a devotional chant set to a particularly evocative classical Indian melody. I remember being surprised by how relaxed and comfortable I was in that space as the chant started. Though I was in a hall with hundreds of people and a spiritual master sitting before me, somatically and psychologically, it was as if I were relaxing in my living room on a Sunday morning.

As the chant unfolded, I casually watched my Guru sing. I noticed that she was giving her entire self to the chant and to the reality it invoked, and in that act of giving herself, nothing was held back. She was giving absolutely everything. I had never witnessed any one give like that. I had never seen such total love before in my life. As soon as this recognition dawned, a constricting knot on my heart, which I was not previously aware of, unraveled. One after another massive waves of bliss started to rise through my being. In this outpouring of bliss, I become aware of my own deepest self, the very core of my being, and realized with utter clarity its true value. I simultaneously became viscerally aware, by contrast, of the way I had treated my own self throughout my entire life and how utterly misguided and painful that self-conception had been. Tears began rolling down my face. The awakening experience was an explosion of love, the unleashing of indescribable bliss, and a recognition of inestimable value of my own essential nature.

Later the same day, this new revelation continued to unfold. During the afternoon festivities of the Guru's birthday celebration, I became possessed by an unbounded devotion and lost all inhibitions and normal self-consciousness. I marveled as an intoxicating love that knew no boundaries expanded, swallowing up all my conventional notions of self and world. At the conclusion of the celebration, I encountered a young man whom I had just met for the first time, and marveled as wave after wave of love for him flowed through me. With a great force, this love was radiating from the center of my body. The only reference point I had for this experience was falling in love romantically for the first time, but the magnitude was a million times more powerful, with no explicit connection to any one person or source.

The next day during a chant, I became powerfully absorbed in each round of singing and when I silently listened to the call of the lead chanters, my thinking mind disappeared completely. Then, when it was time to sing, I would move from that silence and merge with the sound of the chant, and as soon as the response ended, my mind again disappeared. For the entire duration of a thirty-minute chant I did not have a single thought, only an immersion in the sound punctuated by total stillness. Immediately after, while marveling at this new experience, I set out for a walk around a lake on the Ashram property; as I did my awareness began to open out naturally in all directions. The boundary of my self-sense was no longer limited to my body. All the objects in my field of vision—the lake, hillside, and trees—were vividly clear and I experienced them as shining inside me. This enlargement of my awareness persisted for four hours.

Overall, the most important transformations of these awakening experiences have been a consistent sense of trust in life itself and an affinity with the beauty of the whole. I have also noticed an expanded receptivity to the profound pain and tragedies of life and have continued to endeavor to not become numb to that dimension of reality. The transformation also precipitated a career change, from running a small business to pursuing a PhD in Sanskrit and Indian religions, and now teaching, researching, and writing as a professor in that field. This experience and the process of transmission from a living teacher both animate many of the research questions I am currently pursuing in the history of Indian religions.

A final anecdote. While consolidating my dissertation topic a few years into my PhD program, my advisors invited me to present some of my initial research in a public talk at the University. What was interesting about the event is that many friends from the local meditation community attended the event, as well as the faculty on my dissertation committee and academic friends and colleagues. As I read the talk, while I was carefully explicating the liberating vision of the philosopher and mystic who was the subject of my doctoral research, I made eye contact with a dear friend and fellow practitioner in the audience. As I shared the quintessence of the view, his eyes widened in recognition and wonder, and as they did the entire field of my vision was suddenly flooded with light.

After a brief pause, I continued the task of delivering the talk, but my perceptual field was now completely altered. The paper I read from, the podium in front of me, all the bodies in the room, and the entire space, were saturated with a blazing radiance, and the boundaries between people and objects were but a faint outline. I remember looking out at my advisors, sitting attentively, and seeing this exquisite light enveloping them. Thankfully, I remained calm and focused, and completed the talk gracefully. Before going to sleep that night, as I reflected on the experience, I had the thought: "maybe I didn't choose to write a dissertation on this particular luminary of medieval India; maybe he chose me." As soon as I posed this question, a bolt of energy shot up my back into my head and my entire being was filled with a benevolent energetic current that seemed to resound with a "yes."

Chapter Twelve

Awakening and Transformation

Duane Elgin, MBA, MA

Duane Elgin, MBA Wharton Business School, MA Economic History University of Pennsylvania is Co-Director of the Choosing Earth project: www.ChoosingEarth.Org and author of the book, **Choosing Earth: Humanity's Journey of Initiation Through Breakdown and Collapse to Mature Planetary Community**. *Other books include:* **Voluntary Simplicity, Awakening Earth**, *and* **The Living Universe**. *In the early 1970s, Duane was a senior social scientist on the "Presidential Commission on the American Future" and then a senior researcher in the futures group of the think-tank, SRI International. This description of awakening was taken from the second appendix of* Awakening Earth *originally published by William Morrow and Company in 1993 (ISBN 0-688-11621-3) and is available as a free download from my website: www.DuaneElgin.com.*
See: https://tinyurl.com/k57qjvk1

In late 1977, I reached a crisis in my life and I decided to take a half-year retreat from the work I had been doing (primarily strategic planning, futures research and policy studies for government agencies) and devote myself wholeheartedly to self-directed study and meditation. My goal was to come to the deepest understanding possible regarding insight into age-old questions: What are we doing here? What are our highest potentials? Where is evolution headed?

Intensive meditation over the previous ten years had given me glimpses of insight into these questions. This meditation practice was based primarily on Buddhist approaches but included study of a number of other spiritual traditions—in particular, contemplative Christianity, Zen, Hinduism and Taoism. In addition, for several years I had been a subject in a range of parapsychology experiments at a major think tank (SRI International) and had the opportunity to learn, first hand about the nature of our energetic connections with the ecology of consciousness permeating the universe. Finally, I accepted understanding that the structure of the universe becomes self-evident when we come into authentic union with it. As I entered this self-directed retreat, I was confident that if I approached the cosmos with purity of intent and a one-pointed desire "to know," the universe would meet me half-way with insights commensurate with my intention—and intensity—to know.

Throughout the winter and spring of 1978, I spent weeks at a time alone in my home. Approximately half of this time was invested in formal meditation and quiet contemplation. The remainder of the time was invested in reading dozens of books on subjects ranging from the world's spiritual traditions, physics, history, anthropology, psychology and systems theory. Over a period of months, I put up notes, charts, lists, diagrams, poetry, and pictures on the walls of my kitchen, living room, and bedroom. Gradually, my entire home was transformed into a single quest and question.

By late spring, the coherent picture of reality, identity and social evolution that I was seeking had not emerged. Instead of clarity, I was more confused than ever. I felt overwhelmed with the mountain of disconnected information and ideas that had accumulated over the years. Missing was the wisdom and insight that could make sense out of all the disorganized knowledge. Day by day and week by week I searched for clarity. Increasingly, I felt that I was wasting precious time in a fruitless, idealistic pursuit.

With my allotted time running out, I finally made a decision based on roughly equal measures of unshakeable confidence and utter desperation. I resolved to go to the end of this path by holding in consciousness the felt experience of all the questions now burning in my mind, body and soul regarding the nature of reality, life and evolution. I decided to hold fast to the experience of these questions until genuine insight and unifying awareness emerged, no matter what.

Physically rested and psychologically settled, on the morning of May first, I proceeded with irrevocable determination and concentration. Moment by moment by moment I nurtured the felt experience of knowing (and intending to know) until it became a continuous thread of resonant experience that filled every aspect of my consciousness. With immense difficulty—second by second, minute by minute, and hour by hour—the pressure and sensation of this conscious intention "to know" was nurtured and focused.

Toward the end of the first day, my experience was analogous to being inside a lighted hollow ball with fragments of mirrors covering the entire inner surface. Everywhere I looked there was a mirror of consciousness to reflect back every aspect of my life and existence. Mundane and profane, loving and indifferent, caring and cruel, intellectual and emotional everything was equally suitable for reflection in the mirror of consciousness. Only with utmost determination and unconditional self-acceptance could "I" stay with my self-experience and avoid endless distractions of judgment and imagination. Gradually, the pressure of conscious intention began to penetrate through layer after layer of my mentally constructed being. That night I slept lightly and arose early to continue with meditation.

With single-minded concentration, I moved ever deeper into this raw process of self-inquiry. Stripping away uncountable layers of self-pretense and returning, again and again, to the core intention, a humbled being gradually emerged. By the evening of the second day, all was constantly dissolving—even the mirror of consciousness that reflected my experience was dissolving and reconstructing second by second. All that existed was an ocean of living process in constant change. Nowhere was there anything that I could hold onto, or rely upon, or build upon. There was no fixed meaning, no fixed self and no fixed reality to be found anywhere. Again and again and again I was forced to abandon everything I had formerly known and simply trust the purity of my intention to carry "me" through the constantly disassembling reality. The unbroken silence of these seconds, minutes, hours and days now penetrated ever deeper, asking me to yield ever more until it felt as if nothing more could be surrendered. The second night seemed as if it could be the last of my life.

By the third day, the thread of intention had grown into a living field of awareness with a distinct and palpable presence and texture. With growing ease, I moved within a flow of self-referencing knowing that had acquired a life and momentum of its own. Eternities of time passed as morning moved into early afternoon. Then, in a sudden and unexpected rush, the seeking of the past six months and the concentration of the past three days finally burned a hole through the "ego-I." In an instant of grace, the years of accumulated questions and yearnings opened into a joyful, sacred and crystalline space of Knowing. Within a single, exhilarating moment, everything became transparently self-evident—throughout the entire range of my experience, all was in its proper place and "made sense." This knowing was direct, non-conceptual, self-evident and unmistakably clear. Accompanying this inner experience was a subtle radiance that bathed all that I could see with a soft light—the furniture, plants, and walls were all infused with a golden lustre and glow.

For the next several hours I stood virtually rooted in one place, physically stunned and mentally shocked to the deepest core of my being. Everywhere I looked, I saw an infusing radiance of immense intelligence, creativity and love. I saw, and directly experienced, that everything, including "empty space," is visibly alive. Space is not simply the absence of form, but the formless expression of infinite possibility. I also saw that the entire fabric of material reality is arising in a flow of continuous creation, that a reflective capacity is present throughout the universe, that an organizing geometry of elegant symmetry and simplicity infuses the universe, and that our cosmos exists within an ocean of boundless compassion. From mid-afternoon until early evening, with utter simplicity and breathtaking directness, every question about human evolution that I had ever imagined was effortlessly answered. Again and again, I was overwhelmed by the miracle of "ordinary reality"—by the immensity and depth of Life in which we are immersed, by the aesthetic and functional structure of existence, by the infinitely deep and compassionate Knowing that permeates the cosmos, and by the visible presence of Life-energy in the flow of continuous creation. This experience left me feeling unshakably confident in the deep integrity of creation, profoundly grateful, inexhaustibly happy—and finally home.

In the days following this experience, transparent insights coalesced into symbolic patterns representing the major stages of human evolution, both personal and civilizational. These symbolic patterns became living seeds of insight with a life of their own that coalesced into specific concepts, ideas and life-objectives.

Day-by-day, my entire life for the past 44 years has been transformed by this awakening experience.

PART TWO

STEs Occurring During or
Awakening From Sleep

This second category of essays includes STEs that were triggered in some relation to the sleep state, including during sleep, upon awakening from sleep or during lucid dreaming. Though the experiences themselves varied widely, the noetic aspect of expanded awareness was consistent across all. One author shared that after awakening from a lucid dream, she felt a "spontaneous, noetic sense of absolute Oneness activating every fiber in my body, with an embodied sense of interconnection with everything." Another said, after awakening in the middle of the night, that he was "filled with a marvelous warm sense of well-being. The darkness seemed alive, pervaded with a powerful harmonious force.... The force filled the whole universe. It was the essence and the source of all things." And, in this ongoing theme, a third said, "I suddenly experienced my sense of self – both physically and mentally – gently dissolving, and I began to experience a sense of 'oneness' with everything around me."

How could a sleep state engender a sense of expanded awareness? We propose that during a sleep state the conscious mind's control relaxes, there is a decrease in activity in the Default Mode Network, and thus the brain's filtering processes are reduced, allowing a more expansive state to be experienced.

Though these initial experiences were often somewhat similar in their noetic quality, the individuals' worldviews or frameworks in which they interpreted the experiences were often varied and in stark contrast to each other. In one essay the experience resulted in a change in "the root core of my belief system..... It was the closest I have ever come to touching infinity". In contrast another labelled the STE as an "anomalous experience...a momentary lapse in my perception of reality, not to be pursued or appreciated." As you see in these two examples, the interpretation was sometimes influenced by the individual's worldview when they entered into the experience. Though some worldviews crumbled, like a house of cards, when met with the noetic experience, others, though they gave a glimpse into an alternative lens on reality, remained in place for many years, as further experiences and evidence were required, in order to shift to a new framework.

As you read these essays, we invite you to notice your initial reactions to the experiences described. Do these reported experiences seem trustworthy and reliable encounters with an expanded state of awareness, or do you feel yourself dismissing them or even pathologizing them? Your initial response is often an indicator of your underlying world view, consciously or unconsciously held, that establishes boundaries for how you interpret the veridicality of anomalous experiences.

Chapter Thirteen

That Night

Jeffrey J. Kripal, PhD

Dr. Jeffrey Kripal is the J. Newton Rayzor Chair in Philosophy and Religious Thought and the Associate Dean of the Humanities at Rice University. He is also the Associate Director of the Center for Theory and Research at the Esalen Institute in Big Sur, California, where he also chairs the Board of Trustees. Jeff is the author of eight monographs, including, most recently, **The Flip***: Epiphanies of Mind and the Future of Knowledge (Bellevue Literary Press, 2019). He is presently working on a three-volume study of paranormal currents in the history of science and esoteric literature for the University of Chicago Press collectively entitled* **The Super Story***. His full body of work can be seen at http://jeffreyjkripal.com.*

I have written explicitly and many times of what I call simply "that Night." By such a simple phrase, I mean to point back to early November of 1989, when I was living in Calcutta and personally immersed in the fall festival of Kali-Puja, a major ritual cycle in West Bengal dedicated to the Hindu Goddess Kali, who is depicted in the spectacular art as "standing" on her prone, sleeping, or meditating husband Shiva, her four arms outstretched in various poses, her tongue sticking out in something between fury, ecstasy, and arousal.

I went to bed one night in the middle of the festival and did not wake up. Or better, I woke up, but my body did not. A conscious intelligent energy emerged from, well, from somewhere. As I lay there on my back, like Shiva, this Force, Power, or Energy (shakti) interacted with me erotically, spiritually, and physiologically all at once (maybe it came from "below" that horizontal line). I thought I was dying. Actually, I thought I was being electrocuted or having some kind of heart attack. It was that physical. It was not just a dream, though, yes, of course, it was clearly dream-like.

Maybe I was dying, or almost dying. Then the Conscious Energy imploded into my heart region, and I experienced myself floating to the ceiling, as if drawn "up" by some kind of invisible metaphysical magnet. Eventually, I got "back" and regained control of my body and muscles. I now felt this intense and immense Energy in my body, in my cells, as it were, that was now somehow encoded with too many thoughts and insights to manage or express consciously. It was terrifying. And it was great. And the event had some very practical results: my little library of books written over thirty years now, each and every one of them still trying to express something, anything of whatever that was.

Honestly, if you asked me today what that Night was about, I would say that I think it was all my future books flowing into me, at once, at that moment. I could not understand them, of course, because I had no context for them, but they were all "there," all at once, in that Night. It was this future flowing back into that past, which was my present in November of 1989. It was one gigantic premonition, inspiration, precognition, or time loop (Wargo, 2018).

(Excerpted with permission from the chapter, The Future of the Human(ities), by Jeffrey Kripal, in *Consciousness Unbound*, Kelly & Marshall, Eds., Rowman and Littlefield, 2021, pp 359-405. All rights reserved.)

Chapter Fourteen

Coming Home

Jessica Corneille, MSc

Jessica Corneille, MSc is a research psychologist specialised in spontaneous spiritual awakening experiences. She graduated with a Masters Degree in Psychology (Distinction) from the University of Greenwich, where she focused her studies on altered states of consciousness. Her mission is to challenge the default pathologisation of awakening experiences by helping to inform and encourage mainstream psychology to look beyond the current designated spectrum of 'normality', to encompass the transpersonal as something that is intrinsic to the human experience. Jessica has presented at a number of academic conferences, including with the British Psychological Society. She works for the Scientific and Medical Network, is part of the Galileo Commission steering committee, is a collaborator of the Emergent Phenomenology Research Consortium and Spiritual Crisis Network, and a certified Kundalini Yoga teacher.

February 20th 2016, at around 9.30 am.
Corner of Calle del Espiritu Santo and Calle de las Pozas, above J&J Books and Coffee, second floor – 28004 Madrid, Spain.

These are the coordinates for the time and space that I touched infinity.

I had moved to Madrid for work one month prior to my experience, and found myself in a very exciting period of my life. I went to parties, made new friends – lived as a standard 23-year-old embarking on a new adventure far from home. I had never considered myself 'spiritual' up until that point. In fact, whilst I had always been sensitive and grew up with a deep sense of curiosity (particularly towards the cosmos), frequently engaging in profound philosophical thought from a very young age, I had always rejected anything loosely pertaining to the religious and the spiritual. I was a proud atheist and had no intention on having my mind changed about that.

That's until that sunny, crisp February morning, when I woke up from the most intense lucid dream of my life, to a new day - and a new reality.

As I opened my eyes and scanned around my room, I was suddenly overcome and overwhelmed by a tremendous sense of deeply embodied interconnection with everything and everyone in the entire universe. A spontaneous and noetic sense of absolute Oneness imbibed and activated every fibre in my body, and it felt as though a veil had been lifted from my eyes, or as though my lens of perception had been cleansed, and I was finally able to perceive the true nature of reality beyond all layers of conditioning - a reality that had been staring at me in the face my whole life, but that I had been blinded to until that very moment in time. I was bathed in the clearest 'understanding' of an all-pervading, infinite, and benevolent 'intelligence' that not only permeates the universe, but is the very essence from which it is made.

Every cell in my body was suddenly overwhelmed with a love I had never previously experienced, in a state which remains indescribable after all these years. Of course, words are rather useless at conveying the experience, because it is not something that can be conveyed through active thought, but rather, through felt experience. It is the closest I have ever come to touching infinity: something so impossible to fathom with the mind, yet that paradoxically, felt so deeply familiar within the soul. It was coming home.

Much like awakening from sleep, it felt as though I had awoken from reality - to Reality. Having said this, I was equally aware of the existence of multiple 'layers' of reality or perception through which one could experience life, and of their equal importance as derivatives of the same, One truth. I was also filled with the deep realisation that the universe exists both outside and within each and every one of us, and that the answers already lie within. Through self-realisation, therefore, one could finally remember their true god-nature – not as a 'god' intended in religion and dogma – but as the connecting force that makes this universal dance possible.

An overwhelming tsunami of gratitude hit me that morning, and I cried for what felt like hours, but in hindsight was probably more like minutes – time and space entirely ceased to make sense in that state. Everything around me, both the animate and the inanimate, gleamed with life, and felt so quintessentially innocent and benevolent - and yet so deeply wise. In many ways it was like being reborn - seeing life through child-like eyes, with a child-like heart. Colours and shines, touch, sounds, smells and taste were amplified, and I felt as though my cells were vibrating with new life-energy. I had an overwhelming and acute physical sensation in my heart-space, third-eye and crown of my head, accompanied by a clear sense of pure white light emanating from these areas in my body, despite not having ever been exposed to spiritual or esoteric concepts alluding to energy centres prior to my experience. I felt totally electric and in awe, and yet at the same time in deep, limitless and oceanic peace, equanimity, bliss and satisfaction. I ran to the mirror in my bathroom to crystallise the moment: "This is real", I said to myself. "Always remember that".

I found it almost impossible to concentrate on the past or dream of the future in the midst of the peak of my experience. The very concept of doing so seemed utterly futile. I realised intuitively from that day onwards that the perfect state lies in the complete surrender to the ongoing, infinite 'now', and that the essence of this universe is Love - a Love that could only truly reveal itself in full immersion and dedication to the present moment.

The experience, which peaked for several months after that morning, is now fully integrated into my everyday existence - but it changed my life in almost every single measurable and immeasurable way possible.

The realisation of my position within an interconnected, alive, pure and conscious universe has intensified my connection to other people, leading me to become a lot more understanding of human tendencies, behaviours, patterns and conditionings. It has enabled me to become infinitely more accepting, trusting, empathetic and compassionate towards myself and towards others, and has made me more altruistic and better at communicating (and especially at listening). The experience also catalysed a deeper sense of connection towards other life-forms, strengthening my relationship with trees, plants and animals, enhancing my sense of duty towards protecting the environment, and thus leading me to make certain lifestyle changes to better support my mission.

My awakening also undoubtedly enabled me to cultivate a more harmonious relationship with my own life. The experience liberated me from a sense of conformism, freeing me from much of the anxiety that I used to hold around what others would think, or what was expected of me. It has led me to adopt more authentic behaviours, and enabled me to make more radical lifestyle choices which in turn have made me feel more confident, inspired and alive. I am now much more able to notice the detail, beauty and opportunity in every moment, whilst also being able to appreciate more clearly the bigger picture at play. I have become infinitely more sensitive to noticing the opportunity in every moment, even when things don't go according to 'plan'. I now find it much much more pleasant to flow in the chaotic stream of life, rather than to try and control it.

Practically speaking, my awakening has made me less materialistic, and more engaged in spiritual literature and contemplative practices - which continue to enhance my quality of life. It also left me with a deep sense of mission to serve and spread love to others. I let go of my aspirations of becoming an art curator, and quit my job in the contemporary arts and cultural heritage preservation in Madrid to move back to London and acquire the scientific tools to enable me to play a part in helping to better understand and reframe these experiences - typically misunderstood, stigmatised and pathologised by default in mainstream psychology - as experiences which carry the potential for deep healing and transformation, and which can lead to the unravelling of essential human qualities so desperately required in today's fragmented world.

Finally, from being a proud atheist, I came to understand that there is more than meets the two eyes and the five senses.

And that all that exists, is Love.

Chapter Fifteen

A Process of Uncovering: How I learned to Understand and Accept My Spiritual Nature

Steve Taylor, PhD

Steve Taylor PhD is a senior lecturer in psychology at Leeds Beckett University, UK, and a past chair of the Transpersonal Psychology Section of the British Psychological Society. He is the author of several best-selling books on psychology and spirituality, including **Extraordinary Awakenings, The Clear Light, Out of the Darkness** *and* **Spiritual Science***. His books have been published in 20 languages, and he writes blog articles for* **Scientific American** *and* **Psychology Today***. Eckhart Tolle has described his work as 'an important contribution to the shift in consciousness which is happening on our planet at present.'* www.stevenmtaylor.com

There has been an innate spiritual sensibility inside me for as long as I can remember, which just seemed to be there naturally. My spiritual development was all about understanding this part of myself, accepting it and allowing it to express itself.

When I was a teenager, I loved to spend time alone, reading or listening to music, or walking the streets. I was attracted to nature and to quietness, but there was very little nature in my city. In the evenings, when it was dark, I would often go back to my school, climb over the gates and wander around the school fields, simply because it was the only quiet and natural place near to me, where I knew I wasn't likely to encounter other people. The open space of the fields and the open space of the sky and the quietness around me filled me with a sense of calmness and wholeness. The clouds looked so real and alive that they seemed to be sentient and the black spaces between them amazed me with their deep richness. The sky was very important to me, since it was the only untouched open natural space I had access to.

I felt exhilarated by these states of well-being and wonder but I also thought there was something wrong with me. I didn't understand why I couldn't function the way I was supposed to. I was very introverted. I would sit in groups of people in a pub or youth club but find it impossible to speak. As a result, people began to think I was 'weird.'

At the age of 18, I went to university, and started a daily routine which I would follow for many years afterwards — I would stay up very late, usually till around 4 or 5 o'clock in the morning, and get up around lunchtime (or later) the next day. I loved going on walks when the streets were deserted and everyone else was asleep, enjoying the stillness and spaciousness. I felt a strong connection with trees and felt that in some way the trees 'came to life' when the rest of the city was asleep. I could sense their sentience, and felt that they were communicating with each other, as well as with me. However, I still suspected that there was something wrong me, and wondered if I would ever be able to fit in or live a normal life.

It wasn't until I was 22 that I began to understand my spiritual sensibility. I found a book called *Mysticism: A Study and Anthology* by F.C. Happold. It contained short excerpts from spiritual texts, and from the writings of Christian and Eastern mystics, and most of the passages resonated deeply with me. I recognized my own experiences in them. After that, I read Walt Whitman's '*Song of Myself*', D.H. Lawrence's '*Selected Poems*' and many other spiritual books.

Now everything began to make sense. I felt like I had arrived home and began to trust and accept my spiritual sensibility. It was a wonderful period — I felt ecstatic, uplifted, in touch with my own essence and in communion with the world. I still had no idea where I was going in my life but it didn't seem to matter. All that mattered was to be alive in the glorious present. It was wonderful to finally understand and accept myself.

It wasn't all plain sailing from this point though. Music was one of my passions, and at the age of 24, I was invited to join a friend's band — as bass guitarist — which led to my moving to Germany. There I began to disconnect from the framework I'd built up. I started to follow a typical musician's hedonistic lifestyle, smoking and drinking too much, surrounded by other people who did the same. As a result, I lost myself a little. After struggling for so long to connect with the core of my own being, I became disconnected from it again.

One night in Germany, I had the most powerful spiritual experience of my life. I woke up in the middle of the night, for no apparent reason, filled with a marvelous warm sense of well-being. The darkness seemed alive, pervaded with a powerful harmonious force. The darkness seems so thick with this force that I felt I could reach out and touch it. But it wasn't just in my bedroom. The force filled the whole universe. It was the essence and the source of all things. I knew that all was well in the world, that there was nothing to worry about. No matter how messy and frustrating life can be, no matter how much trouble there is in the world – in some way all of that is just on the surface. Below the surface the whole universe is gently vibrating with warm radiance and is filled with harmony. And I was part of that harmony. I was being carried along by it, out there in space, surfing on the waves of an ocean of bliss.

The experience was a recalibration, a realignment with my spiritual nature. Not long afterwards, I returned to the UK. Although I had always an impulse to be a writer, I now realised exactly what I was supposed to write about: spirituality, psychology and philosophy. Then I learned about the field of transpersonal psychology – in a book by Ken Wilber – and knew that I belonged there. I returned to university to study transpersonal psychology at master's level, which led to a PhD, then a role as a university lecturer and researcher.

Ever since, I have felt that I'm doing exactly what I'm meant to be doing, researching and writing about spiritual awakening, as well as exploring other unusual phenomena, such as psi and near-death experiences. Since I understood and accepted my spiritual nature, and found that the right avenue to express myself, my life has unfolded naturally and easily, as if I'm being carried along by the current of a river.

Chapter Sixteen

From a Sense of Oneness to Interacting With the Divine:
Empirical Evidence?

Gary E. Schwartz, PhD

Dr. Gary E. Schwartz has been a Professor of Psychology, Medicine, Neurology, Psychiatry, and Surgery at the University of Arizona for more than thirty years. He was an Assistant Professor of Psychology at Harvard University and a tenured Professor of Psychology and Psychiatry at Yale University. His integrative research bridging mind-body medicine, energy medicine, and spiritual medicine has been funded by the National Science Foundation, the National Institutes of Health, the National Institute of Mental Health, and numerous private foundations. He has published more than 500 scientific articles and chapters and authored or edited 25 books. He directs the Laboratory for Advances in Consciousness and Health at the University of Arizona (www.lach.arizona.edu) and served as the founding president of the Academy for the Advancement of Postmaterialist Sciences (www.AAPSglobal.com).

It was the late 1970's, and I had recently learned of emerging findings in astrophysics that the fundamental constants in the universe were too finely tuned to have likely occurred by chance per se. Such findings challenged my Western, materialist framework, and I was confused.

Early one morning around 3 am, I was up thinking about astrophysics, and I was looking out of a large picture window in our living room. I was on a sabbatical from my professorship at Yale University, and I had some free time to ponder. Being mid-winter, the trees were bare of leaves. I could see hundreds of stars peeking through in the sky.

And then, completely unexpectedly, I suddenly experienced my sense of self – both physically and mentally – gently dissolving, and I began to experience a sense of "oneness" with everything around me. Not just the stars, black sky, and dark trees, but the walls and couch in the living room. "I" felt completely at peace and somehow "at home," and I reveled in the wonderous experience for a few minutes.

However, having no background in religious studies or mystical experiences, and being well-trained in clinical psychology and psychiatry, I labelled this "anomalous" experience as a momentary lapse in my perception of reality, not to be pursued or appreciated. It would take anomalous experiences that were "evidential" and could be "independently validated" to awaken me to the existence of a greater reality.

Of the subsequent spiritual events I have experienced over the course of my fifty-year academic career (from my PhD at Harvard in 1971 to 2021), probably the most challenging and awakening was the first time I was inspired to "ask the Universe" a question, and I received an answer that I could verify.

I shared this unexpectedly evidential awakening experience in my book *The G.O.D. Experiments: How Science is Discovering God in Everything, Including Us.* The acronym G.O.D. stands for "Guiding, Organizing, Designing" process (Schwartz, 2006), what Larry Dossey refers to as One Mind (Dossey, 2014), Sri Aurobindo calls Supermind (see Pradhan, 2020), and Ervin Laszlo calls Source (Laszlo, 2020).

My transformative awakening experience was triggered by a suite of astronomically improbable, seemingly inexplicable synchronicities which I initially included as an Appendix in *The G.O.D. Experiments* book, and later was featured in my book *Supersynchronicity: Where Science and Spirit Meet* (Schwartz, 2017). Very briefly, here is my transformative awakening experience.

It was the mid 1980's, and my atheistic / western science supported / materialist framework was being shattered not only by emerging evidence for the existence of extraordinary organization and order in the laws of nature and the cosmos (from physics to astrophysics), but also by personal experiences that suggested that the human mind was part of, and could interact with, a greater mind. One night around 2 am, I was inspired to do something I had never considered nor tried before; I decided to mindfully "ask the Universe a question."

My question was very simple: Could the Universe give me another name for God?

My reason for asking this question was that I had been raised in a reform Jewish household where I was taught that God – if 'he' existed – was an angry white man with a beard and cane who sometimes spread insects on people (i.e., one of the plagues claimed in the Passover). When I heard or thought the word God, my mind functioned like a classically conditioned dog. The automatic and primitive "angry white man" association interfered with my envisioning the Source in terms of 'It' being abstract, complex, universal, caring, creative, infinite, and whole.

Before I finished asking the question (silently and somewhat sheepishly), I immediately heard in my head the name "Sam," and I began laughing. Would you have thought the name Sam was another name for God? Also, do you know what the origin of the word Sam is? I said to myself "This is either my creative unconscious, or I am experiencing a Woody Allen movie."

Startled by hearing the seemingly silly Sam name, I felt compelled to get out of bed, go into my study, and look up the origin of the word Sam in my old, Webster's 2nd edition, unabridged dictionary. Of course, I knew that Sam was short for Samuel. However, to my utter amazement I discovered that the root of the word Samuel came from the Hebrew "Shemuel" which literally translated means "The Name for God."

When I read this fact, my jaw metaphorically dropped to the floor.

I wondered, what were the odds that upon asking the Universe for another name for God, that (1) the word Sam would pop in my mind, and (2) its origin would refer to the name for God, by chance alone? Was there some rational explanation for this coincidence? As Yogi Berra once said, "Some things are too coincidental to be a coincidence," and as the medium Susy Smith rephrased it, "Some things are too coincidental to be accidental."

As I explain in detail in The G.O.D. Experiments books, I carefully analyzed at least eleven possible alternative hypotheses, beginning with chance and prior knowledge[2] hypotheses and ending with potential paranormal hypotheses.

---

[2] For example, did I know Hebrew? The answer was no. Or, had a read a book that discussed the origin of the word Samuel? Again, the answer was no.

However, the hypothesis that I found most disconcerting was the possible spiritual explanation, stated in the form of a wisdom lesson, "Be careful what you ask for." What I had done was in a state of deep genuineness and humility, I had purposely asked 'the Universe' a meaningful question, and maybe the hypothesized One Mind / Supermind / Source mind had intentionally given me an answer that I could verify empirically.

Honestly, I was so shaken by the Sam / name of God experience that I decided I would not touch it with a 10-foot pole (or even a 110-foot pole), and I resisted repeating the secret personal experiment of asking another question of the Universe for over a decade. When I was finally mature (and brave) enough to repeat the secret personal experiment, I began to cautiously ask the Universe questions. I experienced numerous instances where novel responses popped into my head that I could verify empirically (e.g., see the "Remember the Diamond" evidence in *The G.O.D. Experiments* book).

It would take a combination of a couple of decades of empirical research, integrated with complimentary personal experiences, for me to release my materialist identity and become a postmaterialist scientist and person. In the process, this required that I lose credibility with many of my mainstream materialist colleagues, a sometimes painful but ultimately positive (and peaceful) consequence.

I predict that it is only a matter of time before some scientists will become brave enough to address the human interaction with the Divine hypothesis in a formal and sacred scientific way (Plante and Schwartz, 2021). Can you imagine how humanity might change if we knew, scientifically, that human interaction with the Divine was not only possible (in principle, for anyone), but was part of the very fabric of the Universe itself?

References

Dossey, L. (2014). *One mind: How our individual mind is part of a great consciousness and why it matters.* Hay House.

Laszlo, E. (2020). *Reconnecting to the source: The new science of spiritual experiences, how it can change you, how it can transform the world.* Griffin.

Plante, T. G. & Schwartz, G. E. (Eds.). (2021). *Human interaction with the divine, the sacred, and the deceased: Psychological, scientific, and theological perspectives.* Routledge/Taylor & Francis.

Pradhan, R. (2020). Supermind and the supramental consciousness: Sri Aurobindo's integral metaphysics. In: *Metaphysics of consciousness.* Springer. https://doi.org/10.1007/978-981-15-8064-2_8

Schwartz, G. E. (2006). *The G.O.D. experiments: How science is discovering God in everything, including us.* Atria Books.

Schwartz G. E. (2017). *Super synchronicity: Where science and spirit meet.* Waterside Productions.

Chapter Seventeen

'No More Searching'

Paul Marshall, PhD

Paul Marshall is an independent researcher with interests in mysticism, religion, philosophy, and science. He studied natural sciences at the University of Cambridge and received his MA and PhD in religious studies from Lancaster University. He is author of **The Living Mirror: Images of Reality in Science and Mysticism** *(1992),* **Mystical Encounters with the Natural World: Experiences and Explanations** *(2005),* **The Shape of the Soul: What Mystical Experience Tells Us About Ourselves and Reality** *(2019), and coeditor of* **Beyond Physicalism** *(2015) and* **Consciousness Unbound** *(2021). Details of his publications can be found at https://mystical-encounters.com*

In 1981, during a holiday break from university, I had an expansion of consciousness that revealed previously unsuspected depths of self and world—or so it felt at the time. As a teenager, I had been enthusiastic about science, captivated by the beauty of nature, given to philosophical musings, and, in my later teens, dedicated to writing poetry and fantastical short stories. The atomic theory of matter enthralled me early on, with its promise of explaining everything in terms of a few basic particles arranged into a hundred or so elements. However, I grew uneasy with confident scientific claims, although unable to identify where the problem lay. Certainly, a growing realization of the incompleteness of scientific theory was a factor, and also the troubling thought that science could portray living beings—myself included—as nothing more than complex chemical reactions.

I embarked on an adolescent phase of pervasive doubt, questioning what it means to 'know' and 'understand'. Another puzzle that caught my attention could be expressed as 'Why now?' Given the vast multitude of moments that make up time, it seemed improbable that my present moments in the mid 1970s should be the ones that happen to be actual, all others gone or yet to be. Whether or not the puzzlement was justified, it did lead me to think that all moments are equally actual, a moment a hundred years ago just as existent as my current one—all times coexist. The puzzle of time led to the puzzle of self-identity—is today's I the same as yesterday's or tomorrow's?

So it was that when I arrived at university to study the natural sciences, I brought with me a bundle of intellectual and existential questions. I was intent on coming to grips with the strange new physics, relativistic and quantum, but disappointment set in. It soon became clear that there would be no questioning of fundamental ideas. I therefore looked outside the course and found a creative outlet in the writing of a novel. The central character seeks an awakening but, in the final chapter, abandons the search as futile.

A turning point came when I read a little about Zen Buddhism. From here I was led to Carl Jung, and during the Christmas break I began to read his *Memories, Dreams, Reflections.* The book inspired me to record my dreams, and the expansion of consciousness followed a few days later, while I was asleep. When I woke up, I was left with an extraordinary sense of wholeness, far beyond anything I could have imagined possible. At first I did not remember the core experience, but memories appeared soon after. I have described the experience at length in my book *The Shape of the Soul.* Here I can give only a brief account.

Gazing at a vast world of light, I think with tremendous relief, 'No more searching', as if at long last I've found what I'd always sought. I realize that I know everything, understand everything, and it's so simple, so obvious—how dim-witted I've been not to see it before. The world is packed with detailed luminous structures, and I take notice of several human figures, some located in other times. The nearest figure is myself, my body, including head and face, consisting of a trail of images. It is a shock to see myself like this, with no life of my own but animated by the great life and intelligence of the world. There is dismay and humour at the discovery, my ordinary self put in its place. Yet while I am this flimsy, dependent thing, I am also the mind that supports and contains everything. My worries fall away, and I tell myself not to forget what I've discovered—it is too important. There is some sense of my life ahead, but I remember little or nothing about it later.

The realization that everything exists within myself is now tempered by the discovery of very many others for whom the same is true. I am aware of numerous centres of consciousness, like little rings, and I'm amazed that such tiny beings encompass everything. As I view them, a tremendous feeling of love arises, pictured as light streaming from the centre of my body, reaching out to all. By comparison, how impoverished is my usual capacity to love. I feel impure and uncomfortable in this atmosphere of love. Perhaps it is now that the experience comes to an end.

But the searching had not finished. When memories emerged, I tried to repeat the experience through meditation, so attractive was it, but without success. Nevertheless, the experience had a great impact on me, affecting the course of my life as I laboured to understand it and take in its most important lesson—the possibility of inclusive love. While I still struggle with that lesson, I have hopefully made progress towards the understanding. Initially I could barely find the words to express what I'd discovered, so far outside my ken was it. I struggled to say 'mind is fundamental' or 'everything exists in consciousness', but that was the gist of it. I had inadvertently become an idealist.

A few years later I came upon an idealist philosophy that promised to make sense not only of the experience but the puzzling physics. This was the metaphysics of Gottfried Wilhelm Leibniz, according to which the world consists of a multiplicity of perceptual agents, each of which expresses the entire universe in its perceptions. The philosophy sits well with the frame dependence of special relativity and the holism of quantum physics. So I set about looking into the matter, and the first fruit of my labour was *The Living Mirror* in 1992. Doctoral research on mystical experience at Lancaster University followed, published as *Mystical Encounters with the Natural World* in 2005. Since then, as an independent researcher, I have continued to delve into the application of mystical insights and idealist metaphysics to the mind–body problem and the puzzles of modern physics.

Chapter Eighteen

Awakening

Federico Faggin

Federico Faggin received a Laurea degree in Physics, summa cum laude, from the University of Padua, Italy, in 1965, and moved to Silicon Valley in 1968. He developed the MOS Silicon Gate Technology in 1968; the world's first microprocessor, the Intel 4004 in 1971, and several highly successful microprocessors, like the Intel 8080 and the Z80 produced by Zilog, his first startup company. Faggin was CEO of several high-tech startup companies he founded and directed since 1974. He is currently president of Federico and Elvia Faggin Foundation, dedicated to the science of consciousness. Faggin has received many international awards, including the 2009 National Medal of Technology and Innovation, from President Barack Obama. In 2021 he published his autobiography Silicon.

My interest in consciousness was sparked in 1987 when I was studying neuroscience as background material for the R&D work on artificial neural networks that I was conducting at Synaptics Inc. As cofounder and CEO of that Silicon Valley company, I wanted to develop silicon chips that could emulate neural networks, thus creating the basic building blocks for cognitive computers.

All the neuroscience books I was reading were describing brain operation in terms of electrochemical activity as if that movement of molecules and signaling were identical to sentient perception. Surprisingly, the word consciousness was never mentioned, and I was asking myself: "How can electrical and biochemical signals become sensations and feelings? Clearly the two cannot possibly be the same thing."

The computer can neither be aware nor consciously know anything. It can only translate the complex pattern of electrical signals generated by the sensors of the odor molecules into another electrical signal: the name "rose." The comprehension brought by consciousness is not accessible to a computer. And herein lie the crucial limitations of artificial intelligence. Science cannot explain why we have feelings. Based on science, consciousness should not exist either in computers or humans.

During the time I was struggling to understand how to make a conscious computer, I also found myself in a deep existential crisis. I had achieved everything that common wisdom says should make me happy, and I was beset with a deep dissatisfaction. I had reached a stage of quiet desperation. I was wondering, "What do I live for?" And, at the same time, I felt compelled to maintain a facade, given my responsibilities as husband, father, and head of a promising company. But I almost felt dead inside.

I realized that I was preventing myself from experiencing my despair. I lived hiding in an artificial cocoon that I had constructed to protect myself from feeling my deepest and most genuine feelings. I only imitated being happy. I asked for help. I prayed, not verbally, and not even consciously, searching for an answer to my fundamental questions: "What is the meaning of my life?", "Is death really the end of everything?"

In December 1990, while I was with my family at Lake Tahoe during the Christmas holidays, I woke up around midnight to drink a glass of water. When I went back to bed, while waiting in silence to fall asleep again, I felt a powerful rush of energy-love emerge from my chest, the like of which I had never felt before and couldn't even imagine was possible. This feeling was clearly love, but a love so intense and so incredibly fulfilling that it surpassed any possible idea I had about what love is. Even more unbelievable was the fact that I was the source of this love. I perceived it as a broad beam of shimmering white light, alive and beatific, gushing from my heart with incredible strength.

Then suddenly that light exploded and filled the room and then expanded to embrace the entire universe with the same white brilliance. I knew then, without a shadow of a doubt, that this was the "substance" of which all that exists is made. This was what created the universe out of itself. Then, with immense surprise, I knew that I was that light! The entire experience lasted perhaps less than one minute, and it changed me forever. My relationship with the world had always been as a separate observer perceiving the world as outside of me and separate from me. What made this experience astonishing was its "impossible" perspective, because I was both the experiencer and the experience.

For the first time in my life, I was simultaneously the world and the observer of the world. I was the world observing itself! And I was concurrently knowing that the world is made of a substance that feels like love. And that I am that substance! In other words, the essence of reality is a substance that knows itself by self-reflection, and its self-knowing feels like an irrepressible and dynamic love.

This experience contained an unprecedented force of truth because it felt true at all the levels of my being: at the physical level my body was alive and vibrant like I never felt it before; at the emotional level I experienced myself as an impossibly powerful source of love; and at the mental level I knew with certainty, and for the first time, that all is "made of" love. That experience also revealed the existence of another level of reality never before experienced: the spiritual level, in which I felt one with the world.

This was direct knowing, stronger than the certainty that human logic provides—a knowing from the inside (gnosis) rather than from the outside. A knowing that involved for the first time the concurrent resonance of all my conscious aspects: the physical, emotional, mental, and spiritual. I like to think that I have experienced my own nature both as a "particle" and as a "wave," to use an analogy with quantum physics impossible to comprehend with our ordinary logical mind.

The particle aspect was the ability to maintain my unique identity despite being also the world, which was the wave aspect. Thus, my identity is that unique point of view with which One—All that is, the totality of what exists—observes and knows itself. I am a point of view of One. This experience maintained its original intensity and clarity over time, and it changed my life from the inside out, continuing to have a powerful impact to this day.

After the awakening experience, I started reading books like the Tao Te Ching and the Bhagavad Gita. These ancient texts were reflecting and enriching the understanding of my own awakening, revealing that since time immemorial humans' personal journeys had been illuminated by experiences like mine. Prior to my awakening, those books would have only fed a superficial literary interest, since "soul" had little real meaning to me. Afterward, soul meant that alive scintillating loving and self-knowing substance of which everything is made: it became a lived experience rather than an intellectual idea.

That awakening also opened the door to a stream of other spontaneous and extraordinary experiences of consciousness that have continued to this day. They included vivid dreams, deep intuitions, expansions of consciousness, out-of-body experiences, and other states of consciousness that greatly expanded my previously limited concepts about reality, constrained by preconceived ideas.

A little at a time, I began to realize that the truly important journey is the inner one. And with the same dedication I had showered upon my technological and scientific research, I committed to discovering the truth about myself, beyond the perceptual distortions fostered by prejudices. I had the opportunity to see how deep my "rabbit hole" was and how much my life had been conditioned by false beliefs and ideas. These experiences also made me relive many emotions and events I had repressed and forgotten.

After twenty years during which I spent 30 to 40% of my time doing personal work, I began to take seriously the idea that consciousness could be a fundamental aspect of nature already present in some fashion in the atoms and molecules of which everything is made. This idea emerged gradually, due to the impossibility of explaining how consciousness could arise from the material complexity of our brain. I kept thinking: how can a physical inert structure that possesses only outer aspects give rise to inner experiences? The concept of complexity has nothing to do with the sensations and feelings that populate our inner world. In fact, today's computers, which are very complex, do not have a shred of consciousness.

There was no logical alternative: the inner world of meaning must also be an irreducible property of all that exists from the very beginning. Meaning and matter must be like the two faces of the same coin.

This topic fascinated me because it had the potential to explain and unify the existence of the outer and inner realities that I had been experientially exploring for twenty years. Science and spirituality, until now irreconcilable, could find a deep union rather than a simple juxtaposition of convenience. So, I decided to withdraw completely from all my other activities and for the next few years, focused on developing a model of reality based on the assumption that consciousness is fundamental rather than deriving from matter. The model I developed, the CIP framework (Faggin, 2021), is based on quantum field theory—the most accurate model of reality we currently have—adding to it the idea that consciousness exists before the Big Bang, which is considered the beginning of our universe.

References

Faggin, F. (2021). *Silicon*, Waterfield Publications. and see www.siliconthebook.com

Chapter Nineteen

Strange Dreams, False Awakenings and Spiritual Surges

Bernard Carr, PhD

*Bernard Carr writes: my professional area of research is cosmology and includes such topics as the early universe, dark matter, black holes and the anthropic principle. For my PhD I studied the first second of the Universe, working with Stephen Hawking at the Institute of Astronomy in Cambridge and the California Institute of Technology. I was elected to a Fellowship at Trinity College, Cambridge, in 1975 and moved to Queen Mary in 1985. I am the author of around three hundred scientific papers and the books **Universe or Multiverse?** and **Quantum Black Holes**. I am also developing an expanded paradigm of physics which accommodates mind and spirit. I was President of the Society for Psychical Research in 2000-2004 and am currently President of the Scientific and Medical Network.*

In this essay I will describe some experiences which I've not discussed openly before but which have profoundly altered my life. Although I would describe them as 'psychical' rather than 'mystical,' I still regard them as 'awakenings' in the sense that they have made me aware of non-material domains and prompted me to think more deeply about the nature of consciousness. Indeed, since many of them have occurred in the aftermath of some powerful dream, they have literally involved awakenings. I will describe a series of experiences rather than a single one because they are interconnected. In my case at least, the expansion of consciousness has been a gradual process, involving many steps.

My first inkling of an awakening – though I didn't recognize it as such at the time – was at the age of eight at my preparatory school (St Chad's School in Lichfield). I was lying in bed in my dormitory in the dark, discussing with a friend the strange electrostatic effects of rubbing a comb, when what felt like surges of electricity started to flow through my body. They became more and more powerful and I thought I would be electrocuted. So I became frightened, jumped out of bed and ran to the matron, whose bedroom was down the corridor. When I explained the problem, she fetched one of the masters, who lay on the bed and found nothing wrong.

A decade later, shortly before going to Cambridge as an undergraduate, I developed an interest in out-of-the-body experiences (OBEs) as a result of reading *The Projection of the Astral Body* by Sylvan Muldoon and Hereward Carrington and *Techniques of Astral Projection* by Robert Crookall. These books discussed techniques for inducing the experience, which I was eager to try. This led to several episodes of sleep paralysis and I recall waking up one night in the lounge of my home, while my physical body was still in bed. With hindsight this was what I term a false awakening (i.e. a type of OBE in which one awakes in one's familiar physical environment but not in one's physical body) but I was sufficiently frightened by the experience to stop my experiments for a while.

When I went up to Cambridge University in 1968, I joined the University Society for Psychical Research (CUSPR) and the Buddhist Society (CUBS). With the CUSPR, I conducted ESP experiments, visited haunted houses and investigated mediums under the guidance of Tony Cornell, a leading ghost-hunter who was to become a close friend. I also carried out an experiment to investigate whether a person's weight is reduced when they fall asleep as a result of their astral body temporarily leaving their physical body. The results were not very convincing but this illustrates my early desire to address spiritual questions scientifically.

With CUBS, I took up Samatha meditation and studied Buddhist philosophy. I was a poor meditator, although I did experience a 'nimmita' image (an intense blue light) during a visit to Vietnam several decades later and long after I'd stopped this kind of meditation. However, in 1976, shortly after completing my PhD and returning from a year in California, I became interested in Kabbalah and started another type of meditation involving chakra visualisations. This had a stronger effect on me and one night I had a powerful dream in which I encountered a 'being', whom I was sure represented death. When I awoke, I felt waves of energy passing through me and experienced the same 'electrical' surges which I had experienced at St Chad's, along with intense imagery associated with the dream. I was convinced that I was either dying or being possessed, so in a panic I phoned Tony Cornell, who despite the time (3 am) calmed me down. Although I didn't die or become possessed, this was the start of a series of powerful dream encounters, which have continued for most of my life, so I regard this episode as my key awakening.

Most of my psychic experiences have occurred in the strange threshold state between waking and dreaming. A key feature is the aforementioned electrical surges and I've found that recollecting the dream image immediately triggers further ones, so I have to blank my mind in order to stop them. There have also been various other effects, such as the shaking of my body, hearing a high-frequency vibration and whooshing sounds, chakra activation, a slowing of my heart-beat and cracking sounds in the room. I would also sometimes see figures, hear voices (on one occasion I heard the recitation of a poem), be entranced by ethereal music, and perceive text (although the words never made much sense). Such impressions might be dismissed as hypnopompic or hypnagogic hallucinations but they felt very real.

I have the impression that these experiences are sometimes the after-effects of an OBE but I rarely experience an astral exit of the traditional kind. More often, I seem to get out of bed in the usual way and only realise that I'm not in my physical body when something strange happens. For example, the light may not go on when I flip the switch or my bedside radio stays on when I reach out and turn it off. Or I look in a mirror and my body is deformed in some way. Sometimes I get out of bed and open the curtain but find the wrong view. Once this happened while I was staying in a hotel in New York in 1969. When I opened the curtain I was surprised to see the view from my bedroom at home in England.

These experiences are distinct from lucid dreams, which I experience more frequently and involve another sort of awakening (i.e. cognitive awakening while still in a dream). However, these may also contain anomalous features. For example, sometimes I meet myself – on one occasion an older future self and on another I met myself at a party and the other me pointed out that there was a third me sleeping in the bed next door. Once I dreamt of having a conversation with my Kabbalah teacher and was awoken by a knock on the door. This was my teacher and I was amazed when he told me about our dream conversation since this was clear evidence of telepathy. However, I then awoke again, so this was another kind of false awakening. Sometimes I encounter dead people in lucid dreams, although I accept that they may just be projections of my imagination. My most convincing evidence for survival came when Tony Cornell – who'd always promised to 'return' if possible – appeared to me in a dream shortly after his death. He was in his car and talking about his will. A week later I visited his wife, who told me that she'd been looking for his will and eventually found it behind the sunshield in his car.

Occasionally I've had threshold experiences during the day but this worries me. I'm happy to encounter transcendental realms at night (when safely tucked up in bed) but it feels dangerous during the day. Indeed, I gave up meditation for many years on this account. My failure to confront the fear provoked by some experiences has doubtless impeded my spiritual progress but their influence on me has been profound. They have increased my interest in spiritual matters, convinced me that consciousness is not just the froth of the brain and awakened me to the existence of 'higher' realms. Although they've not impacted my professional work as a cosmologist, they have certainly motivated my attempts to find an extension of physics which can accommodate such phenomena. For if consciousness really can leave the body and visit non-material domains, this is clearly a challenge to the standard physical paradigm. My own 'hyperspatial' proposal invokes extra dimensions going beyond ordinary space and time. This idea is already invoked by mainstream physicists, although most would surely dismiss both my experiences and the theories proposed to explain them.

I've been reluctant to write about these episodes until now, partly because I suspect it may stop them happening but also because it might result in my academic colleagues regarding me as deranged. Nowadays the experiences only happen rarely, so the first factor is not so relevant, and the opinions of colleagues are of less concern now that I'm retired. Sometimes I harbour doubts about the authenticity of my experiences. But then I'm reassured by the fact that thousands of people have reported similar experiences, including some other contributors to this volume, so maybe it's time to come out of the closet!

Chapter Twenty

Puerto Angel

Shantena Augusto Sabbadini, PhD

Shantena Augusto Sabbadini is a physicist, philosopher and a scholar of Chinese classics. As a physicist he worked at the University of Milan on the foundations of quantum physics and at the University of California on the first identification of a black hole. In the 1990s he was scientific advisor of the Eranos Foundation, an East-West research center founded by C.G. Jung and Olga Froebe-Kapteyn in 1933. Presently he directs the Pari Center, an international institute located in the small medieval village of Pari, Tuscany. He is the author **of Pilgrimages to Emptiness, Rethinking Reality through Quantum Physics, Tao Te Ching: a guide to the interpretation of the foundational book of Taoism** *and* **The Original I Ching or Book of Changes: The Eranos I Ching Project**.

In 1972 I was working on the first identification of a black hole (Cygnus X-1) at the University of California Santa Barbara under the guidance of Jim Hartle. It was very exciting work, because it was the first concrete evidence of the existence of those weird celestial objects that showed up as mathematical consequences of Einstein's general theory of relativity. By the end of that year the theoretical part of the work was done and I decided to spend the winter break vacationing in Mexico with my wife.

We drove down from California, visiting archeological sites, churches and markets and taking many pictures, like the good tourists we were. But the last part of that journey took a surprising turn and was the seed of much subsequent development.

It started while we were travelling across the mountains from Oaxaca to Puerto Angel, a small fishing village on the Pacific coast. The road joining those two localities was at the time an unpaved track across a mountainous region covered with a splendid jungle.

The jungle is what first impressed me. It was my first time in a tropical forest and its intense aliveness felt awesome. From time to time we would drive by adobe houses with their milpas (fields of corn and beans), pigs and chickens running about, food cooking on clay stoves, women weaving on hand looms.

It was a new world to me, and I felt like this was what I had been seeking in all my previous journeys, longing to escape from the grip of European civilization. In some deep sense I had arrived home.

And yet I could not be at home there. A barrier was separating me from that world. It was as if I was wearing an armour of metal and plastic: my car, my camera my maps. I was cruising through that world enclosed in a hard shell.

Two events that happened during that journey intensified that feeling and contributed to the crisis that was to come in the following days.

The first was spending the day with a family of local indios. A young Mexican man to whom we had given a ride invited us to meet his friends, who most kindly welcomed us into their home and shared their food with us, sitting on the ground inside the house. The food was chewy goat meat that I would have found repulsive in other circumstances, but in that heartful context seemed the most delicious food I had ever tasted. At sunset we took leave from our hosts, both of us deeply touched by their kindness, simplicity and earthliness and continued on our way to the coast.

The second encounter took place a few hours later. A truck had fallen off the road and was lying on its side on the escarpment. Its lights were still on, so we descended to inspect it. Inside were a young man at the wheel and a middle-aged woman, who turned out to be his mother. The son was unconscious, the mother badly bruised but otherwise ok.

We loaded them both into our car and spent the rest of the night trying to find medical assistance for the young man. I omit the various adventures of that search. We did not find a doctor, but at dawn we could finally deliver mother and son into the care of a nurse in a rudimentary medical ward. Meanwhile the boy had recovered consciousness, so we felt ok continuing on our journey. Around noon we arrived in Puerto Angel.

The angel's harbour: the place is idyllic. We lodged in a palm leaf hut and swam in the crystal clear water. All was perfect. Except me. The emotions experienced during our arrival kept stirring inside me. The sense I had of being locked in a hard shell of ego and separation intensified. The simplicity of the environment made all my defenses stand out. I felt a stranger there. More fundamentally I felt a stranger in life, in the fragile and splendid exuberance of everything.

Thus, a descent to hell began. I could not stand myself, I wished I could sink into the ground, knowing well that that was impossible, there was no escape from the curse of being me. I felt I was losing my mind.

That hell lasted for three days. Then suddenly a radical change happened. One morning (it was Christmas Eve) I woke up in a space of pure light. It was as if a veil had fallen from my eyes. The fight with my ego of the previous days had become utterly irrelevant. I was no longer there. All around me glistened as if just created. Everywhere existence celebrated the wonder of being. And I felt part of that celebration, I felt I was that celebration. Washed of all my sins, I felt innocent like a newborn. I was not there and yet I was more present than ever.

The whole day passed like that, a day of blessing and deep peace. Everything, both life and death, was utter perfection.

But the next day, Christmas day, I woke up with a high fever. It was as if my body was incapable of containing so much intensity. By the evening I was delirious. My wife set out to look for a doctor. The one she found was drunk, but still better than no doctor at all. The drunk doctor injected me with something powerful and the fever started to decrease. Slowly I returned to the world of the living.

I do not remember how many days I lay on my bed in the hut. But I remember well the cemetery across the palm leaf wall of the hut. Through the spaces of the wall I could see the tombs, utterly simple, pink, light blue, yellow. They were inviting, they said: come rest with us.

At last the fever subsided. I felt extremely weak, but alive and able to walk. I remember an image of that convalescence. My wife and I were sitting on top of a cliff. Big waves crashed on the rocks below us. Each wave was an explosion of foam and the splashes rose up to us. There was so much energy in those waves that just looking at them I felt fragile. They were beautiful, but too strong for me. Contemplating them I felt it was time to return. I suddenly longed for the routine of everyday life. I thought of the university almost with nostalgia.

But beside that feeling there was another one, just as clear. However much I might wish to return to normality, the former normality was no longer there.

Something radically new had entered my life and nothing would ever be the same again.

In the following years, experiences and readings provided me with a language to think about 'mystical experiences'. But at the time of Puerto Angel I still did not have such a language. A few months later, in a letter to my closest friends in Italy, I was still trying to explain the Puerto Angel epiphany in Hegelian terms.

The impact of that experience on my work and career was not immediate, but it was profound. It opened up a perception of our existence in this vast and mysterious universe that was far from being reducible to rational models. And it brought to my awareness a large gap between the profound mystery we scientists (and especially we astrophysicists!) were trying to capture in our equations and the daily reality of our academic life. The realization of the mystery was confined to the scribbles on our blackboards and completely forgotten in our daily life, where publishing, competition and career were much more relevant concerns.

Puerto Angel was the turning point of the inner process that five years later would bring me to leave academia. In the meantime, I completed my work on the identification of Cygnus X-1, I returned to Italy and for a few months I worked in the astrophysics department of the University of Milan.

But my heart was not in it any more. I was dreaming a very different dream, a dream involving nature, community, self-sufficiency, inner exploration. Every morning I went to my office and fell asleep with my head on my desk. It was time to give up habit and security and follow the call of my heart.

By the end of 1977, with a small group of friends, I founded a spiritual community in the hills of Tuscany. The community has gone through many transformations since then, but it still exists and flourishes.

My life also went through many transformations. I traveled to the East and did many menial jobs. Eventually I became scientific advisor of the Eranos Foundation, an East-West research center co-founded by Jung in the 1930s, and in that context I translated various Chinese classics.

Then in the early 2000s I went back to the Tuscan hills as Director of the Pari Center, an international institute devoted to the exploration of the interactions between science, art and the sacred. And at present, together with my wife, I am creating an eco-spiritual center called The Valley Spirit on the Sierra Nevada in Southern Spain.

It all links back to Puerto Angel. Would I have lived a different life if that journey had not happened? An impossible question of course. But I feel a deep sense of gratitude when I remember that experience.

PART THREE

STEs Occurring Spontaneously During Daily Activities, Often Without a Specific Triggering Event

The essays in this category most often represent a series of gradual insights that bring the individual closer and closer to a sense of unity with all that is around them. One person wrote, "There was no 'Road to Damascus', no blinding light ... just a gradual opening to a presence in the heart." The experiences often seemed to happen in the midst of "ordinary" activities, which were suddenly perceived as "extraordinary." During this experience the usual ordinary state of awareness was transformed into a wider, expanded awareness.

This shift in consciousness happened in many contexts, from a jail cell in Spain to the bush of Africa. We include here the classic example of Arthur Koestler's epiphany in a jail cell in Spain (Koestler was an early Member of the Scientific and Medical Network). He said, "I was standing at the recessed window of cell No. 40, and, with a piece of iron-spring that I had extracted from the wire mattress, was scratching mathematical formulae on the wall... I was trying to remember how to derive the formula of the hyperbola, and was stumped; then I tried the ellipse and the parabola, and to my delight succeeded.... Now, as I recalled the method and scratched the symbols on the wall, I felt the same enchantment. ...And then, for the first time, I suddenly understood the reason for the enchantment: the scribbled symbols on the wall represented one of the rare cases where a meaningful and comprehensive statement about the infinite is arrived at by precise and finite means..... The significance of this swept over me like a wave."

In another essay the author talks about his experience as a 19-year-old in a beautiful part of South Africa. He says, "There, at Sengwa was the beginning of the long trail that has brought me to new ways of being in nature which encompass academic biology and science, but which are in fact much older and wiser.... This feeling of being in the midst of the deepest sacred and of the most wise never left me for a moment during the five months or so I spent at Sengwa."

It is possible that as in other types of STEs, when one is intensely engaged with an activity or with the natural environment, there is a reduction in activity in the Default Mode Network and a suspension of the egoic narrative of the mind, allowing an experience of unfiltered expanded awareness.

We invite you to look back at your own experiences to see if you also may recall a moment when you were engaged in an activity and shifted to an experience of "flow." Perhaps it was a moment when there was a loss of "self" consciousness and you experienced a movement into an expanded state of awareness, where you appeared to be effortlessly engaged.

Chapter Twenty-One

The Light of Love

Janice Miner Holden, EdD

*After 31 years on the University of North Texas (UNT) Counseling Program faculty, Jan Holden retired in 2019 as Professor Emerita of Counseling. Beginning in 1988 with her doctoral dissertation, her primary research focus has been counseling implications of near-death and related experiences. In this research area she has over 50 refereed journal publications; several chapter and book publications, including lead editorship of the **2009 Handbook of Near-Death Experiences**; and over 100 national and international presentations. Among Jan's numerous recognitions is the 2019 UNT Eminent Faculty Award, one of the university's highest honors. Since 2008 she has served as editor-in-chief of the International Association for Near-Death Studies' scholarly **Journal of Near-Death Studies**, and she serves currently as that association's President. Her website is www.janholden.com.*

So far in my 71 years in this lifetime, I've had four mystical experiences. This was my first.

The year was about 1979, making me 29 years old, living in the Chicago, Illinois area where I had grown up. My husband, George, and I had been married for about a year, I had been a high school psychology teacher for about five years, and I had just finished my master's degree in counseling. I had recently read Raymond Moody's book, *Life After Life*, about near-death experiences (NDEs). George and I had signed up for a Psychosynthesis weekend workshop. In the interim, we had bought a house. As it turned out, the first day of the workshop was our first day of access to our new house. We had paid for the workshop, so we were going, but my heart wasn't in it; I was anxious to begin life in our new house.

The second day of the workshop, our leader, Tom Yeomans, led us in a guided imagery exercise. He instructed us to identify some as-yet unresolved challenge in our life. At the time, I and my psychology course were very popular with the students, but I had had a problem with one type of student. He—always a male—sat in our lecture hall up and away from the rest of the students. In an attempt to engage him and encourage his involvement with the rest of us—for his own developmental good—I would urge him to come down and join the rest of us, and he would resist. We would get into a power struggle that ended in discord. The only time I had sent a student to the principal's office was as a culmination of one of these struggles. I sincerely wished to know how to handle the situation differently but was genuinely stymied as to how I possibly could.

That was the challenge I had in mind when, after standard induction of relaxed breathing, etc., the eyes-closed guided imagery went something like this:

> You are outdoors, sitting under a tree on a lovely day. In the distance, you see a mountain. You stand and begin walking toward it. As you walk, a symbol of innocence appears, and you bring it with you as you walk. Upon reaching the mountain, you see a winding path upwards and follow it, accompanied by your symbol. When you reach the top, you turn a corner, and before you is your symbol of the ultimate benevolent source of wisdom in the universe. You present your problem and wait to receive anything the source might offer you. (Pause of a few silent minutes.) As the time approaches for you to leave, you convey gratitude for anything the source offered, and you turn to descend the mountain path. As you walk back to your place beneath the tree, your symbol of innocence vanishes, and as you sit back down, you reflect on anything you want to take with you and keep from this experience.

In my experience, my symbol of innocence appeared as a three-year-old girl who took my hand as we walked. When I got to the top of the mountain, I had no idea what symbol of wisdom would appear, but when I turned the corner, there was the Being of Light from NDEs. I presented my challenge, and as I waited, the imagery took on a life of its own. First, the Light entered the little girl, and I was amazed to see it fill her and emanate from her chest. As I held her hand, I felt its power—and then the Light came into me, filling me and emanating from my chest.

As I lay there on the floor, eyes closed, I wept profusely. At one point, my face was so tear-and-snot-covered that I opened my eyes, got up, stepped over other people, got to my purse to retrieve and use a tissue, went back to my place, laid down, closed my eyes—and was right back in the experience of the Light. Even as I write these words right now, I'm overcome with chills to remember the overwhelming sense of love I experienced. There were no words, no verbal message—just this experience of profound embodied and emanating, exuding Love.

If I had to put words to the "message" of this experience, it was: Just love him. Let him be as he is. See him in a broader developmental context: just because he is isolating now doesn't mean he always will. The best way to foster his development is to accept him now where he is, and just love, Love, LOVE him.

After that experience, I was transformed—in the most subtle yet profound way. I didn't "try" to be different; I just WAS different. During my remaining six years as a high school psychology teacher, I had "that student" a few more times. But I never again had a problem with him.

I also credit that experience with my subsequent effectiveness as a counselor. No matter where my individual or couple clients were, or where I hoped they would ultimately arrive, developmentally, I more fundamentally just loved them where they were. Although I did not restrict myself to a person-centered counseling approach, I resonated experientially with a favorite saying of its founder, Carl Rogers (1980) who quoted Lao Tsu (c 600 BC), author of the *Tao Te Ching*:

If I keep from meddling with people, they take care of themselves;
If I keep from commanding people, they behave themselves;
If I keep from preaching at people, they improve themselves;
If I keep from imposing on people, they become themselves.

Though Rogers did not attribute this attitude to a transpersonal source, for me, its true source is a wisdom that transcends the usual personal limits of space, time, and identity. The attitude is not chosen and cultivated; it is the product of a transformation resulting from an encounter with an ultimate divine force: the Light of Love.

Reference

Rogers, C. R. (1980). *A way of being.* Houghton Mifflin.

Chapter Twenty-Two

Spiritual Transformation and Evolving Frameworks

Anne Shumway-Cook, PT, PhD

Anne Shumway-Cook, PT, PhD, FAPTA is Professor Emerita in the Department of Rehabilitation Medicine at the University of Washington, Seattle, Washington. Her research focused on understanding the physiologic basis for balance and mobility disorders in neurologic and geriatric populations, and the translation of this research into best clinical practices for assessing and treating balance in order to reduce falls and optimize mobility function. She has published extensively, and with Dr. Marjorie Woollacott co-authored the textbook **Motor Control: Translating Research into Clinical Practice**. *She has practiced meditation for more than 50 years.*

I grew up in a Catholic family. My Mother converted to Catholicism as a young adult and frequently shared her faith and beliefs with my sisters and myself. My Father identified himself as an agnostic. Growing up in the Catholic church, I was taught to believe that because of original sin (the fall of Adam and Eve), we were all sinners, but through faith in Jesus Christ I was saved from my sinful nature. The key to salvation was belief in the savior. While raised in the fixed beliefs of the Catholic church, my Mother strongly encouraged me to explore and form my own spiritual beliefs as I grew older.

God Is Love: My first spiritual transformation. It was a beautiful sunny spring morning. I was 36 years old walking in a park near my home, pushing my recently adopted son in his stroller. I was filled with a sense of wonder and gratitude for the amazing gift of my son. While walking I had an extraordinary experience. Time seemed to stop. I felt an intense sensation of fullness, I was filled and overflowing with joy and extraordinary happiness. I felt an intense sense of love surrounding me, filling me, flowing through me, connecting me to my son and to the world around me. I felt the spatial boundaries of my body dissolve, I was one with the love surrounding me, the love spilling through me, I was one with the world.

I felt this profound "knowing" that I was experiencing God. I knew it was God's love that I felt surrounding me and flowing through me. I "knew" without a shadow of a doubt that God knew ME, loved ME, intimately, personally and unconditionally. I knew that my deep unconditional love for my son was exactly how God loved me. That it was God's unconditional love flowing through me that gave me the capacity to love unconditionally too. I knew that God's unconditional love filled the world, it flowed through me and through all aspects of the world, deeply connecting all of us to God and to each other. God's true nature was unconditional love and it filled the world, all was sacred.

As I think about that experience, I realize that my spiritual framework at the time was deeply Christian so my interpretation of the experience in the park was that I was experiencing God, and God's true nature above all else was unconditional love. I believed (and still do) that Jesus also experienced God's unconditional love for him personally and for the world. The metaphor he used to articulate his experience was that God was like a loving Father (Mother), and God's love was like a Father/Mother's unconditional love for a beloved child. What transformed for me in the moment of that experience was my understanding of the true nature of God; that God was not a harsh, condemning judge of humanity who sent his son to save us from our sins, but instead was pure and unconditional love. I felt God's unconditional love for me personally and the entire world. The experience changed my understanding of God, but did not necessarily impact my understanding of my own true nature.

God Dwells in You as You – My second spiritual transformation – Ten years later I was visiting a friend who was staying at a Spiritual Ashram. As I walked in the front door of the Ashram I saw a large banner hanging overhead that said "God Dwells in You as You". My eyes were transfixed on this sign, time seemed to stand still for me. I was immediately transported back to the park and my experience of God's love filling me and surrounding me. I realized in that moment that unconditional love was not just God's true nature but mine as well. Suddenly I had a new understanding of Genesis 1:26 "Then God said, "Let us make man in our image, after our likeness." I realized that if I am in fact created in the image and likeness of God, then like God, my true nature is unconditional love. In that moment my spiritual framework changed; the Christian concepts of original sin, humanity as sinners needing a savior, disappeared like smoke dissolving. It was replaced with a profound sense of knowing that God dwelled in me, and the entire cosmos. I knew that my true nature and the true nature of everything is this world was unconditional love.

Impact of spiritual transformations on daily life. The intensity of these two spiritual experiences has not lessened over time. The emotions associated with these experiences continue to this day to range from intense joy, when I remember who I truly am, to despondency that I cannot seem to live that understanding in my day-to-day life. What has changed is the priority I give to my spiritual practice day to day and a better understanding of the underlying intent of that practice. I believe the intent underlying my spiritual practice is to help me remember the truth of who we are and endeavoring to manifest that truth in each moment. A quote by Rumi perfectly describes this intention: "Your task is not to seek for love, but merely to seek and find all the barriers within yourself that you have built against it." I don't need to seek Divine unconditional love; my true nature is unconditional love. My spiritual practice is designed to help me understand and remove the barriers within myself that keep me from living this truth.

Paloutzian suggests that "spiritual transformation constitutes a change in the meaning system that a person holds as a basis for self-definition, the interpretation of life, including the overarching purposes, ultimate concerns, values, meanings, and corresponding life directions of an individual" (2005, p. 334). For many people, an experience of spiritual awakening results in both a shift in self-definition and a change in life direction, perhaps a career change. While my spiritual experiences changed my self-definition, they did not result in a change in my career path. They did however change the underlying intention that I brought to my career. I was raised by parents who stressed the importance of service. "We are here to serve" was a constant message I heard while growing up. At the age of 13 I met a group of physical therapists (PTs) and knew I would serve through this profession, whose theme is "Physical Therapy: The science of healing. The art of caring". I did in fact become a PT and spent 40+ years in clinical practice, getting a PhD and teaching as well. My subsequent spiritual experiences did not alter my career path, but strengthened my understanding of why I was a PT, it was to serve each patient with compassion and skill. My spiritual path has been and continues to be essential to my ability to serve the world compassionately.

Some thoughts on the nature of transformation. There is a common belief that "time" changes our understanding of the nature of an experience, and the impact of that experience on our lives. For example, when an individual experiences a sudden catastrophic medical diagnosis or trauma, the immediate interpretation is often an overwhelming belief in the devastatingly negative impact of that experience on one's life. Over time the interpretation of the effect of that experience can shift dramatically. As the individual begins to see the positive effects of that same experience, they begin to understand that their life has been utterly transformed for the better because of that experience. It is not "time" per se that changes the experience, but rather the underlying framework (belief system) used to interpret the impact of that experience on life that has changed dramatically. Thus, transformation occurs because of a shift in the underlying framework used to interpret experience. To understand spiritual transformation, we need to understand shifts in the underlying framework used to interpret spiritual experiences.

My spiritual experiences have taught me that subsequent transformation can manifest in many ways. An experience can result in an immediate transformation, that is an instantaneous change in an underlying framework used to interpret the experience. But transformation can also occur repeatedly over an extended time frame. With every significant spiritual experience, our underlying spiritual framework changes, thus the lens through which we see and understand all prior experiences changes as well. Thus, there is not a single "awakening", but many "awakenings", as one's underlying explanatory model evolves and changes. For some people, an underlying spiritual framework is grounded in fixed immutable beliefs, and thus not readily subject to change. But for others, an underlying spiritual framework is dynamic and evolving, subject to change and modification in response to curiosity, self-inquiry and experience. The key to spiritual transformation from my perspective is summarized by Ravi Ravindra's advice: be a searcher, rather than a believer!!

Reference

Paloutzian, R. F. (2005). Religious conversion and spiritual transformation: A meaning-system analysis. In: R. F. Paloutzian & C. L. Park (Eds.), *Handbook of the psychology of religion and spirituality* (pp. 331-347). Guilford.

Chapter Twenty-Three

How I Learned About the Limitations of Science

Sarah S. Knox, PhD

Sarah Knox received her PhD and MS degrees from Stockholm University in Sweden; and began her career as a Principal Investigator at Stockholm University and the Karolinska Institute, where she did epidemiologic research using the Swedish Twin Registry. She subsequently returned to the United States, to the National Institutes of Health, where she focused on cardiovascular research before assuming a leadership position to guide the implementation of the National Children's Study. Dr. Knox is currently Professor Emerita at West Virginia University School of Public Health and a member of the WVU Cancer Institute and the Galileo Commission. Her current research interests focus on biophysical signaling in cancer and the integration of physics, consciousness, and spirituality in healing. For further information see:
https://www.researchgate.net/profile/Sarah_Knox4

The two spiritual experiences that I am about to relate have been difficult to integrate into my scientific work but have guided its direction and reinforced my conviction that the tenets underlying the current biomedical paradigm are grossly inadequate for understanding the nature of human reality (Knox, 2010; 2018; 2020).

The first occurred before graduate school. Without any active efforts such as meditation, I was suddenly transported into a state where I experienced universal love. I felt unconditional love for every person I met and had no fear of anything or anyone. I could have gone anywhere by myself in the dark of night and felt absolutely no fear. This "state of grace" persisted for about two and a half days. I understood with clarity that the only reason societies need laws and prisons is because we lack this sense of universal love. At the time it occurred, I was agnostic and had no idea how to interpret it, other than as some vague notion of "humankind's potential." I have never been able to recreate that experience.

In graduate school, I was interested in pursuing consciousness studies and decided to begin by focusing on the physiological effects of EEG biofeedback. The literature was full of claims that changing one's brain wave frequency could change one's state of mind by triggering an altered state of consciousness called the "alpha state." This was reported to be a state of relaxation that evoked feelings of inner peace. Despite these claims, no one had actually measured the physiology or the subjective experience of a random group of people taught to increase alpha using biofeedback; however, experiments had been done on meditators and non-meditators, showing more alpha in the meditators.

After improving the biofeedback technology, I measured heart rate, skin conductance, muscle tension and the QRS and T-wave components of the ECG on participants being trained in alpha enhancement. I compared people who were able to successfully increase their alpha waves by 15% or more to those who weren't. There were no physiological or psychological differences between the two groups. These results taught me a valuable lesson. The materialist assumption that changing a single physiological parameter related to brain waves could change consciousness was not supported by the data. The assumption underlying the hypothesis was that the cause of mind is matter. In the meditation studies, there was a correlation of alpha brain frequency with subjective experience, but correlation is not equivalent to causality. There are basically four primary frequency ranges in the human EEG (alpha, beta, theta and delta). How could they possibly differentiate between the innumerable feelings and subjective states that humans experience?

After graduate school, I pursued a traditional academic career. But I was living a double life. I had been doing 'hands-on" healing since I was a child (on myself). I was brought up in a Christian church and believed what Jesus said about hands-on healing that "all this you can do and more." When I was 9, I had a large birth mole on my leg that I eradicated simply by repeatedly putting my hands on it. As an adult, I practiced only within my family. I was agnostic and thought that the healing worked through a simple transfer of energy and that if I could just figure out the mechanism, I would be able introduce it to science. I never told any of my university colleagues about it for fear of losing my scientific credibility.

All that changed one Sunday morning when my daughter woke with a stomach ache and couldn't walk and couldn't eat. She rarely got stomach aches, but I didn't see it as an emergency. She had been up at 5:00 am but by 10:00 am when she was still lying listless on the couch, I called the triage service and made an appointment to see a pediatrician at 2:00 pm. She was clearly ill, so I decided to do some "hands-on" healing on her in the meantime. I did this simply by picturing the energy flowing from my hands into her body. Because she was my child, a natural feeling of love intensified as I did this, and as the love increased, the energy flow from my hands intensified, building to a crescendo that felt as if a dam had burst. I did this for several minutes and about 10 minutes after I had finished, she hopped up and started to play. The stomach ache was gone. We went to the doctor at the appointed time. As I described how the pain had started and progressed, the pediatrician said decisively that I was describing appendicitis. She was perplexed as to why it had stopped. I said I didn't know, and we left.

This should have been a positive experience but it was not. The implication that something so subjective as love could influence the flow of energy, totally contradicted my left brain need for objective science. I remember that as the energy burst with the increasing intensity of the love I was feeling, I silently screamed to the universe: "you don't seriously expect me to tell them that!?" I was still convinced that energy healing was real but concluded that I had no idea what I was doing and would stop. I decided to stay on the research side of things. Unfortunately, this research doesn't get funded by traditional sources because they haven't understood the implications of quantum mechanics and don't even know that the body is full of voltage potential networks that serve important somatic functions (Knox, 2020).

Over the years, I have personally been healed of a myriad of conditions by acupuncture, including breast tumors (my mother died of breast cancer) (Knox, 2010). However, my observations are that despite the fact that acupuncture is an exact science (Knox, 2021), the clinically most effective acupuncturists are those who integrate some form of spirituality into their practice. In the underlying tenets of acupuncture, not only matter but also personal consciousness and emotional state are theorized to play an important role in the flow of energy and health. Based on repeated quantum physical experiments, we know that the observer is never separate from the observed phenomenon, implying that the consciousness of the healer and the patient are critical components that need to be integrated into clinical research.

References

Knox, S. S. (2010). *Science, God, and the nature of reality: Bias in biomedical research.* BrownWalker Press.

Knox, S. S. (2018). Wave / particle duality in biomedical research design. *Molecular Biology,* 7, 3: DOI: 10.4172/2168-9547.1000215.

Knox, S. S. (2020). Why the biomedical research paradigm must change if we are to win the "war on cancer". *American Journal of Biomedical Science & Research.* DOI: 10.34297; ISSN: 2642-1747.

Knox, S. S. (2021). The science of acupuncture: Biomedicine, physics and beyond. Submitted for publication.

Chapter Twenty-Four

Mystical Awakening

Arthur Koestler

Arthur Koestler (1905-1983) was a scientifically educated writer, born in Budapest. He studied science and psychology at the University of Vienna. As a correspondent for a British newspaper, he covered the Spanish Civil War, during which he was imprisoned and sentenced to death. However, he was later freed as part of a prisoner exchange and returned to Great Britain. He wrote about science, including research on the paranormal, on the creative process, mysticism, and synchronicity. This essay is an excerpt from Arthur Koestler's autobiography, **The Invisible Writing***, in which he relates his own mystical awakening under the severe conditions of imprisonment during the Spanish Civil War in 1937. Koestler was an early Member of the Scientific and Medical Network and endowed the Chair of Parapsychology in the University of Edinburgh.*

I was arrested on February 9, kept for four days incommunicado in the prison of Malaga, and was transferred on February 13 to the Central Prison of Seville.

I was standing at the recessed window of cell No. 40, and, with a piece of iron-spring that I had extracted from the wire mattress, was scratching mathematical formulae on the wall. Mathematics, in particular, analytic geometry, had been the favorite hobby of my youth, neglected later on for many years. I was trying to remember how to derive the formula of the hyperbola, and was stumped; then I tried the eclipse and the parabola, and to my delight succeeded. Next I went on to recall Euclid's proof that the number of primes is infinite....

Now, as I recalled the method and scratched the symbols on the wall, I felt the same enchantment.

And then, for the first time, I suddenly understood the reason for the enchantment: the scribbled symbols on the wall represented one of the rare cases where a meaningful and comprehensive statement about the infinite is arrived at by precise and finite means. The infinite is a mystical mass shrouded in a haze; and yet it was possible to gain some knowledge of it without losing oneself in treacly ambiguities. The significance of this swept over me like a wave. The wave had originated in an articulate verbal insight; but this evaporated at once, leaving in its wake only a wordless essence, a fragrance of eternity, a quiver of the arrow in the blue. I must have stood there for some minutes, entranced, with a wordless awareness that 'this is perfect-perfect'; until I noticed some slight mental discomfort nagging at the back of my mind-some trivial circumstance that marred the perfection of the moment. Then I remembered the nature of that irrelevant annoyance: I was, of course, in prison and might be shot. But this was immediately answered by a feeling whose verbal translation would be: "So what? Is that all? Have you got nothing more serious to worry about?" – an answer so spontaneous, fresh and amused as if the intruding annoyance had been the loss of a collar-stud. Then I was floating on my back in a river of peace, under bridges of silence. It came from nowhere and flowed nowhere. Then there was no river and no I. The I had ceased to exist.

It is extremely embarrassing to write down a phrase like that when one has read The Meaning of Meaning and nibbled at logical positivism and aims at verbal precision and dislikes nebulous gushing. Yet 'mystical' experiences, as we dubiously call them, are not nebulous, vague or maudlin - they only become so when we debase them by verbalization. However, to communicate what is incommunicable by its nature, one must somehow put it into words, and so one moves in a vicious circle. When I say 'the I had ceased to exist', I refer to a concrete experience that is verbally as incommunicable as the feeling aroused by a piano concerto, yet just as real - only much more real. In fact, its primary mark is the sensation that this state is more real than any other one has experienced before-that for the first time the veil has fallen and one is in touch with 'real reality', the hidden order of things, the X-ray texture of the world, normally obscured by layers of irrelevancy.

What distinguishes this type of experience from the emotional entrancements of music, landscapes or love is that the former has a definitely intellectual, or rather noumenal, content. It is meaningful, though not in verbal terms. Verbal transcriptions that come nearest are: the unity and interlocking of everything that exists, an inter-dependence like that of gravitational fields or communicating vessels. The 'I' ceases to exist because it has, by a kind of mental osmosis, established communication with, and been dissolved in, the universal pool. It is this process of dissolution and limitless expansion which is sensed as the 'oceanic feeling', as the draining of all tension, the absolute catharsis, the peace that passeth all understanding.

The coming-back to the lower order of reality I found to be gradual, like waking up from anaesthesia. There was the equation of the parabola scratched on the dirty wall, the iron bed and the iron table and the strip of blue Andalusian sky. But there was no unpleasant hangover as from other modes of intoxication. On the contrary: there remained a sustained and invigorating, serene and fear-dispelling after-effect that lasted for hours and days. It was as if a massive dose of vitamins had been injected into the veins. Or, to change the metaphor, I resumed my travels through my cell like an old car with its batteries freshly recharged.

Whether the experience had lasted for a few minutes or an hour, I never knew. In the beginning it occurred two or even three times a week, then the intervals became longer. It could never be voluntarily induced. After my liberation it recurred at even longer intervals, perhaps once or twice in a year. But by that time the groundwork for change of personality was completed....

The 'hours by the window', which had started with the rational reflecting that finite statements about the infinite were possible- and which in fact represented a series of such statements on a nonrational level-that filled me with a direct certainty that a higher order of reality existed, and that it alone invested existence with meaning. I came to call it later on 'the reality of the third order'. The narrow world of sensory perception constituted the first order; this perceptual world enveloped by the conceptual world which contained phenomena not directly perceivable, such as gravitation, electromagnetic fields, and curved space. The second order of reality filled in the gaps and gave meaning to the absurd patchiness of the sensory world.

In the same manner, the third order of reality enveloped, interpenetrated, and gave meaning to the second. It contained 'occult' phenomena which could not be apprehended or explained either on the sensory or on the conceptual level, and yet occasionally invaded them like spiritual meteors piercing the primitive's vaulted sky. Just as the conceptual order shoed up the illusions and distortions of the senses, so the 'third order' disclosed that time, space and causality, that the isolation, separateness and spatio-temporal limitations of the self were merely optical illusions on the next higher level....It was a text written in invisible ink; and though one could not read it, the knowledge that it existed was sufficient to alter the texture of one's existence, and make one's actions conform to the text. ....

I feel that this present account gives a far too tidy and logical description of a spiritual crisis with its constant ups and downs, advances and relapses; its oscillation between new certainties and old doubts; its sudden illuminations, followed by long periods of inner darkness, petty resentments and fear. My stay in cell No. 40 was a protracted, compulsory sojourn on the 'tragic plane' where every day is judgment day. When I got out, the process continued. It had started at the unconscious foundations, but it took many years till it gradually altered the intellectual structure.

....I do believe that one can suddenly 'see the light' and undergo a change that will completely alter the course of one's life. But a change of this kind takes place at the spiritual core of the subject, and it will take a long time to seep through to the periphery, until in the end the entire personality, his conscious thoughts and actions, become impregnated with it.

...In the years that followed I wrote a number of books in which I attempted to assimilate the experiences of cell No. 40. Ethical problems had hitherto played no part in my writing; now they became its central concern....Finally, in *The Yogi and the Commissar*, I tried once more to digest, in the form of essays this time, the meaning of the solitary dialogue of cell No. 40. This book, written in 1943, closed the cycle; it had taken five years to digest the hours by the window.

Note: Koestler's later writings focused on science, creativity and mysticism. He had a strong interest in parapsychology and explores this in his book *The Roots of Coincidence* (1972). He later reviewed possible connections between quantum physics and parapsychological phenomena in his book *The Challenge of Chance*. He participated in conferences of the Parapsychological Foundation and at the 1974 conference, he stated, "So there is now a radical wing in parapsychology, a sort of Trotskyite wing, of which I am a member, with Alister Hardy and others, who are trying really radically to break away from causality, not only paying lip service to the rejection of causality, or confining this rejection of causality and determinism to the micro-level, but who really wonder whether a completely new approach, indicated in holism, Jung's synchronicity, and so on, might not be theoretically more promising." He asked that a part of his estate be donated to a British university for the study of paranormal faculties. This was awarded to the University of Edinburgh, to establish the Koestler Chair of Parapsychology.

(Essay excerpted with permission from ***The Invisible Writing***, by Arthur Koestler, MacMillan Press, all rights reserved).

Chapter Twenty-Five

Transformation as a Continuing Spiritual Experience

Joan Walton, PhD

Joan writes: My first degree was in Social Theory and Institutions (University of Bangor, North Wales). Following University, I travelled for a year in India and South East Asia, including working in one of Mother Teresa's children's homes in Calcutta. My early professional career was in social work, mainly working with children and families in residential and community settings. In 1995 I established an independent centre for action research and education, which enabled me to be involved in a wide range of staff development and research projects in the public, private and not-for profit sectors. Following completion of my PhD in 2008, I had a career change, and entered the academic world, initially at Liverpool Hope University, and now at York St John University in the School of Education.

Spiritual awakening has not, for me, been the unexpected, extraordinary experience, which has – in an instant – radically altered the way I live in and understand reality. Rather, I would say that my life has contained a number of 'significant events', each of which has resulted in a subtle shift in consciousness. Perhaps the kind of transformations that most people contributing to this book are writing about are as spectacular as a caterpillar metamorphosing into a butterfly. My experience has been incremental in nature, to be compared more to a child growing up – the changes are definitely happening and are progressive, with notable milestones, but no exceptional turning point.

If I were to summarise what the process of spiritual awakening has been for me, I would say that it has felt as though I have moved from an initial sense of being enclosed within my own body, completely separate from any external entity, whether that be a person, nature, or the wider universe. I felt strange, lonely, trapped in a life which seemed full of tragedy and misery. Over the course of nearly 50 years, though, there has been the sensation of boundaries dissolving, leading to the present day, when I feel integral to an eternal and infinite reality, where separation is an illusion, and love and creativity are infused throughout.

There have been many events that have contributed to this gradual dissolution of boundaries, and the subtle shifts in consciousness that accompanied them. In the early days, when the experiences appeared more 'amazing' (perhaps because I was not used to them), I kept a journal, in which I wrote at length and great depth. I think that the process of transmitting what was going on inside me into the written word, made a substantial contribution to the transformational process. On many occasions, I would read what I had written, and think: "Oh, so that is what was going on for me!". Through reading my own words, I was able to gain a greater understanding of the meaning and possible explanation as to what was happening.

It is not possible in this short account to provide details of all significant occurrences. I will briefly introduce four. The first was reading Carl Jung's *Memories, Dreams, Reflections* at age 19. I was raised as the daughter of Christian missionaries, in a strict Church of Scotland faith, with parents who loved me, but did not understand why I did not conform to what they believed was 'right' behaviour. I was very unhappy and depressed, feeling a huge dissonance between my inner sense of self and the external expectations placed on me. My reading of Jung's autobiography was exhilarating and mind-blowing. The main outcome was that I no longer felt on my own. There were so many similarities between Jung's early experiences and mine, that suddenly, I felt that perhaps I was not so odd after all.

The second key event was a year later, when I started university, and went to the first session of a year-long optional class entitled Study of Religions. Up to that point, I had thought that Christianity was the only religion, and my choice was to accept or reject it. As a result of brilliant teaching, and being introduced to Huston Smith's classic *The World's Religions*, a huge vista of possibilities opened up. I walked out of that first session feeling completely disorientated and quite faint; it took me a while to return to a balanced state of mind. My sense of the world, and what it was all about, totally changed, and led me onto a different road to the one I had been on.

Amazing synchronicities have played a central part in my life, allowing me to experience for myself Jung and Wolfgang Pauli's claim that the physical and the psyche are two aspects of the same reality. One particularly startling synchronicity was when, as a young family travelling to France for a holiday, we had our 20-year-old blue and orange 6-person tent, marred by a few small holes, stolen from under our caravan, where we had put it when stopping for breakfast in a layby in Devon, UK. Our friends, with whom we were meeting up later in the journey, were going to borrow this tent, and had little money for alternative accommodation. When we reached our campsite in France, we somewhat helplessly asked the campsite owner whether she could offer any suggestion that would help us with our plight. She told us that just that morning, a family had left her their tent, saying they had no need of it now, and to give it to someone who could make use of it. She then fetched a blue and orange, 6-person tent, which was virtually identical to the one that had been stolen. I thought at first that it was ours, but although it also had small holes, they were in different places. It was a hugely powerful experience – it seemed an impossible coincidence – and I found myself thinking that, if ever I doubted there was a transcendent power, to remind myself of this occasion.

More recently, over 40 years after reading Jung's autobiography, I was in Snowdonia, North Wales, on a week-long meditation course. I spent many hours walking and running in the mountains, as I loved to do, feeling completely at one with nature. One evening, I sat in a guided group meditation, towards the end of which the teacher told us to connect to the infinite and eternal reality to which we belonged. I realised in that moment that I was already there, and my permanent state of being was to feel that we are all expressions of an infinite and eternal, loving and creative reality. I had, over time, experienced a complete transformation of consciousness. I may not have undergone an exceptional spiritual awakening that has provided me with amazing psychic abilities or sensitivities, but this does not detract from what continues to feel like a profound and exciting spiritual journey.

This inner journey has inevitably influenced the choices I have made in the external world. Personally, the main significance has been in my relationship with my daughter, and other significant people in my life, seeking to connect with their essential selves, and to support what they feel is right for them in their lives. Professionally, the challenge has been to create a good balance between ideas and action: how to learn intellectually about this world and the purpose that energises our lives; and at the same time, what this means for action we take to put our learning into practice. For most of my professional life, I have developed and led my own education centre, allowing me to be responsive to the invitations to work with individuals and groups in different organisations, in ways that focused more on action than theory. Following completion of a PhD, which was a narrative account of my spiritual journey, I chose to join a university, looking for ways to introduce and integrate a post-materialist worldview into academic settings. At the same time, I have for many years connected with groups and organisations, such as the Scientific and Medical Network, and the Galileo Commission, who are also aiming to achieve a post-materialist worldview. My ultimate belief is that the way we interact with others, both individually and collectively, will be critical in how the future of humanity unfolds. My ultimate hope is that we can be guided in what this means by the spiritual presence which so many of us experience.

Chapter Twenty-Six

Circumnavigating the Soul: Experiences of Presence That Shaped My Beliefs

Les Lancaster, PhD

Les Lancaster is a Founding Director and Dean of the <u>Alef Trust</u>. *He is Professor Emeritus of Transpersonal Psychology, Liverpool John Moores University, Honorary Research Fellow in Religions and Theology, University of Manchester, and Associated Distinguished Professor of Integral and Transpersonal Psychology at the California Institute of Integral Studies. He has previously served as Chair of the Transpersonal Psychology Section of the British Psychological Society, as President of the International Transpersonal Association, and as a Board member of the Association for Transpersonal Psychology. Les' research interests focus on the cognitive neuroscience of consciousness and the connections between this topic and mysticism, specifically focusing on kabbalistic psychology. His published works include* **The Essence of Kabbalah** *and* **Approaches to Consciousness: The Marriage of Science and Mysticism**.

There was no "Road to Damascus", no blinding light ... just a gradual opening to a presence in the heart. Over many years I was taught practices—meditation, visualisation, developing skill in ritual—but it took some years before a finer quality of awareness brought experiences that were off limits to my normal range of senses.

So, the question is: why did I stay the course? In those early years, when others around me reported experiences of which—to tell the truth—I was cynical, why did I continue to foster the practices? There were three factors that held me in that discipline. First was the person who introduced me to the Kabbalah, the tradition that has taken centre stage in my life for more than forty years. A man of insight, compassion, and penetrating presence (Oliver, 2020), the like of which I had not experienced before. Second was the integrity of the tradition. As I explored writings of the great kabbalists in the Jewish rabbinic tradition, I found myself encountering minds that towered way above any that I met in the context of the research in psychology that was my academic career. I have written about the path of intellectual mysticism elsewhere (Lancaster, 2018); here I simply want to mention the intense experiential encounter that can arise from the subtle complex of meanings in which these authors were immersed. This is not "intellect" in the way we generally conceive it; rather an inspired wisdom to imaginatively build connections beneath the surface of what the "unenlightened" take to be a text's meaning. This "mystical intellect" convinced me that there was something worthy of my commitment.

The third factor that kept me on the path that had seemingly opened by chance was precisely that—the notion of "chance" was changing dramatically! I discerned that events in the world around me formed a pattern nudging me in the direction. I had read Jung, so knew the word "synchronicity" ... but the way in which my world was becoming enlivened by meaning seemed so real, so subtly interconnected—beyond occasional events that were synchronistic. Nuances of meaning that kabbalists found woven within the fabric of the sacred text were finding their parallel in the unfolding tapestry of my life.

These three elements—the "being" of my teacher, the realisation that a form of "higher intellect" was attainable, and recognition of patterns in my life that bridged apparently psychological and physical realms—were the trunk and branches to which the leaves of specific experiences adhered. The heart awareness came through my involvement in ritual practices. I have a vivid memory of when I first noticed it; the only words that can approximate the feeling are openness, space and compassion—but they seem hackneyed. Part of the experience was my reflection at the time: "Ah ... so this is what the teachings are referring to ... now I know!"

Further distinctive experiences arose when I spent many years in movement training—both in the tradition of Gurdjieff and Sufism. The Sufi turning dance brought a range of positive, even ecstatic, experiences—not to mention an initial nausea! But the experience that endures was that of achieving a change of perspective—from the whirling, personal-centred perspective to one of stillness, the "still point of the turning world." Whilst the sense of the world blurring past never really faded visually, its dominance became supplanted by a finer emotion associated with a growing, firmer centre. And this centredness continued beyond the turning movement itself. A different centre of gravity had taken root.

For many years the two realms—on the one hand, my academic career and on the other, my spiritual practices and studies in the mystical literature—were rigidly demarcated. But I had a conviction that a bridge should be possible. After all, kabbalistic teachings explore the nature of thought, albeit the unfolding of divine thought. Given the central maxim of correspondence above and below—that the human as microcosm reflects the macrocosm—kabbalistic insights into God's thought relate also to the human mind, and therefore carry relevance to psychology (Lancaster, 2021). And it was clear to me that spiritual practices had tangible psychological effects and would therefore play a core role in building the bridge.

Consciousness provided the initial foundations for the bridge. In the late 1970s I introduced into the psychology curriculum a course on consciousness. It took some years before the ground was sufficiently prepared for a postgraduate programme that added transpersonal psychology to the mix. Raising my head increasingly above the parapet, I introduced spiritual and mystical content into a book exploring self from the perspective of neuroscience and psychology (Lancaster, 1991).

My studies in the Kabbalah and other traditions had sensitised me to a world of meaning and experience irreducible to the material. Engaging with kabbalistic texts while trying to fit the ideas into the predominant functionalist and materialist assumptions in psychology was like operating with one hand tied behind my back! I increasingly hold that what truly counts is the "as if" imaginal stance that enables exploration of the other worlds of mysticism; this stance opens doors and brings richer ways of being. Such "fruit for life" is more important than debate over ontology.

That bridge linking spirituality with academic psychology is completed when the quest towards transformation is included. The educational model that underpins postgraduate provision at the Alef Trust focuses on study as "journey"—not only in terms of curricular content but also in the more spiritual connotation of working with integral practices. "The MSc was life-changing" is a comment we hear often from our graduates, and it is a comment that takes me full-circle back to my initial encounters with mysticism: "If you're not prepared to change, don't touch it", warned my initial guide into the labyrinthine world of the Kabbalah. And bringing that transformative imperative into my academic work has been the enduring legacy of my encounter with mysticism.

References

Lancaster, B. L. (1991). *Mind, brain and human potential: The quest for an understanding of self.* Element. (ISBN 1-85230-209-7).

Lancaster, B. L. (2018). Re-veiling the revealed: Insights into the psychology of 'enlightenment' from the Kabbalah. *International Journal of Transpersonal Studies,* 37(2), 73–87. doi.org/10.24972/ijts.2018.37.2.73

Lancaster, B. L. (2021). The faces of God: A kabbalistic "myth" and its implications for consciousness. In P. Dennison (Ed.), *Perspectives on consciousness* (pp. 277-317). Nova Science.

Oliver. L. (2020). *Tessellations: Patterns of life and death in the company of a master.* Matador.

Chapter Twenty-Seven

Toward Panpsychic Experience:
A Sentient World on Our Pulses

Peter Reason, PhD

Peter Reason was Director of the Centre for Action Research in Professional Practice at the University of Bath, England, and an international leader in the development of participative approaches to inquiry. He co-edited the **Handbook of Action Research: Participative Inquiry and Practice** *(2006, 2008) and co-founded the journal* **Action Research**. *Since retiring from full time academic work, Peter's two books* **Spindrift: A wilderness pilgrimage at sea** *(2014) and* **In Search of Grace: An ecological pilgrimage** *(2017) weave explorations of the human place in the ecology of the planet into the stories of sailing voyages. His most recent publications (with artist Sarah Gillespie) are* **On Presence** *(2019) and* **On Sentience** *(2021); and (with Jacqueline Kurio),* **Voicing Rivers through Ontopoetics: A Co-operative Inquiry**. *River Research and Applications, Special Issue: 'Voicing Rivers' (2022).*

I am seventy-seven years old. I have studied with many teachers and worked in many disciplines, including humanist and transpersonal psychology, Ch'an Buddhism, Tai Chi, Medicine Wheel, Gaia practice. I was happy to respond to the invitation for this collection, but as I approach this writing, I find myself wondering: is it appropriate to describe such experiences, out of context, in a public domain? As I reflect, I find that the very idea of a 'spiritual awakening' disturbs me. The word 'spiritual' points tacitly toward a transcendence of this worldly realm; for me that which is sacred is immanent on Earth. And the metaphor of 'awakening' harks back to the conceit of Enlightenment: my experience is that the dark is as full of meaning as the light. Further, my experience is not of one turning point but an unfolding process over decades. I can, however, trace some moments of grace, of subject-to-subject encounters, that lead me tentatively to experience the world as sentient.

I was brought up firmly within a modernist, masculine, rational worldview. The non-living world was composed of insentient things; the living world was there for human use; any other view was for the fairies. Over approaching eighty years, my perspective has changed radically. At times, I am quite alarmed at myself.

Maybe my first major step away from this was my engagement in the human potential movements in the 1970s. In encounter groups and co-counselling, I began to confront the rigidities in my character and beliefs and the impossibility of purely rational understanding.

A significant insight came when I was searching for a design for my PhD research. I can vividly remember the moment, the footfall on that particular paving stone, when I realized that in order to study two-person relations in authentic depth, I needed to invite people to the inquiry not as 'research subjects' (i.e., the objects of my research) but as co-inquirers. In doing this I undercut the separation of researcher from the object of inquiry that underpins the Cartesian worldview and thus much science. This set me off on a quest for a 'participatory paradigm' and to articulate the theory and practice of participatory action research.

When I look back at this time, I see my understanding was intellectual and anthropocentric. I talked and wrote about participation rather than feeling it 'upon the pulses' as poet John Keats put it. Over the decades, through influential encounters with teachers and several confounding experiences, I moved toward a deeper sense of living as a participant in a sentient world, 'a world of persons, only some of whom are human', to borrow animist Graham Harvey's phrase.

These experiences include:

A night on a hilltop in Wales, when, as part of my Medicine Wheel Apprenticeship, I was charged to summon a shooting star to confirm my 'sacred name'. When a vivid and indisputably real star streaked across the sky, my preconceptions of a world of insentient objects was shaken to the core, and with it my sense of my own identity: how could such a thing happen to a rational white male like me?

Two long ecological pilgrimages sailing a small yacht alone in the waters around the British Isles brought profound encounters. In particular, when becalmed on moonless nights, I looked beyond the bright stars into the smoky haze of starlight that filled the sky, faint but dense, profoundly dark and brightly lit at the same time. And with the gazing I was drawn into the infinity of the space above me, so that I felt I was both disappearing into and becoming part of the whole of everything.

On the same pilgrimages I sailed on the west coast of Scotland, for days on end doing little but watch the transit of moon and sun across the heavens, absorbed in the generative silence that underpins our everyday world. As I travelled north, I anchored alongside ancient rocks: first the 500-million-year-old granite on Mull, then the more than two-billion-year-old Torridonean sandstone, finally reaching the over three-billion-year-old Hebridean gneiss. Through this, I found myself experiencing the reality of Deep Time.

My current practice is to initiate and participate in co-operative inquiries with humans and Rivers. These inquiries draw on Freya Mathews' 'living cosmos panpsychism': if we invoke a world of sentient presence, calling to other-than-human beings as open to our communicative gesture, might we receive a response? We find that our invocations may on occasion elicit 'moments of grace', responses that strongly suggest a subjective presence. Such responses are poetic, not in human language but in synchronous material gestures. These may be subtle—the breath of wind or the falling of leaves; or dramatic events whose unexpected timeliness confirms their veracity.

I visit the River I am working with at dawn. I prostrate myself in a ceremony of atonement, expressing grief and sorrow for the damage modern humans inflict on the world. As I complete this, the Sky flames into colour and, quite unexpected, I hear the rhythmic thrum of wings. Looking up, I see two Swans flying across the orange morning clouds. Necks outstretched, wings beating, they fly east across River. I imagine they will fly away, but they circle round and fly back right overhead. The timing and choreography of their flight is a strong indication that this is a gesture from the other-than-human in response to my call. I am left sitting with my mouth open. A moment of grace.

I remain ambivalent about placing these narratives in a collection such as this. I worry about exhibiting what Chögyam Trungpa called 'spiritual materialism'. For years I refrained from speaking about my encounter with the shooting star, seeing the experience as private, between me and the Cosmos; but gradually I came to see that as a 'teaching story' it might stimulate wider imaginations.

We are asked also to say how our 'spiritual awakening' has contributed to our career and our relationships with others. This is, once again, no easy task. As I look back, I see that my life has been overshadowed by the gathering ecological catastrophe. I have a childhood memory, strangely both clear and hazy, that was an intimation of things to come. As a small boy in the 1950s I am sitting at the kitchen table turning the pages of a weekly magazine— possibly *Life* or *Picture Post.* I come to a double page spread featuring a dramatic black and white photo of a filthy smokestack, illustrating an article predicting a future environmental crisis. I ask my mother about it, and her reply lovingly brushes my concerns aside, forbidding even the thought that lies behind the question: "You don't want to think about that, dear". But clearly the notion that life on Earth was precarious lodged in my mind.

We now know that we live in what some call the Anthropocene; others, maybe more accurately, call it the Capitalocene. Whatever we call it, this is the epoch in which the activities of humans—actually a small minority—dominate, destroy, and overwhelm, the processes of the planet both locally and globally. It is also the Sixth Extinction, in which the loss of life forms is up to 1,000 times the background rate. It is clear that those of us in that small minority have a practical and moral obligation to lower our impact on the Earth system, individually and collectively. In particular, we have the now critical task of stopping the emission of anthropogenic greenhouse gases into the atmosphere.

In addition to this, we must understand this devastating impact is driven by a worldview, developed again within that minority culture, that sees the other-than-human world as purely material. This worldview channels our thinking and perception in significant ways. It tells us that that the world is made of separate things. These objects of nature are composed of inert matter operating according to causal laws. They have no subjectivity, consciousness or intelligence, no intrinsic purpose, value and meaning. And it tells us that mind and physical reality are separate. Humans, and humans alone, have the capacity for rational thought and action and for understanding and giving meaning to the world. And until very recently, this view was applied equally by this small minority to the greater part of humanity.

My life's work has been to contribute to an alternative: to deepen my understanding of what I have called a 'participatory worldview' both intellectually and 'upon the pulses'; and to smuggle these insights into everything I do, to temper everyday life with a participatory perspective. This included my work at the University of Bath teaching 'sustainable business' to students; developing the theory and practice of participatory action research; contributing to a range of 'alternative' institutions. Post retirement, liberated from the obligation to make scholarly contributions to the University research profile and materially supported by a generous pension, I hope my work has taken a more radical turn. Over the last few years, I have invoked the presence of Rivers sentient beings, drawing other humans into a series of co-operative inquiries: if we invoke a world of sentient presence, calling to other-than-human beings as persons, might we elicit a response? The extent to which these endeavours make any significant contribution to the catastrophe of our times is unknowable. But the work feels worthwhile.

The point is, very simply, we are already part of it all. We don't have to work at it: we belong in the Cosmos, always in relation to each other and the more-than-human world, glorious and flawed yet temporary centres of awareness and action within an interconnected sentient whole. And since we are part of it all then the moral and practical issue for all humans is to learn to live in a way that does justice to this participation.

Chapter Twenty-Eight

Belonging to More Than Myself

Andrew Powell, FRCPsych

Dr. Andrew Powell MA, MB, BChir, MRCP, FRCPsych. Formerly: Consultant Psychotherapist and Senior Lecturer in Psychiatry, St. George's Hospital and University of London; and Consultant Psychotherapist and Honorary Senior Lecturer, the Warneford Hospital and University of Oxford. Founding Chair of the Spirituality and Psychiatry Special Interest Group of the Royal College of Psychiatrists, UK. Co-editor of **Spirituality and Psychiatry** *(2009) and* **Spirituality and Narrative in Psychiatric Practice: Stories of Mind and Soul** *(2016). Author of two volumes:* **The Ways of the Soul. A Psychiatrist Reflects: Essays on Life, Death and Beyond** *(2017), and* **Conversations with the Soul: A Psychiatrist Reflects: Essays on Life, Death and Beyond** *(2018).*

My first 'awakening' was in my infancy, a memory that remains vivid and profoundly compelling. Lying in my pram and staring up at the azure sky, I was irresistibly drawn up into that luminescent blue with prescience of something mysterious, greater and ineffable that lay beyond.

The second occasion took place when I was four years old, at my day nursery. It was a hot summer's day and we children were playing in the garden, a large one, surrounded by trees. Everything was going on as usual. Then I looked up and saw this giant tree – the picture is still absolutely clear in my mind – standing motionless before me. The leaves shone brilliant green in the sunlight and within there was deep shade. Suddenly, I became one with the depths of that shade. All sound ceased, time stood still, and although what happened may have lasted only seconds, it might as well have been forever.

The third time I was in my mid-forties, taking part in a Zen Enlightenment Intensive. On this retreat, my assignment had been to spend every waking minute dwelling on the koan 'What is life?' We comprised a group of about twelve, working non-stop in pairs. One person would reflect aloud on their koan for half an hour, followed by listening in silence for half an hour while the other person did the same. Then a bell would ring, partners would change and then the process would repeat, hour after hour. By the end of the first day, I was running out of all imaginable descriptions for 'What is life?'

During the second day, time started slowing down and I found myself uttering strange half-familiar words as the mind emptied itself. My intellect was running out of steam while the cracks in my thoughts were growing wider and wider. I had been given an apple to hold and observe while reflecting aloud. Without warning, my mind did a kind of somersault and just like before, when I was four years old, everything stopped. I could still see the apple in my hand, yet I was everywhere all at once! There was no 'me' or, I could equally say, everything was me! All was unity, all in its right place, unbounded, timeless and shimmering with is-ness.

After what seemed an eternity, I watched a thought unfolding before my eyes, like a piece of ticker tape. It 'said' to me, 'Now you know what it is to be truly conscious – without anxiety'. A moment later, the whole thing was over. Tears sprang to my eyes and I felt a rush of great emotion – of love and gratitude. I was back in the everyday world of duality, in self, mind and body. The experience had been abrupt and very powerful. There was no worship, no Imago Dei, no spiritual path to climb and nowhere to go. It had been more like falling off a mountain, which would seem to be characteristic of Zen Satori.

How did these three events influence my life? It's hard to say. Although the human ego likes to set everything in order, in truth, cause and correlation are inextricably entangled. Given that every incoming soul is born unique, with its own path and purpose, perhaps I was possessed of a disposition that prepared me for such experiences beyond space and time.

I know that I was a sensitive and somewhat introverted child. As a small boy, saying bedtime prayers with my grandma was very special – I could now describe it as feeling lovingly and safely cradled in the embrace of the universe. Soon, I would be swept up in the challenge of getting to grips with the wider world, sometimes pleasurable and other times decidedly painful. Well-loved at home but lonely and homesick at boarding school from the age of seven, I sought refuge in books and music. By the age of fourteen, and now widely read, I determined to study the mind and unravel its strange commingle of joys and sorrows. I went on to do so by becoming a doctor, later specialising in psychiatry and psychotherapy – thereby taking the well-trodden path of the wounded healer.

My early professional years were devoted to mainstream healthcare. But I had always sensed myself to be part of an infinitely greater Creation, one that I had first glimpsed at the very start of life. In my middle years, spurred on by reading Carl Jung, and the forward-thinking climate of the Scientific and Medical Network, I brought the transpersonal dimension to my clinical work. I found that many of my patients were open to, and in need of, a wider and deeper frame of understanding than the one offered by the reductive psychology and neuroscience of the day. For some, it was important to have their faith-based tradition acknowledged and included in their therapy. For others, spirituality in its wider meaning was of the essence - at its most simple, to know that 'I belong to more than myself'.

The various therapeutic approaches I explored, including spiritual healing, spirit release therapy, soul psychodrama and past life therapy, could all be subsumed by the heading of soul-centred psychotherapy. At the same time, with the help of several like-minded psychiatrists, I started a Special Interest Spirituality Group in the Royal College of Psychiatrists. Over the years, the group has steadily grown to some 4,500 members, more than one in five of UK psychiatrists.

Of my 'awakenings', rather than count them as turning points, I would see that first prescient yearning as finding its fulfilment in my mid-life epiphany. Necessarily, there had been many life challenges between times, for the soul incarnates with good reason! To paraphrase TS Eliot, I had now arrived where I started and could know the place for the first time. Besides which, it's good to be reminded, as the saying goes, that God never promised a smooth crossing – only a safe landing.

Chapter Twenty-Nine

From Proof to Purpose: Parapsychology as a Meaningful Lived Experience

Chris Roe, PhD

*Chris Roe, PhD, holds a Chair in Psychology at the University of Northampton, UK, and is Director of their Centre for the Psychology and Social Sciences. He is the International Affiliate for England of the Parapsychology Foundation and a Vice-President of the Society for Psychical Research, and served terms as President of the Parapsychological Association and as Chair of the British Psychological Society Transpersonal Psychology Section. He is an Associate Editor for the **Journal of Parapsychology** and is on the editorial board for the **Journal of the Society for Psychical Research** and the **Transpersonal Psychology Review**. His research interests are around the phenomenology of paranormal experience, particularly as it affects wellbeing, as well as experimental approaches to test claims for extrasensory perception and psychokinesis.*

When I was director of an MSc programme in transpersonal psychology and consciousness studies, we ran an orientation meeting with each cohort to introduce the research project they needed to complete in order to graduate. We emphasised that for the work to be truly transpersonal it wasn't enough for it to focus on a transpersonal topic, or to adopt more creative transpersonal research methods; it needed also to have the potential to transform them as researcher (and perhaps also as a human being). Similarly, my own transformative process has not been grounded in profound spontaneous experiences or years of spiritual practice, but rather has been prompted by my experiences as a researcher and mentor of others.

For someone with a very public interest in a 'fringe' area such as parapsychology my training began very traditionally. My first degree is in biological sciences, and its focus on quantitative-experimental methods carried through to my PhD, which explored the ways in which people can simulate psychic or mediumistic abilities by subtle exploitation of psychological principles using a collection of strategies called 'cold reading' (e.g. Roe & Roxburgh, 2013). That training emphasized rigour and control, with the expectation that if experiments are conducted competently then 'real' effects will be replicated with high fidelity. My first inkling that this was unrealistic in the social sciences came about during one of my PhD studies, when I discovered that some participants had been conducting their own experiments within my experiment!

They were asked to draw a house, tree and a person which would be interpreted by an analyst to give a personality description. In fact, there was no analyst and everyone received the same personality description compiled from statements recommended by pseudo-psychics. As expected, participants were impressed by these character descriptions and rated them as accurate and particular to them. However, they disclosed that they had created their own hypotheses about the study and they had sought to test them via the drawings they produced; for example, to see if drawing a person with large eyes might be interpreted as a sign of paranoia, or drawing a large person relative to the size of the house and tree might suggest egocentrism. I realised that participants are not passive 'data generators' in an experiment, but are sentient beings with their own agendas and expectations. If 95% of the experiment exists only between the participant's ears rather than in the equipment or instructions that the researcher has control over, then the nature of the experiment can differ enormously from person to person. This has instilled in me an appreciation that conducting research is as much an art as a science, and flourishes only when the approach is person-centred and mindful.

At about the same time a fellow PhD student, Tony, gave a conference presentation in which he admitted that despite his life-long interest in parapsychology, and the huge effort he had made to develop a thorough understanding of what we knew about psi (the collective term for phenomena that seem inexplicable in materialist terms), when he actually encountered people who reported a rich history of personal psychic experiences, this made him feel deeply uncomfortable. It was one thing to accept in abstract terms that extrasensory perception or psychokinesis might be demonstrated in the laboratory as tiny but statistically significant effects, and quite another to be confronted by people for whom the phenomena that Tony had studied were a pervasive feature of their lived experience. To his credit, he recognised that it was his reaction that needed to be corrected. As researchers who are interested in psi as it occurs in situ, we have a responsibility to engage with the flesh-and-blood experiences of practitioners if we are to have a true appreciation of them. In consequence, an essential part of my work has been to reach out to practitioner communities, to get to know healers, psychics and mediums, and to spend time within their subcultural milieu.

This shift from a dualistic perspective that makes a hard distinction between the researcher and the researched, to a nondual perspective in which we are inextricably linked was also facilitated by a meeting with Patrice Keane, Director of the American Society for Psychical Research. As we chatted about our research interests and activities, I happened to bemoan the difficulty in finding reliable and committed participants to work with. Patrice asked if we had thought of being our own participants, or otherwise looking to develop our own psychic abilities. That was certainly one way to ensure that the participant wasn't cheating! To our shame, we admitted we had not, but on our return to the UK set about rectifying matters. We began a series of dream ESP experiments that could include ourselves as participants — the computer-based system allowed us to be both experimenter and participant without compromising either role. This provided a wonderful opportunity for me to become more familiar with my inner world, to recognise habitual thoughts and feelings but also to notice unusual responses that were potentially the result of an ESP influence. Over time I have become more successful as a participant in those controlled experiments, reflecting, I think, my increased sensitivity to my inner experience.

It has become clear to me that a characteristic feature of a first-person perspective is meaning; human beings are naturally meaning makers rather than fact finders. This realisation has affected the perspective I adopt when presented with a new case to study or participant to interview. When I started out as a researcher my intention was clearly to map exceptional experiences in a way that allowed us to identify any possible conventional explanations and test whether the experient's (usually 'paranormal') interpretation was tenable. The focus was very much on whether the experience could be construed as proof of some kind of anomaly (a contradiction to the prevailing materialist worldview).

This has become less important to me as I have shifted to a meaning orientation, and I am more likely to begin by asking what meaning the experience has for the percipient, what lessons do they draw from it and how might it have changed their lives. Much of my time is now devoted to normalising 'paranormal' experiences, explaining that while they might be rare occurrences for many they are so common across the population as a whole that they clearly fall within the range of healthy human experience. Common or garden variety exceptional experiences (if that isn't an oxymoron) are not indicative of credulity or pathology, so people should not fear disclosing them to others, or be wary of reflecting on and processing their experiences so that they can be an impetus for spiritual growth and self-realisation.

References

Roe, C. A. (1995). Pseudopsychics & the Barnum Effect. *European Journal of Parapsychology*, 11, 76-91.

Roe, C. A., & Roxburgh, E. (2013). An overview of cold reading strategies. In C. Moreman (Ed.) *The spiritualist movement, Speaking with the dead in America and around the world: Volume 2, Belief, practice, and evidence for life after death.* (pp. 177-203). Praeger.

Chapter Thirty

Wondering What I Am

Ravi Ravindra, PhD

Ravi Ravindra obtained an MTech from Indian Institute Technology, Kharagpur; MSc and PhD in Physics from the University of Toronto, and MA in Philosophy at Dalhousie University. At different times he has held post-doctoral fellowships in Physics (University of Toronto), History and Philosophy of Science (Princeton University) and in Religion (Columbia University). He is now Professor Emeritus at Dalhousie University in Halifax (Canada) where he had taught courses in the departments of Physics, Philosophy and Comparative Religion. Ravi was a Member of the Institute of Advanced Study in Princeton, a fellow of the Indian Institute of Advanced Study in Shimla, the Founding Director of the Threshold Award for Integrative Knowledge. He has authored many articles and books in a variety of fields. www.ravindra.ca

On one occasion, at age 18, after winning a badminton match, I was very tired, almost exhausted, and I simply lay down by the side of the court. I don't think I was asleep, but certainly not very awake. Then suddenly my whole body shook, and I found this sound resonating in the whole of my body, "Ravi, you don't know who you are. You did not create yourself. Your body is not only yours." I stood up, completely bewildered, not knowing where I was, and who was speaking to me, or rather in me.

This was soon after India became independent and there was a great social pressure to develop expertise in science and technology. It was simply assumed that a good student should specialize in technology. A recently initiated institute, Indian Institute of Technology (IIT) in Kharagpur, was considered the best place for education in technology. I graduated from IIT in 1961 with a BSc (Hons) and MTech degrees. I could now get a good job, but something in my soul was not at all satisfied with my technological education which had nothing to say about my question about why I had been created. All the necessary life requirements and academic demands needed to be attended to, but some mysterious part of me kept coming back to the questions such as "What am I? Why have I been created? By whom?" None of my fellow students or professors were interested in questions of this sort, but I could not set them aside.

Imagining that science may provide some clue, I ended up in Canada on a Commonwealth scholarship and obtained an MSc and PhD in Physics at the University of Toronto. As I got closer to finishing my PhD, I became sadder and sadder: the more I was certified as an educated man, the clearer I was about my ignorance of myself. Several months later, I had the privilege of a private meeting with Jiddu Krishnamurti at Rajghat in Varanasi. My heart was touched by his presence exuding wisdom and love. He remarked that Philosophy means love of wisdom, not love of thought. It became clear to me there are levels of reality subtler than the usual analytic mind, and that to connect with the trans-personal Real the mind needs to be quieted and a radical transformation of the whole of my being is needed to be free of me-my-mine occupations of my ego-self.

Physics has been considered the queen of the sciences since the 17th century. I could never understand why so many intelligent people have concluded that only science can lead to true knowledge of the universe, and that music, poetry or any of the arts may be entertaining but do not lead to real knowledge. So, while teaching Physics in Canada at Dalhousie University in Halifax, I did an MA in Philosophy, and took a leave of absence from the Physics Department to be a post-doctoral fellow in the Philosophy Department at Princeton University. At Princeton I developed a fairly close friendship with some eminent philosophers and physicists and a few years later I was invited to be a Fellow in the Institute of Advanced Study there. I was invited to join the Faculty in the Department of Philosophy at Princeton, but sadly, I did not feel that in the midst of all the on-going philosophical arguments there was any search for wisdom. Also, the Dean of the Faculty of Arts and Science at Dalhousie University was keen to make sure that I returned there and therefore offered to me the position of a Professor jointly in the Departments of Physics and Philosophy.

Imagining that Religious Studies might bring some clarity to my search I obtained a post-doctoral fellowship in Religion at Columbia University, and on returning from there a year later I shifted from the Philosophy Department to the Department of Comparative Religion, becoming a Professor in the Departments of Physics and of Comparative Religion. Although there are exceptions, in general in my experience, the professors of religion are not religious. Finally, I retired in 2001 as a Professor Emeritus at Dalhousie University having taught courses for several years in the Departments of Physics, Philosophy and Comparative Religion.

There is no reason to be against any of these academic studies. Each of these disciplines has its charm and its occupation. But for me it became increasingly clear that the search to connect with the mysterious Spiritual Energy—for which many labels are used—requires an impartial and steady self-inquiry and a radical transformation of the worldly self, usually occupied with desires and fears of one sort or another. Of course, serious philosophical and scientific engagements can also lead one to see the limitations of these disciplines. Here are brief remarks of two well-known physicists:

"Religion's true domain is far beyond anything in reach of scientific explanation." - Erwin Schrödinger (*Nature and the Greeks*)

"Everyone who is seriously involved in the pursuit of science becomes convinced that a spirit is manifest in the laws of the Universe--a spirit vastly superior to that of man, and one in the face of which we with our modest powers must feel humble. In this way the pursuit of science leads to a religious feeling of a special sort." -Albert Einstein ("*Purpose in Nature*")

For me, while over decades engaged in teaching and research in the fields of Physics, Philosophy and Religion, the main inner occupation has been how to connect with the Spirit manifest in the laws of the Universe—both outer and inner. I have been drawn to the scriptures and the writings of the sages in several traditions and I have written books on the *Yoga Sutras*, the Bhagavad Gita and the Gospel of John, as well as several others. Owing to my own need and search, and the benediction of subtle spiritual energies, I have been blessed with many very helpful meetings with Jeanne de Salzmann who was the main expositor of the Gurdjieff teaching after his death in 1949 until her own death in 1990 at the age of 101. I had helpful meetings with many other spiritually exalted persons such as J. Krishnamurti, Kobori Nanrei Sōhaku Roshi who was the head of Rinzai Zen in Japan for decades, and Archimandrite Father Vasileios on Mount

Athos.

It is increasingly clear to me that a spiritual undertaking is not against any of the academic disciplines. In fact, it can even be assisted by these studies if one can be a little free of winning or losing an argument or a prize. Also, it is clear that the spiritual journey is without end. But I need to find more and more freedom from attachment to any end since whatever I imagine the goal or the end of the journey to be, it is inevitably at least partly conditioned by my mind. So, I begin to find more and more interest in the journey where everything— including the very difficult times-- is true and engaging. The mystery remains and I keep wondering what I am.

Chapter Thirty-One

How Did I Reawaken to the Natural Inclusion of the Intangible Within the Tangible?

Alan Rayner, PhD

Alan Rayner is an evolutionary ecologist, writer and artist. He was born in Nairobi, Kenya and gained BA and PhD degrees at King's College, Cambridge in 1972 and 1975. He was a Reader in Biological Sciences at the University of Bath from 1985 to 2011 and has published numerous papers and books, the latter including, most recently, **The Origin of Life Patterns in the Natural Inclusion of Space in Flux.** *He was President of the British Mycological Society in 1998 and President of Bath Natural History Society from 2012 to 2018. Since 2000, he has been exploring 'natural inclusion', the co-creative evolutionary flow of all forms of life in receptive-responsive spatial and energetic relationship. https://admrayner.medium.com*

Towards the end of 1998, when I was 48 years old, I began a return journey. Up until then, my life had taken me along a course that became devoted to the study of fungi and their relationships with other life forms and habitats, especially trees and woodlands. This study was made, however, within the context of a scientific and academic culture from which I felt increasingly alienated and that nibbled away at my confidence. Feeling very far from home, I abandoned ship in mid-ocean. I took 6 months sick leave and considered a career change. In the end I persisted as an academic for a further 11 years at the University of Bath. During these years both my research and my teaching changed radically, and by no means with the approval of my peers. Something had happened within me that made me want to re-soul science and in the process re-soul myself.

Within 2 years of breakdown, I had become explicitly aware, in a visionary moment, of what I now call 'natural inclusion' (by way of distinction from 'abstract selection'). I embarked on a new voyage of discovery – or rediscovery – which, as it turned out took me even further from mainstream thought. But this voyage also brought me much closer to home and what I feel I have always known, since early childhood, but suppressed in a vain effort to conform with societal expectations.

When I was around eight years old, having recently made the trip with my family back 'home' to London from where I was born and lived my earliest years in Nairobi, Kenya. I contracted measles, the first of many childhood illnesses that confined me to bed and disrupted my schooling. My father sat by my bedside and read stories to me about the planets and outer space, infecting me with his love of scientific exploration. I was given books to read about natural history and I learned to identify the garden birds alighting in the tree that grew outside my bedroom window. I was taken on my first 'fungus foray' to a place called Burnham Beeches, west of London. I was awestruck by what I many years later described as 'The Fountains of the Forest' as they erupted from ground and rotting wood in manifold shapes and colours, not least the legendary 'fly agaric' (Amanita muscaria), the 'parasol' (Macrolepiota procera) and numerous 'brittle gills' (Russula spp).

Over following years, I became familiar with more and more of the British flora, fauna and fungi, filling my head with thousands of Latin names and associated mental images not only of the organisms themselves but also of the habitats in which they flourished and the ground-shaping processes that formed them. I loved the companionship of others on natural history walks and fungus forays, and the thrill of new finds and sharing knowledge. I met the love of my life, Marion, on a fungus foray at Oxford in 1969. The same year I began my University studies in natural sciences, specialising in botany and eventually doing PhD research in fungal ecology at King's College, Cambridge.

However, there was a problem. To study biology as a 'science' was not the same as experiencing 'life in the wild' in the caring companionship of others. If anything, it was wild life's antithesis: a competition to be first or best while following strict codes of practice designed to eliminate subjective human 'error' and conform to an unquestionable norm prescribed by prior authority. This kind of biology, I discovered, was obsessed with technicalities, reproducibility, quantitative data and removing variables as well as a Darwinian view of evolution as purposeless competition between selfish genetic survival machines. To me it felt soulless and unforgiving and made no sense, in sharp contrast to my own empathy for the organism and associated fascination with qualitative patterns, processes and relationships in Nature. And I felt increasingly unnerved by inconsistencies between my own findings and experience and those described by others in what was supposed to be an objectively predictable and technically standardised field of study. I began to lose trust in both myself and my peers. Eventually, I made a farewell gesture by presenting a painting of the 'Fountains of the Forest' to the British Mycological Society. Here is how I described its imagery:

> 'A tree is a solar-powered fountain, its sprays supplied through wood-lined conduits and sealed in by bark until their final outburst in leaves ... Within and upon its branching, enfolding, water-containing surfaces, and reaching out from there into air and soil are branching, enfolding, water-containing surfaces of finer scale, the mycelial networks of fungi ... which provide a communications interface for energy transfer from neighbour to neighbour, from living to dead, and from dead to living'

Since childhood, painting had been a source of respite for me as a way to express my feelings for the natural world, and as an antidote to the rigidity of scientific objectivism. Now I began painting again in earnest. And not only painting, but writing verse – sometimes alongside or as an inspiration for a painting. And with that move, and some prompting from friends, my awareness of 'natural inclusion' came back to me.

Although I did not initially realise it, all my paintings made since 1969 represent a shift from the abstract perception of space, time and material boundaries as sources of definitive separation between independent objects, to recognising them instead as mutually inclusive sources of natural continuity and dynamic distinction. Correspondingly, the simple process of moving paint around in response to the inviting presence of a blank canvas for me expresses the mutually inclusive relationship between intangible receptive spatial influence and energetic current in all tangible material forms.

It was this recognition of naturally inclusive relationship between tangible and intangible occurrences that resonated so strongly in the cavity of my heart and made such sense of my feeling for qualitative pattern, process and relationship. And with that bringing of intangible occurrence to centre stage, my scientific understanding was transformed from one that shuns to one that includes art and spirituality. I could now appreciate that life evolves in response to receptive invitation, not selective exclusion. We are called to evolve, not forced. Life is a gift of natural energy flow, which we receive with grace, care for protectively, and pass on – not a competitive struggle for existence in a sealed box. We breathe life, we don't suffocate it. What a relief!

The immediate effect of my reawakening was a shift to a very different mode of academic activity. From the point of view of my department I became 'research inactive', no longer receiving any grant income or publishing in respectable books and journals, and instead writing many on-line essays and articles in 'fringe' journals. To compensate, I was required to take on a heavy teaching commitment. This included a truly innovative trans-disciplinary final year course entitled 'Life, Environment & People', which I managed to keep going for 11 years, despite much disapproval from colleagues and examiners, until the stress finally became too much and I retired in 2011. In retirement I have continued to do all I can to bring natural inclusion to wider attention, publishing numerous essays and papers, as well as two significant books, '*NaturesScope*' and '*The Origin of Life Patterns in the natural inclusion of space in flux.*'

Chapter Thirty-Two

Epiphanies: Extraordinary and Everyday

Etzel Cardeña, PhD

*Dr. Etzel Cardeña received his PhD at UC Davis and was a postdoctoral fellow at Stanford University and faculty at various places including Georgetown University. He holds the endowed Thorsen Chair in psychology at Lund University, Sweden, where he directs the Center for Research on Consciousness and Anomalous Psychology (CERCAP). His areas of research include alterations of consciousness and anomalous experiences, dissociative processes and acute posttraumatic reactions, and the neurophenomenology of conscious states. He has around 400 publications, some in top journals, and his work has been covered by various media including the **New York Times**, the **New Yorker**, and the BBC. He is the founding editor of the **Journal of Anomalous Experience and Cognition**, and has worked professionally in theatre as director, actor, and playwright.*

I call this little essay Epiphanies: Extraordinary and Everyday because revelations of the exuberance of being have manifested themselves in a variety of circumstances throughout my life, from extraordinary events in my past to the everyday miracles shared with my wife and 3-year-old son. As to the first, training in ritual experimental theater gave me two major insights that changed my life.

The first one was gradual. Up to that point I had been a <u>very</u> cerebral person whose intellectual precocity (e.g., I gave a lecture as a 13-year-old in México's Museum of Anthropology) overweighted a disconnection with my body, which I took mostly as a clumsy vehicle for my ideas and feelings. Becoming a member of Mexico's National University Taller de Investigación Central (which has been going on strong for decades) changed that. Our psychophysical exercises challenged our inhibitions and limitations, from running to exhaustion and past it while remaining present, through touching others and being touched by them for the sheer experience of contact, to exercising balance while trying to climb a loose piece of wood that might fall down and hurt me if I lost focus.

As time passed, I noticed that instead of my thoughts being intermediaries between an impulse or a perception and an action, I could increasingly act immediately in an organic, unmediated way. Gradually I started feeling more and more at vibrant home in my body. There were also jolting events. One of them occurred in the very cold skirts of a volcano outside of México city (the Ajusco). The group leaders (Nicolás Núñez and Helena Guardia) took us to climb it during sunset, perhaps as a recreation of the symbolic novel *Mount Analogue* (Daumal, 1959; see also the depiction of this novel in a painting of the same name by Remedios Varo). I recall that some members smoked a bit of pot before ascending, but I was at that time reluctant to try any substance that might affect me.

As we were about to start the climb a sense of harmony within my body and with the volcano overtook me. I took off all my clothes, which I experienced as hindrances, and started climbing, my mind silent letting my body move as it saw fit, with an agility and speed that I would have thought of as impossible, at least for me. I recall that some members of the group told me that I should put my clothes and shoes back on, or I would get sick. I responded that as long as I was in the state I was, nothing bad would happen to me. Which is exactly what happened (or not happened, if you will). Later on, I read about the concept of "body wisdom," sometimes expounded by people who seemed to be as alienated from their bodies as could be, but that afternoon (and a few other times) I lived that concept as my bare feet moved around sticks and stones with exquisite, flowing precision, without being bothered by the cold until I came back down and started interacting with my friends and experiencing matters as usual.

There was another experience, while performing a play in which the boundaries of the inner and outer erased, this time in an explosive way. Some actor friends and I prepared a performed invocation of the Devil using a text that actually had very little to do with it. I recall two moments very distinctly. In the first I (playing a magician) was rehearsing with my best friend (who played the Devil). During an improvisation, he seemed to be taken over by evil and grabbed a poker, lifting it to strike me. At that moment I was not sure whether he would go ahead and attack me. I never found out because at that precise moment the phone rang, breaking the spell. To complicate matters, there was no one at the other end of the line. Was I (or we) somehow affecting the circumstances to break a dangerous moment? I cannot be sure.

The second moment occurred during the actual performance of the play in front of an audience. I was holding a large mirror to see the arrival of the Devil into a drawn-up pentagram, because we thought that it would be too dangerous for me to see him directly. Suddenly, without any reason I can think of, the mirror broke and one big sliver entered my hand. I bled profusely but felt no pain as I continued with the performance. It was one of the most intense moments I have experienced and I could not explain then my lack of pain nor, considerably more challenging, how the mirror could have broken. It has been through my body, not through imagery (despite researching hypnosis) that the most dramatic transgressions of consensual views of reality have occurred in my life.

At that time, I was also studying clinical psychology in the university and sought in vain for anything that my discipline could tell me about the alterations of consciousness and ostensible direct mind-matter interactions I had lived. Thus, I left México to study with the world's foremost authority in altered states of consciousness, Charles Tart, and built a career seeking to integrate into the scientific mainstream research and theory on alterations of consciousness and ostensible psi phenomena (e.g., Cardeña, 2014, 2015).

As for the Quotidian Epiphanies swirling in my life now, it would take far more than the space allotted for this essay to try to do them minimal justice. And, then again, I prefer to keep them personal and intimate. Suffice it to say that moments of eternity and blessedness have imbued me since being one with Sophie and our radiant little León.

References

Cardeña, E., Palmer, J., & Marcusson-Clavertz, D. (2015). *Parapsychology: A handbook for the 21st century.* McFarland.

Cardeña, E., Lynn, S. J., & Krippner, S. (Eds.) (2014). *Varieties of anomalous experience: Examining the scientific evidence* (2nd ed.). Washington, DC: American Psychological Association. Doi: 10.1037/14258-000

Cardeña, E. (2019). Snapshot 3: What the Taller de Investigación Teatral revealed to me. In N. Núñez, *Anthropocosmic theatre: Theatre, ritual, consciousness*. University of Huddersfield Press.

Daumal, R. (1959). *Mount analogue*. Vincent Stuart.

Chapter Thirty-Three

Chinsembwe

Stephan Harding, PhD

Stephan Harding holds a doctorate in behavioural ecology from the University of Oxford. He is Deep Ecology Research Fellow and Senior Lecturer in Holistic Science at Schumacher College in Dartington, UK, which he helped to found and where coordinated the MSc in Holistic Science for almost 20 years. He is the author of **Animate Earth: Science, Intuition and Gaia** *and editor of* **Grow Small Think Beautiful: Ideas for a Sustainable Planet from Schumacher College**. *His most recent book is* **Gaia Alchemy**, *published by Bear and Co for release in February 2022.*

It was straight out of A level Zoology, Physics and Chemistry and into the African bush for me, to a remote wildlife research station on the Sengwa river about 350 km east of Musi oa Tunya (Victoria Falls) in what is now Zimbabwe in Southern Africa. I was only 19 years old. There, at Sengwa was the beginning of the long trail that has brought me to new ways of being in nature which encompass academic biology and science but which are in fact much older and wiser and which are now so vitally important for enfolding deep ecological consciousness into our culture.

This feeling of being in the midst of the deepest sacred and of the most wise never left me for a moment during the five months or so I spent at Sengwa in the delicious wall to wall sunshine of the Southern African dry season, all graciously gifted me by the red sandstone cliffs and soils, the animals and plants, the fungi and all the invisible ones in the soils and in the air. Sengwa has left me with a powerful, life-changing imprint which I have carried all the way through my scientific training as a field ecologist, to my ecological work at the National University of Costa Rica and then to Schumacher College which I helped to found at Dartington Hall, England, in 1990.

This imprint was most clearly transmitted to me one sun-swept dry season afternoon sometime in 1972 after a long and dusty journey through the bush to Chinsembwe, a humble spring of water tumbling down a steep quite high red sandstone escarpment in the wildest and most remote Sengwa bush country consisting mostly of elegant thinly scattered Mopani trees with large patches of tall, dried out yellow grasses shooting upwards between them.

Here in this remote region of Mopani forest, the sense of the sacred was particularly strong, full of the living presences of birds, kudu, impala, bushbuck and other large ungulates. Elephant and black rhino too. There are also plenty of lions, leopards, jackals and hyenas. And let's not forget the wonderful diversity of reptiles, insects and even, but only once, a lovely porcelain-beige tree frog, glistening with moisture in the garden at the research station.

At any moment, perhaps, a glimpse of a little group of zebra amongst the yellow grasses. Or a small gang of impala, there in the trees, gazing us at us with no fear, in wonder. In the heat of the dry season, it's cool in the shade of these big widespread Mopani trees. There's animal dung here and there, elephant, buffalo, antelope - they all come to drink Chinsembwe's life giving water. It is all deeply healthy and at peace, and we sense - now that we have arrived - that Chinsembwe wants to share something of her angst about the planetary impacts of 'modernity' and her give us her wisdom.

We are in a place where life is sustained by the water of life.

This is alchemical water, both psyche and matter together, and is therefore deeply nourishing if only we could find how to drink it. My mainstream attitude of objective, disconnected observation dissolved, and I was with a wise and ancient friend who lives in and is the very rocks and trees and biota and the stream herself as Chinsenbwe's waters plunge down modestly from her heights. An immense yet comforting quality of immense value morphs and changes until a sense of the eternal appears, bringing with it gifts of great warmth, insight and comfort. Looking back now after almost half a century of ecological teaching and research, I like to think that I bowed, and that, with deep gratitude mixed with a powerful nostalgia and a longing to further explore such depths of connection, I offered myself, only 19 years old, suntanned and deeply 'bush happy' in service to Chinsembwe's soul and spirit and to Gaia, our sacred living earth.

Chapter Thirty-Four

A Scientific Awakening

Brenda J. Dunne, MA

Brenda Dunne holds a Master's degree in Human Development from the University of Chicago and an honorary PhD from Ubiquity University. She is President and Treasurer of the International Consciousness Research Laboratories (ICRL) and served as Laboratory Manager of the Princeton Engineering Anomalies Research (PEAR) laboratory from its founding in 1979 through its closing in 2007.

Many scientists speak of how they came to a spiritual awakening as the result of unanticipated and inexplicable experiences. My story followed the opposite trajectory – from a spiritual orientation to a scientific one. Due to an unstable family environment, from a young age my primary reality was a mystical/magical one. My earliest refuge was a fascination with fairy tales, world mythologies, religions, and the spiritual and mystical traditions of different cultures. Pondering questions such as "Who am I?", "Why am I here?", and "What is real?" led me to perceive the outer physical world as being symbolic of the personal inner one rather than some kind of objective absolute.

Married at seventeen, with motherhood following closely, I did not enroll in college until after my two children were in school full time. I earned joint degrees in psychology and the humanities from Mundelein College with two capstone projects: one on altered states of consciousness, and the other replicating the remote viewing experiments of Harold Puthoff and Russell Targ (1976). My remote viewing results were so encouraging that I continued to explore the phenomenon. In 1976 I enrolled in a doctoral program at the University of Chicago with the Committee on Human Development. Although I correctly sensed that this path would mean the end of my marriage, it was very clear that my interests and aspirations would not be met as a suburban housewife.

In 1978 I presented my remote viewing findings at a conference of the

Parapsychological Association, where I first encountered Robert Jahn, Professor of Aerospace Engineering and Dean of Princeton's Engineering School. Bob had recently supervised a student who constructed an electronic random event generator to replicate the PK experiments of Helmut Schmidt (Schmidt, 1972). The startling results of this project prompted Bob to establish a research program at Princeton to investigate the potential engineering implications of these phenomena. When he invited me to work with him, my acceptance was an enthusiastic "yes!"

Despite the recalcitrance of his university, Bob managed to set up a small laboratory in the basement of the engineering school. I joined him in June 1979, and we created the Princeton Engineering Anomalies Research (PEAR) Laboratory. PEAR's two primary foci were studying the effects of human consciousness on the behavior of random physical systems, and developing analytical techniques to quantify information acquired via remote viewing. Over the next 28 years, supported by a small interdisciplinary staff and under rigorously-controlled conditions, we accumulated immense databases that provided statistically significant evidence that these anomalies could not be accounted for by chance. The data indicated that consciousness could indeed play a proactive role in the establishment of physical reality.

Early in our relationship, Bob had asked what I thought was going on in these events. I answered that I thought that the interaction between entities could establish a relationship that transcended either of the individuals. He then described how atoms interact to form a molecule, to which I replied, "You physicists already have the answer, but you don't know what the question is!" This exchange stimulated my interest in science and resulted in a transformation of my world view. Driven by the desire to understand intellectually what I sensed intuitively, I proceeded to learn about the scientific method, experimental design, statistical analysis, and acquire the other skills required of a research scientist.

At one point I attended a graduate class on quantum mechanics that Bob was teaching, and it became clear that I could bring a unique perspective to the topic. We proceeded to have extensive conversations exploring the metaphorical implications of how quantum mechanics, or indeed any model of reality, is not simply a description of the physical world per se, but a product and reflection of the mind, a description of how consciousness experiences and shapes its environment. We discussed similarities between the principles of quantum mechanics and the processes underlying human consciousness, and in 1986 we published a paper titled "On the quantum mechanics of consciousness, with application to anomalous phenomena" in *Foundations of Physics* (Jahn & Dunne, 1986). Nearly two decades later we expanded the article into a book, *Quirks of the Quantum Mind*, which contains an extensive collection of relevant quotations by many of the patriarchs of modern physics (Jahn & Dunne, 2012). This book was published by the ICRL Press, a division of International Consciousness Research Laboratories (ICRL), a not-for-profit organization that Bob and I established when it came time to close the PEAR Laboratory.

The accomplishments of the PEAR lab have been published in many reports, journal articles, and books. Two of particular significance are *Margins of Reality: The Role of Consciousness in the Physical World* (Jahn & Dunne, 1987), and *Consciousness and the Source of Reality: The PEAR Odyssey* (Jahn & Dunne, 2011). But the essential dynamic that drove PEAR was the complementarity central to Bob's and my relationship (Jahn & Dunne, 2015). He brought incisive scientific skills, and I a spiritual perspective, and we learned a great deal from each other. Like the covalent bond, the relationship was more than either of us alone, but together we were able to achieve what neither of us could have done alone. Ultimately, it was the balance of these two dimensions that transformed me into a spiritually-oriented scientist, recognizing that any comprehensive understanding of reality requires a balance of both.

References

Jahn, R. G. & Dunne, B. J. (1986). On the quantum mechanics of consciousness, with application to anomalous phenomena. *Foundations of Physics*, 16 (8), 721-772.

Jahn, R. G. & Dunne, B. J. (2012). *Quirks of the quantum mind.* ICRL Press.

Jahn, R. G. & Dunne, B. J. (1987). *Margins of reality: The role of consciousness in the physical world.* ICRL Press.

Jahn, R. G. & Dunne, B. J. (2011). *Consciousness and the source of reality: The PEAR odyssey.* ICRL Press.

Jahn, R. G. & Dunne, B. J. (2015). *Molecular memories.* ICRL Press.

Puthoff, H. E., & Targ, R. (1976). A perceptual channel for information transfer over kilometer distances: Historical perspective and recent research. *Proceedings of the IEEE,* 64, (3), March 1976.

Schmidt, H. (1973). PK tests with a high-speed random number generator. *Journal of Parapsychology,* 37, 105-118.

Chapter Thirty-Five

On the Trail of Spirit

Lorna Green, PhD

Lorna Green, MA (metaphysics), PhD (life sciences) is a writer and author about Consciousness, a new Metaphysics, a new system of thought for a world sorely in need of one. A New Scientific Image of Nature, A Universe based on Consciousness, Awakening into Feminism, and the Earth as a living conscious being, like ourselves. She is the author of **Earth Age: A New Vision of God the Human and the Earth; Beyond Chance and Necessity: The Limits of Science and the Nature of the Real; Guiding Principles for the Planet: The New Paradigms, Meditations on Cartesian Themes,** *and* **The Reign of the Holy Spirit: Christ, Self, I Am.**

On a journey every step is appointed
A mystic can be content with a crack
in the wall. - Elie Wiesel

My spiritual awakening has taken place through many different moments over the years, involving both mystical experience, new ideas and insights about the Universe that made them possible.

In a time of trial and tribulation, a certain man showed up in my life and put his arm about me, and whammo! I woke up. I went back and reconnected with the small self I was in the garden of my childhood. My love affair with the Earth came as an infant, in the garden.

My earliest bonds were with the Earth. Whenever I had things to think about or pain to absorb, I would go out and lie down on the Earth. There was always magic, fairy tales and animals. A neighbor boy brought us a salamander. We connected, and I was hooked.

Around seven my friend's mother wrote our names on a piece of paper. I looked at the letters of Lorna and thought is that me?! My love affair with words began, and a life of writing.

My father was a physicist. Science was in my blood from an early age. I had problems with my father's world view. He would say "music is for the spirit," but I did not see any place for spirit, or for his ethics. My fascination was with life.

My questions led me to Science at McGill and graduate work at Rockefeller University.

The term Consciousness came my way at McGill. The library had books on Eastern Mysticism, they were all about Consciousness. At Rockefeller, I began a study of philosophy. I heard the term metaphysics. I knew, that was who I was and what I would write.

My physics teacher wrote Newton's Law of Motion, f = ma on the board: I asked him, just what are the forces, he looked at me incredulous and said, either you are very brilliant or very stupid. In the heart of the Life Sciences, I realized that science could not explain the Universe, which is why I wanted to study Philosophy to find an alternative.

Now that I knew science could not explain the Universe, I did not want to finish my thesis, but Dr. Edelstein said, "if you cannot establish the truth in some small matter in your laboratory, what will you do up there," and he pointed upwards, a telling argument for a seeker after truth.

After several years of dislocation, that left deep scars, I studied philosophy at the University of Toronto. I met Emil Fackenheim, and when he heard the questions I was asking, he said, you are going to be a metaphysician. Philosophers at U of T believed that metaphysics was dead, that science had all the answers. I knew they were wrong. I learned from him: the true task of the metaphysician is the human self-image. The metaphysician must make herself exquisite.

While working on my thesis, I became a tutor in the Great Books program at St. John College in Santa Fe. There I heard the deafening silence of women in history and resolved to break into it. Feminism was just getting off the ground. I would have been considered a radical feminist: they are the ones who come in angling for the patriarchy.

I began looking into spiritual things. I often went to mass, though I was not Catholic. I was spell-bound by the mass no matter how disheveled I was in the day, I always recovered myself.

My third year was darkness. I had been working on my thesis with no answers. I came back to St. John's and saw the heavy structure of the school coming down over me and I went into a deep depression. By that time, I was on the trail of Spirit. A student told me about a monastery in Pecos that I "must visit." I heard Spirit speaking; I went. Entering the monastery, I took one look at the joy on the faces of the men and women, and I knew they had the truth.

I was thinking of giving up my thesis in philosophy and declaring my quest for truth a failure. Abbot David Garrets called the charismatic experience "everyone's mysticism," grounded in a complete experiential connection with the Lord. They prayed over me, and it was as if I stepped fully and deeply into the wholeness of truth.

I returned to the school so transformed a rumor started that I had had a deep mystical experience. I needed to prepare a math class, and a clear voice told me what to do. I told the Abbot about the voice, he said: That is the voice of the Lord, always trust it.

On my third visit I felt some great inner shift happening within me around the thesis. The conclusions that had eluded me for years suddenly burst out of me. I wrote the final section.

That summer, I made a house of prayer at the monastery. My years of dislocation had left me with 10 years of free-floating anxiety. The Abbot taught Jungian Depth Psychology, dream interpretation, symbolism, and deep healing prayer that ended the anxieties. I left academic life to enter a life of writing, prayer, and practical tasks.

At 40 I had picked up most of the learning of this age, and it was time to get serious about metaphysics. I returned to Canada and took up a wilderness life to work the whole thing out for myself. At that point two seminal works came my way: *Seths Speaks,* and Greyson and Flynn, *The Near-Death Experience.* By the time I was 48, I had a pretty good idea about what was what. I told Spirit, I know what everything is, but I am too exhausted to write it. Send me someone with an animus like my father's and I will write it for you.

A man with an animus like my father's showed up in my life. I published *Earth Age: A New Vision of God the Human and the Earth.* I published three other books in 2004. I began meeting with a group of women, my greatest spiritual awakening. We talked about Consciousness and the Earth, as conscious living spiritual beings like ourselves, very different from the scientific version of things.

My four books developed my metaphysical principles, based on the truth of Consciousness.

In this high desert country where I now live, Spirit had given me a privileged standpoint on Being, on the Universe, all Universes, and I started to pay attention.

My true life began meeting with the women. With the accepting affirming presence of these women, my body relaxed, and my pain began to surface. Following a path of inner healing, it was a pivotal moment. As pain released, I opened up powers and abilities. The truth of the Earth around me came in. All the ideas I had taken in as a student came up. A spiritual source told me: you are being asked if you want to be bound by this, and if you don't, just discreate or cancel them.

At that moment the truth of things arose, truly the Earth as the Native people have always understood it - as an incarnation of Spirit.

PART FOUR

STEs Occurring as Synchronistic Transmissions Through the Word

We have included in this category synchronistic transmissions that occur through the written word. One author describes his experience during a visit to the Boston Library, when he was in high school. "On one of the shelves there was a big book with Plato's name on it. I had heard of Plato but had read nothing by him and had no idea what his 'philosophy' was all about. I took the book down and opened it. It opened to his Allegory of the Cave (*Republic*, 514a – 517b). As I was reading the Allegory, my body started to react ...tears flowed freely, chills up and down the spine, and my whole body almost in convulsions. I remember trying to stop it; after all, it was a public space and people were around. But I couldn't stop it. While my body was doing its thing, my mind was understanding Plato's allegory completely. This understanding is not the kind of understanding that comes with effort; the understanding was immediate and effortless."

This theme of awakening through the written word is actually a perennial one, in that many traditions talk about the word as being one with the absolute creative potential of the universe. In India the term that is used for the divine word is *Vak* or *Vac*, often considered as a goddess who is the divine inspiration for poets and visionaries. And in the Christian tradition, logos, the word, is also considered to be divine, as in the phrase, "In the beginning was the word and the word was with God and the word was God." (John, 1:1). In the Tantric tradition of India there is an understanding that when an enlightened teacher shares wisdom through a written text, there can be a direct transmission (*sankrānti*) of the deep meaning of that text to a qualified reader, that is, one who is receptive and becomes deeply absorbed (Williams, 2017).

In reading these essays, we invite you to consider whether the individual was in a state of readiness for this transmission through the written word, which was accompanied by a sense of receptivity, presence and a stilling of the mind, allowing the awakening and expanded state of awareness to occur. Think about times when you have been reading and felt a deep connection to the words or author, perhaps experiencing a direct transmission of meaning going directly to your heart.

References

Williams, B. (2017). *Abhinavagupta's portrait of a guru: Revelation and religious authority in Kashmir. Dissertation.* Harvard University. pp. 248-250. Link: http://nrs.harvard.edu/urn-3:HUL.InstRepos:39987948.

Chapter Thirty-Six

At the Library: A Formative Experience

Neal Grossman, PhD

*Neal Grossman received his PhD in History and Philosophy of Science from Indiana University in 1971. He taught Philosophy at the University of Illinois at Chicago until he retired in 2013. Relevant papers include: (i) Who's Afraid of Life After Death?, JNDS, May, 2002; (ii) Four Errors Commonly Made by Professional Debunkers (JNDS, 26(3), Spring 2008) (iii) Review of "The Self Does Not Die", JNDS, 34(4), Summer 2016. His first book, **The Spirit of Spinoza: Healing the Mind**, (ICRL, 2014) is a readable presentation of Spinoza's remarkable system of spiritual psychotherapy. And his second book, **Conversations with Socrates and Plato** [iff books, 2019] describes "how a Post-Materialist Social Order Can Solve the Challenges of Modern Life and Insure Our Survival".*

Although the event that I am about to describe occurred in my teen years, it was not until fairly recently that I recognized it as a "spiritual awakening" of some sort. Some forty years after the experience I casually mentioned it to Huston Smith, and he was so taken by it that he referred to it in several of his later writings. Huston's reaction caused me to take it more seriously, but it was not until twenty years after that, in discussing the event with Marjorie Woollacott, that I came to recognize it as a spiritually transformative experience. Actually, because the experience happened in my formative years, it didn't so much "transform" me as it "formed" me. That's why, when people would ask me over the years why, unlike the great majority of academically trained philosophers I was so open to spirituality, I did not have an answer, except to say that I was always open to it, in that I could not point to any experience ---like an NDE --- before which I was an atheist/materialist, and after which I was not. But now I can.

My parents were deeply committed to social justice and believed strongly that religion was the "opiate of the people". In my early teens I had completely internalized their beliefs, would have identified as an atheist/materialist, and had my sights set on MIT, where I hoped to study theoretical physics. After all, my teen-age mind reasoned, to understand anything one must know what it is made of, and since everything is made of atoms, the best or maybe only way to understand anything, even human beings, is through understanding what they are made up of. I vaguely recall stating something like this in my application for admission to MIT. Yet when I got to MIT, I took courses on eastern religions and devoured the philosophical and spiritual writings of the great physicists whose equations I was solving in my physics courses. This is hardly the sort of thing a materialist/atheist would do. Now I can understand that at the time I was seeking for external validation for what I had experienced while still in high school.

I need to mention one more influence on me before describing the experience. My parents, in addition to being Marxist/atheists, were avid music lovers, and I grew up with Bach, Beethoven, Brahms and Tchaikovsky. Around the age of 14, Beethoven's music began to affect me viscerally. Tears would come often when I listened to his music, and occasionally I would even experience chills up and down my spine. Although I consciously identified as an atheist/materialist throughout high school, I began to doubt that the materialist paradigm could explain why Beethoven's music had such a powerful effect on me. His music was not just beautiful, it was true. But this is not a "truth" that could be accounted for by materialism.

At the Library. It was the summer between my junior and senior years at high school. I remember spending many days exploring the city of Boston, especially its many historical sites. One day I found myself on the stairs of the Boston Public Library. It was one of those magnificent old stone buildings, many times larger than the public library in Cambridge with which I was familiar. The reader should perhaps bear in mind that in 1958 there was no internet, and all knowledge, the collective knowledge of humankind, was to be found in libraries. Entering the library that day was perhaps, for me, an experience not unlike what a devoted Catholic might have upon entering the Vatican. I was young and impressionable as they say, and was moved to tears by all the books and the knowledge contained in these books. So this was my mindset as I wandered in awe from room to room, each room filled floor to ceiling with shelves of books.

On one of the shelves there was a big book with Plato's name on it. I had heard of Plato but had read nothing by him and had no idea what his "philosophy" was all about. I took the book down and opened it. It opened to his Allegory of the Cave (*Republic,* 514a – 517b). In retrospect, that alone is something of a miracle. As I was reading the Allegory, my body started to react in the same way it had been reacting to Beethoven, except much more intensely. Tears flowed freely, chills up and down the spine, and my whole body almost in convulsions. I remember trying to stop it; after all, it was a public space and people were around. But I couldn't stop it. While my body was doing its thing, my mind was understanding Plato's allegory completely. This understanding is not the kind of understanding that comes with effort; the understanding was immediate and effortless.

I knew without doubt that the worldview expressed through that allegory is true. This worldview is of course the same worldview that is embraced by the mystics of all traditions; and it is the same worldview embraced by deep NDErs. Later, when I took philosophy courses at MIT, and then again in grad school, it seemed to me that no one else, including ---maybe especially ---- the professors (except for Huston Smith), had any real understanding of Plato's allegory. I was puzzled about this for many years. How could they read Plato and not understand what he is talking about? But perhaps the right question to ask is: how could a sixteen-year-old boy read Plato and understand completely what he was talking about?

Reflections. As I reflect on the experience, the understanding that came to me effortlessly that day in the library is akin to the experience of beauty I have while listening to classical music. This kind of understanding is very different from the kind of understanding that academics are familiar with. My understanding of, say the quantum theory, or electromagnetism, or relativity came about after lengthy study over many years. Indeed, my understanding of other philosophers, like Kant, Spinoza, Plotinus, and even many of the dialogues of Plato, came to me in the usual way, after much study, and always more or less tentative. But my understanding of Plato's philosophy came to me at once, without the usual discursive intellect mulling things over (and over and over ....). What was it about that experience that cemented in my mind a complete understanding (and agreement with) the spiritual worldview of Plato's allegory? This understanding never left me, despite being surrounded for 40 years by colleagues who were of the atheist/materialist persuasion, and who, I might add, controlled both my salary and career (or lack thereof, lol). I seriously doubt that what was happening to my body ....chills, trembling, tears ....explains anything.

I am now open to a kind of "explanation" that would not have previously occurred to me. Mediums routinely talk about how they have to raise their vibrations and the spirits have to lower theirs in order for communication to take place. Now, I have no precise idea what this concept of "vibrations" really means, but I suspect we all get the general idea. Maybe something like this happened to me in the library that day. Plato was raising my vibrations, not so much that I could get out of the Cave and see the sun (= God, in the allegory) but enough so that I could "see" with my mind's eye the worldview expressed through the allegory.

This explanation, that Plato himself was involved in my understanding of his allegory, is bolstered by the fact that for the past 15 years or so my writing has taken the form of inner conversations with Plato (and Socrates, Spinoza, and William James). Two rather lengthy books have been completed, one published the other pending. While writing, I did not consciously think or feel I was communicating with deceased philosophers. After all, I had been teaching these guys for decades, and had no doubt internalized their views. It all could be coming from my own sub-conscious mind. Or so I thought. But when I go back and read what I had written, or what was written through me, there is a sense of spontaneity to it, as there would be in a real unscripted conversation among humans. Moreover, the material would always go off in unexpected directions, as if I were not fully in control. And to be complete about this, I should probably mention that several different mediums, independently of one another and without my raising the subject, have stated that they see spirits helping me with a writing project.

Little did that sixteen your old boy know that by opening a book with Plato's name on it, he would be setting an irreversible course for the whole of his life to come.

Chapter Thirty-Seven

Aren't We Here to Play?

Vasileios Basios, PhD

Vasileios Basios (PhD) is a physicist, conducting interdisciplinary research on the foundations of complexity science and nonlinear systems, self-organization and complex matter. During his formative years, he was tutored by Ilya Prigogine (Nobel Laureate) at the Solvay Institutes in ULB and by Emilios Bouratinos on meditation and philosophy. He is interested in the complex interface between action and information and the history of ideas in science and their role in the transformation of science beyond the prevailing naïve materialistic reductionistic world-view. With others from PEAR Lab, he initiated the Mind-Matter-Mapping Project and has since published essays for ICRL where he now serves as a Trustee. He is a member of the Board of the Scientific and Medical Network and the Steering Team of the Galileo Commission.

I remember well the feeling of being devastatingly unfulfilled while I was fulfilling my career's goal studying at a good university, quite protected in my academic bubble. Fresh graduate, young and promising as everybody perceived of me, I still felt the world closing in on me. You see, ever since childhood, the world of science was a world of wonders to me. Early in adolescence I lost my father and the feelings of injustice, fear, grief along with the trauma of loss made me turn to the wonders of science for consolation and meaning. Philosophy also would soothe my wound but I picked physics to study, perceived to be the fundamental science, and it seemed to me that my answers were to be found there.

But this dream would soon exhaust itself. The prevailing materialist-reductionistic world view is devoid of any solace. Physics, we were told, is explaining 'how' not 'why'. It is good for making things, especially atomic bombs but also life-saving surgical lasers and the like. It is also very efficient in reducing everything to random ensembles of mindless elementary particles. Biology on the other hand taught us that we and all animals alike are randomly evolved bags of flesh due to our DNA's meaningless execution of biological commands to survive. So, there is no meaning in trying to find a meaning. Metaphysics is a thing of the past, for the meek of intellect; that was the intended take-home message.

This feeling of existential despair was strongly accentuated at that moment as, together with friendly colleagues, we had finished a round of drinks after participating in the local physics and philosophy club. That day's subject was a discussion on Gödel's, still in these days undeservingly forgotten, results. And I sincerely hoped that learning about the limits of logic would shine some light on the 'inside' of things. In the course of the discussion, someone had mentioned a link to Gödel's work with the problem of measurement and Eugene's Wigner's take on consciousness as a foundational key aspect of quantum reality. The poor guy was severely ridiculed, on the spot, by the crowd. They reached a consensus that we are here to 'shut up and calculate' not speculate, and off we all went for drinks. Nonetheless, I felt even more alone, existentially alone. Every aspect of fun and joy of science's wonders was reduced in front of my eyes to a 'grand partition function' of physical states doomed to oblivion by the second law of thermodynamics. So, I ran away and sought refuge in the library.

Somehow a book with the title "*The Sleepwalkers: a History of Man's Changing Vision of the Universe*" fell on my lap. A certain Arthur Koestler, an unfamiliar name to me at that time, was narrating the big watershed moment of the birth of modern science through the lives of Bruno, Kepler, Galileo and Newton. Awe! That was a moment of revelation for me. My great heroes were deeply spiritual. They too adhered to metaphysical anchors mostly without being aware of them. Like the sleepwalkers, they moved at the boundaries between faith and reason and at the same time they moved these boundaries by their work. I saw traces of perennial philosophy from Pythagoras, Plato and Plotinus guiding their steps. And it dawned on me that the 'modern' denial of metaphysics is itself a metaphysical stand.

This fact having dawned on me I realized that a new sun had also dawned. The library was open 24 hours a day. So, unknowingly to me I had stayed in the whole evening and night. Yet, I was not tired, sleepy, thirsty or hungry. Instead, I had an immense feeling of joy and felt I had tapped into a source of brilliant energy. Everything was clear in my mind; I loved the whole world, even my stubborn colleagues. We are all here to play this wonderful game of self-discovery and learn about the nature of reality by studying the reality of nature. That's science, that's real fun. I knew I had to change things as things have changed in me. For a couple of weeks, I dropped off my courses. I was reading other similar 'stuff' like Koestler's book and, effortlessly, connections with my own Hellenistic and Orthodox Christian upbringing emerged via Koestler's introduction to the Hermetic tradition.

They were luminous days of reading, thinking, daydreaming, reading again and contemplating. This deep contemplation state also seriously affected my dreaming. My dreams during the subsequent nights were changed to vivid and lucid ones. Before, I would occasionally have nightmares of not fitting in or of just a sensation of an undefined fear. Not anymore. Wonderful dreams started transforming me and my choices. There was also a persistent feeling of trust. Trusting the meaningful coincidences that by now I knew were called synchronicities. Trusting more my friends, family and humans at large. I had started to trust wisdom that stemmed from other ways of knowing. Beyond the prevailing group-thinking of materialistic reductionism. I could also trust the 'inside' of things and processes even though I knew that physics and science could not yet, and cannot still, cope with these insights of 'insidedness' or the enfolded part of the whole, as David Bohm would have put it.

This newly discovered joyful trust led me to learn how to better take care of myself and others. I met a wonderful lady, Fotini, my "spiritual mum" as my dear wife would affectionately call her. She took me under her wing and taught me the basics of pranayama (breathwork) and Jungian therapy and introduced me to my mentor and later good and trusted friend Emilios Bouratinos who tutored me in Vipassana meditation and perennial philosophy.

It was Emilios' advice to keep on pursuing my physics studies and to move on by joining Prigogine's group in Brussels. Science, free of scientism, regained its luminous wondrous glory. He was also the one who introduced me to my bosom friends David Lorimer and Peter Fenwick and the Scientific & Medical Network. Emilios is also responsible for me meeting the legendary couple, Robert (Bob) Jahn, the late Dean of Engineering at Princeton University, and the amazing Brenda Dunne founders of the PEAR Lab. Their ground-breaking work has been ever since a source of constant inspiration.

Was it a straight-forward ascent after the initial crisis and transformation?

No, I wouldn't say so. There were and will be a lot of dark corners or dead ends on the road. But this is not so important. What is really important is that there is always this feeling of `Leibnizian optimism' a deep-rooted trust in a fundamental well-being. It is more an evolution akin to `punctuated equilibrium' where long periods of normality - even occasional vicissitudes - are punctuated with instances of illumination, joy, and love.

Another bonus of my speck of spiritual awakening is the healing that comes along with it. Paraphrasing Tony Robbins, I would say: it is never too late to have a happy adolescence. Even the past can change under the light of Love. Abolishing fear, isolation, loneliness, and bondage, there is plenty of room to learn how to enjoy life. We are not here to 'shut up and calculate;' we are here to play and learn. Moreover, we are here to learn how to play without injury or trauma and without hurting the other `kids' in the playground, (i.e. human and non-human animals) that accompany us in this grand game of Life.

References

Bouratinos, E. (2018). *Science, objectivity, and consciousness.* ICRL Press. R. Grant (Ed.), V. Basios (Foreword).

Chapter Thirty-Eight

The Power of Words to Awaken

Stafford Betty, PhD

*Stafford Betty grew up in Mobile, Alabama, the son of an economics professor. CSU Bakersfield hired him to teach Asian religions, and many scholarly publications followed, including a translation of a 16th century Sanskrit philosophical text. Only in the last ten years did his more mature interests find expression. His research books **The Afterlife Unveiled, Heaven and Hell Unveiled,** and **When Did You Ever Become Less by Dying?** established his reputation as a leading analyst and exponent of the non-religious evidence for an afterlife. His novels **The Imprisoned Splendor, Ghost Boy,** and **The Afterlife Therapist** introduced this research to readers of fiction. YouTube lectures and interviews with Jeffrey Mishlove are available online. Stafford is married with five children.*

When I was a young man just back from Vietnam, I decided to test my Catholic faith by reading Bertrand Russell's *Why I Am Not a Christian* to see how it held up. What arguments could this famous atheist produce? What arguments could I counter with? It never seriously occurred to me that he could shake me loose from my convictions. But he did. I was mesmerized as I read along. I felt as if I could hardly breathe or was slogging through a swamp as I kept turning the pages, but I couldn't stop. It was as if I were under the spell of a death wish, and each page sank me deeper into quicksand. But there was also something vaguely exhilarating about it. The utter novelty of it attracted me like a moth to flame. I had no idea that my faith was so vulnerable.

First, he attacked my belief in God: If everything has a cause, as everybody grants, then God must have a cause too. Or if you make an exception for God, then you could just as well make it for the universe. He then looked at the evil in the world—he mentioned the Ku Klux Klan and Fascists—and said that, if all this was overseen and permitted by an omnipotent God, then God must be a fiend. He next attacked Christ. He labeled Christ's teaching on eternal hell "a doctrine of cruelty" and claimed that no one with "a proper degree of kindliness in his nature" could teach it.

But for me the worst offense against right religion was his denial of life after death. He said that "our memories and habits are bound up with the structure of the brain" and that if the brain is injured, the injured man is totally changed. And if the brain dies, that's the end of everything. You're "dissolved at death." As for the soul, he called it a "metaphysical abstraction" and regarded its survival of death "a bare possibility, with much evidence against it." He claimed to be unconcerned about its loss and that a wise man was happiest when he asked nothing of nature it could not supply. He claimed to be at peace with extinction.

I felt spiritual nausea as I considered all this. It was so strange and unexpected that it seemed dreamlike, a nightmare. Yet it was real. I had the feeling of being an outsider, a pariah in God's eyes—if there was a God.

I lived with a badly battered faith for the next seven years, always searching for the answers that would defeat the reasoning of this famous atheist.

In 1975, well along in my new job as a religious studies professor, I came across a new book titled *Life after Life* that presented scientific evidence of an afterlife. I had never heard of a "near-death experience." No one had. I recognized at once that this was a work of historic importance, and my faith in something more took on a vitality denied me since reading Russell. I was impressed by the similarity of the experiences despite the experiencers' drastically different backgrounds, and even more by the ability of some of them to accurately report events that were happening at a distance in the real world despite their comatose condition. Their descriptions of looking down at their body and overcoming their fear of death further solidified my conviction that they were different from their physical body, and that therefore they did not have to share its ultimate fate. All the evidence pointed to survival, and with that my feeling about the world we lived in improved overnight. I could now live my life, as William James famously put it, in a "strenuous mood." My natural inclination toward metaphysical optimism resurfaced. The world smiled at me.

But there was more work to do. I didn't know how to defeat Russell's claim that all our experiences were dependent on the brain, which obviously stopped working at death. In retrospect it surprises me that the answer escaped me for so long.

The answer lay in a different way to conceptualize the relation of the brain to consciousness. It dawned on me—I forget when or exactly how—that our consciousness was not generated by the brain's electrochemical activity, as Russell claimed, but that the brain was the instrument used by the immaterial self until separated by death. In other words, physical matter, the brain especially, is the partner we dance with for as long as we live on a physical planet. The celebrated near-death experimenter, Pim van Lommel, compared the brain to a television set, which converts electromagnetic waves to image and sound: The waves are like consciousness, the TV like the brain. The brain does not produce consciousness; it modulates it.

What happens when the brain is damaged or diseased and the individual's mental life is impaired, as in Alzheimer's? When the instrument is damaged, the consciousness isn't impaired, but it cannot function normally—in the same way that the picture on your TV gets fuzzy or scrambled. There is nothing wrong with the electromagnetic waves, only with the TV. And when the brain stops working altogether, the self can't use it, so it moves on into what we call the afterlife, where physical brains are not needed and do not exist. As for the near-death experience (NDE), it is caused by the temporary separation of the conscious self from the brain.

This reconceptualization is the only way to make sense of the NDE and other types of "paranormal" experience—like deathbed visions, mediumistic reports of spiritual worlds, memories of previous lives by little children, and other phenomena that I've devoted the last 15 years of my life to investigating. Materialist scientists and philosophers cannot account for any of this and usually settle for denying its existence, at great cost to human happiness worldwide.

My spiritual awakening changed not only my feeling about our place in the world, but the kind of research and writing I've done. In the last eleven years I've published three nonfiction books and five novels, all owing one way or another to the spiritual awakening that Moody's book brought about.

My scholarly reorientation cost me the respect of many of my university colleagues who consider what I do "pseudoscience." But that is okay. To live knowing that death opens into a vast and fascinating world is a very desirable trade-off. It feels like a sure bet.

PART FIVE

STEs Triggered by Psychedelic Experiences

Descriptions of spiritual experiences that have occurred through the use of psychedelics have been a part of our human written history for millennia, as these plants have been used as sacramental tools across cultures. For example, Sanskrit texts talk about the legendary Soma, part of Indian sacramental lore, which was possibly an extract of a hallucinogenic mushroom. And the ancient Greeks, in their Eleusinian mystery rites have been said to create a drink which may have included wheat infected with a fungus closely related to LSD. In addition, research on the spiritually transformative experiences associated with psychedelic use has increased during the last century, with individuals such as Aldous Huxley, Willis Harman, Roland Griffiths, and Stanislav Grof being some of the leading contributors to this movement.

In this group of essays, individuals who had taken psychedelics, also called entheogens, report the most exceptional and transformative experiences of their lives. After multiple experiences with psylocibin an author reports: "These experiences were the most ecstatic, most cognitively marvelous, most existentially satisfying experiences of my life." And, "At the time and afterward I realized that this was the most important and most transformative experience of my life – and fifty years later, I still feel the same way." One author, who only ingested it a single time reports, "Not too long after (ingesting the psychedelic), I began a meditation practice, starting practicing yoga, and learned about energy medicine.... My research ever since has been focused on the intersection between spiritual practices, health, and consciousness, with a focus on underlying mechanisms guiding healing and transformation."

Interestingly, research on the change in brain states associated with psilocybin ingestion shows that it appears to act in a way that is very similar to that seen when individuals enter into deep states of meditation. After psilocybin ingestion activity of the Default-Mode Network, which is associated with the narratives or stories we create about ourselves and our relationship to the world and is often considered the source of our egoic identity, is substantially reduced. This quieting of the mind's narratives and the correlated brain areas appears to result in an expansion of awareness beyond the normal default state. As with deep states of meditation, persons often experience a profound transformation of worldview, with terminal cancer patients, for example, losing their anxiety about the diagnosis and their fear of death (Barrett & Griffiths, 2018)). Some individuals have strong opinions, concerning both the advantages and disadvantages of the use of psychedelics. You might ask yourself where you stand now, and again, after you read the essays.

References

Barrett, F. S., & Griffiths, R. R. (2018). Classic hallucinogens and mystical experiences: Phenomenology and neural correlates. *Current Topics in Behavioral Neuroscience, 36,* 393–430.

Chapter Thirty-nine

A Glimpse Beyond the Veil and Seven Years of Transformation

Oliver Robinson, PhD

Oliver Robinson is Associate Professor of Psychology at the University of Greenwich. His research focuses principally on the changes, transformations and transitions of adulthood, and he has written a textbook on this topic entitled **Development through Adulthood: An integrative sourcebook**. *He also writes about the relationship between science, philosophy, history and spirituality, and has recently written a book on this topic entitled* **Paths Between Head and Heart: Exploring the harmonies of science and spirituality**. *He co-organises an annual conference for the Scientific and Medical Network entitled Beyond the Brain (www.beyondthebrain.org). His interests include painting, meditation, dancing and spending time with his wife and young daughter. Dr. Robinson's website: www.oliverrobinson.info*

I am an Associate Professor of Psychology at the University of Greenwich. I have published two books and forty-two journal articles covering topics including the philosophy of science, scientific methodology, developmental crisis, ageing, personality, wellbeing and spirituality. I organise the Beyond the Brain conference each year with David Lorimer and the Scientific and Medical Network. I am President of the European Society for Research in Adult Development. I am also a painter. All of that comes second to being a husband and father.

My spiritual path has been evolving since I was in my early twenties, through many experiences and practices. In January 2015, aged 38, I attended a 3-day ayahuasca retreat in the Netherlands. It was, by a distance, the most spiritually transformative experience of my life. I understand the reservations that people have around psychedelics as a portal to transcendental experiences, and I have reservations too. Using a pharmacological agent to move of the confines of normal waking consciousness comes with risk. Juxtaposed against that risk is my understanding now that ayahuasca is a spiritual catapult, and for those willing to take on the existential G-force of being shot out of the physical realm for a matter of hours, it is one of the great transformative agents. The transformation that it sparks continues for years after the experience itself. The passage below combines two short extracts from the report I wrote several days after the retreat:

"I focused on the love I have for my wife, imagined holding her close, and this appeared in the vision as a light in my chest...The love I was feeling in my chest expanded into an even more intense form, as I was shown my unborn child (my wife was 14 weeks pregnant at the time), as a baby girl in my arms (we did not know the sex of the baby at this point – a scan a month later confirmed that it is a girl). I sobbed out loud with love for this baby for what seemed like hours, and with my tears I was finally released from darkness into light. I was still in realms of total and overwhelming otherness. Now that love and peace were present as the core of the experience, far more order and symmetry was manifest in the visions. The higher worlds that I had emerged into were spectacular. Impossible to describe properly in language, they were constantly-shifting spaces of symmetry-laced geometrical surface and structures, like part-mechanical, part-organic crystalline cities, interlaced with animals, birds, semi-human forms and deity-type figures.

This was no hallucination – no fragmentary perceptual intrusion - I was in these perfectly formed hyper-complex worlds for hours, repeating to myself over and over 'never forget this, never forget this'. Every time I tried to understand what was going on by way of the rational refrains of 'why?' and 'how?', I was informed of something like 'hah, puny human, you cannot understand this! This is far beyond human comprehension'. I felt during the experience that if I were a million times more intelligent than I am, then I still would not understand it...I was shown the nature of my spirit body and the heart centre within this body. What I was shown was that in the spirit body (which is the same shape as the physical body but appears as a coloured lattice of pure energy and information) the heart is a ball of loving light that is located in the centre of the chest. I was informed that our task as human beings is to learn how to love and live from this heart centre, so that it's light and love shines and emanates in our dealings with others and the world."

The shift in understanding that came from this experience was profound. A central realisation was that the intellect can only take us so far. We can theorise scientifically about the nuts-and-bolts functioning of the physical realm, but in understanding the transcendental, we can experience but not explain. The processes that undergird the transcendental order are millions of times too complex for human cognition. It is a bit like a fruit fly trying to reverse engineer a super-computer. No chance. Philosophically speaking, I had already moved beyond materialism, but it is one thing following an argument to a conclusion that consciousness is primary, and quite another knowing it from experience. I knew in a direct and gnostic sense from that point onwards that human consciousness is not confined to the brain or body, and that one can leave the physical body while retaining an individuated sense of being an observing subject.

In terms of behavioural changes following the retreat, the seed that had been implanted in my heart started to take root. The growth was gradual. I started to overcome my workaholic tendencies, which in turn were fuelled by the pervasive myth that work success is the way that one finds meaning in life. I started to realise that I was carrying post-traumatic stress symptoms from my time at boarding school that I was not aware of until that point. I commenced the slow peeling away layers of defence mechanisms that were held together by a superiority complex and a neurotic need to be liked. I did two years of psychoanalytic psychotherapy after the retreat and commenced a dream diary and Jungian dream work. A further four years on, I am still shedding fragments of trauma that were locked into my body and caused me chronic pain for well over 20 years. I am still moving more of myself into the light of consciousness and integrating, bit by bit. It is an inherently slow process, just as jigsaws can only be solved one piece at a time.

Chapter Forty

Another Dimension of Reality

Natalie L. Dyer, PhD

Dr. Natalie Dyer is a Research Scientist with Connor Integrative Health Network, studying the therapeutic effects of integrative medicine practices, including yoga, meditation, and energy medicine. She is also the President of the Center for Reiki Research, where she conducts and educates the public about Reiki research. She completed her Doctorate in Neuroscience at Queen's University and Postdoctoral Fellowships in Psychology at Harvard University and Harvard Medical School. She has published many scientific papers and presented her research to many diverse audiences. Natalie is also an energy medicine practitioner and teacher specializing in Reiki and North American, European, and Tibetan shamanic practices.

It is challenging to map out where and when the spiritual path began for me, as from a very young age I was contemplative and felt a strong connection to God or my Source and true home. However, the trials and tribulations of a tough childhood paired with the cultural programming I was born into tested that innate connection. Life was difficult at home, and I was very sensitive and quiet. To cope, I numbed myself to simply function, whether through mindless activities like television or food, and in my mid-late teens, with alcohol and partying like many others. I was a bit different from other kids in the way I thought about reality, and this weirdness was not helping me socially or mentally. Throughout my early life, I had mystical experiences, including out-of-body experiences, astonishing synchronicities, and verified precognitions, which were all important to my spiritual understanding. However, it was not until I was 23 that I had a profound experience of another dimension of reality.

I was wrapping up my Bachelor of Science degree at the University of Toronto when a writer friend of mine introduced me to a shamanic medicine from Mexico called salvia divinorum, or diviner's sage. He was writing an article about the plant and doing some personal research. He was wrong in his description of the plant extract and its effects, claiming they were mild and just made you feel slightly funny. He left it with me since he did not care for the experience. Later that day I read a little bit about salvia divinorum and with a sitter present, I inhaled a small amount in a water pipe. The effect was instantaneous, and the experience was powerful and elaborate, though it only lasted about 5 minutes. The first thing I noticed was a rhythmic chanting sound, sung by nonhuman beings of some kind. As they chanted the five noted song, the room began to condense into rippled waves and the chanting caused reality to become unzipped. As the unzipping occurred, my awareness transported backwards and outside of my body, behind the couch I was sitting on.

As my awareness was leaving my physical body, I noticed two non-human but humanoid beings behind me. Their job was to limit my awareness by controlling what information entered my brain to be perceived. They seemed almost annoyed that I was there, giving me the impression that I was not ready for this experience. I said to them, though not aloud, "you guys!" as I remembered them from some time before. I ran away from them because I felt uncomfortable having them so close to me. They were not loving celestial beings, they seemed more like neutral workers of some kind. They had shelves behind them with objects of various bright colors on them, similar to a laboratory or a grocery store. In retrospect, it seems that if this were to occur without the influence of salvia divinorum it might have been interpreted as an interdimensional alien abduction experience. The beings sighed in annoyance as I ran away.

The salvia continued to quickly grow in potency, and as I fled the scene, I had a full ego death, merging and existing as nonconceptual awareness, with no subjective sense of self, no life story, nothing but consciousness. It was eternity and there was no "I" to reference. I forgot I had taken salvia, which became frightening as my ego began to return. I remembered who I was eventually and realized I was outside of my body. I saw a rotating sphere in front of me, which was "normal reality," though it was quite small and constrained. I walked along its edge until I saw the back of my body sitting on the couch, which was the view from behind the wall in my living room. I saw a veil, an opening in the sphere and I walked through it and stepped back into my body. As I did, the beings were back, as they appeared to be involved in the operation of my body.

As I reconnected with my body, they began pulling what looked like multicolor ribbons outside of my head, and with each yank a memory or perception disappeared. I yelled, "you are making me forget again!" and they replied, "yes Natalie, you cannot perceive this reality and function there, you would go insane." I somewhat understood, so I frantically wrote down what I could still remember while they continued to unplug me. When I was back in the room and no longer perceiving the beings, I was aware of the multiple positions and parallel realities all around me. I could see that everything was connected by a breathing, alive, rainbow fractal fabric or blanket. It felt like this "normal reality" was a prank played on me. Like I was living on a stage, and I did not realize I was an actor. There is much more that can be written about this experience, but that is for another time and place.

The intensity and lucidity of this experience was transformative for years to come. I had directly experienced a different dimension, nonhuman interdimensional entities, samadhi or ego death, and I was driven toward asking deeper questions. Not too long after, I began a meditation practice, started practicing yoga, and learned about energy medicine. Once I finished my doctorate, the first independent study I conducted in 2013 at Harvard University was on the subjective experience of salvia divinorum, which I presented at Psychedelic Science in 2017, more than ten years after my experience. My research ever since has been focused on the intersection between spiritual practices, health, and consciousness, with a focus on underlying mechanisms guiding healing and transformation. I have had many nonpsychedelic experiences that were also profound and meaningful, and full of universal love, but that salvia experience was a powerful, early catalyst on my journey. I have not taken salvia divinorum since and probably never will again, but I am grateful to the spirit of salvia for her potent medicine.

Chapter Forty-One

The Cosmic Tour

Christopher Bache, PhD

Chris Bache, PhD is Professor Emeritus in the department of Philosophy and Religious Studies at Youngstown State University where he taught for 33 years. He is also adjunct faculty at the California Institute of Integral Studies, Emeritus Fellow at the Institute of Noetic Sciences, and on the Advisory Board of Grof Legacy Training. Chris' passion has been the study of the philosophical implications of nonordinary states of consciousness, especially psychedelic states. An award winning teacher and international speaker, Chris has written four books: **Lifecycles, Dark Night, Early Dawn, The Living Classroom,** *and* **LSD and the Mind of the Universe** *- the story of his 20 year journey with LSD. Chris is a father of three, a Vajrayana practitioner, and lives in Weaverville, NC, with his wife Christina Hardy.*

I've always envied people who have spontaneous mystical experiences, and I honor the inner development this signals. Mine has been a different story. For better or worse, I have actively pursued these deeper dimensions. While I have been a meditator all my adult life, my deepest spiritual experiences have emerged inside my psychedelic practice.

Between 1979 and 1999, I did seventy-three high dose LSD sessions following a therapeutic protocol established by Stanislav Grof (1980). After three introductory sessions, I worked at 500-600 mcg. This is not a regimen that I recommend today, but it took me on a life-changing journey that I describe in *LSD and the Mind of the Universe.*

I would like to share one session from this journey, but the question becomes which one? This odyssey lasted so many years and took me into so many dimensions of consciousness that it is difficult to choose one session to represent them all. The sessions that meant the most to me were often devoid of form altogether save Divine Light, and without the sessions leading up to them, they would lack the context required to comprehend them. So I have chosen an earlier session where the landscape was still visible.

There is not space here to describe what this session meant to me or how it changed my life, but the deeper story in any case is how this entire journey changed me. I offer this one experience to illustrate the communion with cosmic consciousness that psychedelics can facilitate when used responsibly.

I have pruned away the hours of intense purification that took place in the first phase of this session and will skip over the many cycles of death and rebirth that prepared the ground in the preceding four years. Here we move directly to the fruition that opened in the second half of the session. I was 41 years old.

Session 19. After I moved through the collective purification in the "ocean of suffering," I entered an exceptionally clear state that was vast and time-saturated. It felt both ancient and open-ended, a field of infinite possibilities. As I stabilized in this new environment, a circle opened around me and created a space that became an arena of dialogue between myself and a larger Consciousness.

I discovered, much to my surprise, that this experiential field was responsive to my thoughts. When I first discovered this, I had the ecstatic sensation of confronting an enormous Intelligence that included and surrounded my own. "That's right," it said to me. "That's exactly what is happening." I began to ask It questions and It answered by orchestrating my experience in the circle. It was an extremely subtle process.

After some intervening experiences, I was brought to an encounter with a unified field of energy underlying all physical existence. I was confronting an enormous field of blindingly bright, incredibly intense energy. Experiencing it was extremely demanding and carried with it a sense of ultimate encounter. This energy was the single energy that comprises all existence. All things that exist were but varied aspects of its comprehensive existence.

The experience then changed into a moving experience of the Cosmic Tree. The energy became a massive tree of radiant energy suspended in space. Seemingly larger than the largest galaxy, it was comprised entirely of light. The core of the tree was lost to the brilliant display but its limbs and leaves were visible around the edges. I experienced myself as one of its leaves. The lives of my family and close friends were leaves clustered near me on a small branch. All of our distinguishing characteristics, what made us the individuals we were, appeared from this perspective to be quite minor, almost arbitrary variations of this fundamental energy.

I was taken around the tree and shown how easy it was to move from one person's experience to another and indeed it was ridiculously easy. Different lives around the globe were simply different experiences the tree was having. Choice governed all experience. Different beings who were all part of Being Itself had simply chosen these manifold experiences.

At this point I was the tree. Not that I was having the full range of its experience, but I knew myself to be this single, encompassing consciousness. I knew that Its identity was my true identity. I was actually experiencing the seamless flow of consciousness into crystallizations of embodiment. I was experiencing how consciousness manifests itself in separate forms while remaining unified. I knew then that there was fundamentally only One Consciousness in the universe. From this perspective my individual identity and everyone else's appeared temporary and almost trivial. To experience my True Identity filled me with a profound sense of numinous encounter. "So this is what I am." The freedom was sheer bliss.

For the next several hours, this Consciousness took me on an extraordinary tour of the universe. It was as though It wanted to show me Its work. It appeared to be the creator of our physical universe, its generative intelligence.

It would take me somewhere or open me to some experience and I would come to understand some aspect of the workings of the universe. Over and over again I was overwhelmed at the magnitude, the subtlety, and the intelligence of what I was witnessing. "That's incredible. I'm beginning to understand." The beauty of the design repeatedly left me breathless.

Sometimes I was so staggered by what I was seeing that I would stop and It had to come back for me. "Keep up. Keep up," It said, taking delight in my awe. Sometimes I was not sure what I was seeing, and It would do something and everything would suddenly become larger and I would understand. Then It would take me on to something else. These experiences were the most ecstatic, most cognitively marvelous, most existentially satisfying experiences of my life.

My elevation into this field had the subjective quality of remembering, as did all my experiences on the tour. I was reawakening to levels of reality that I had previously known but had forgotten. I was lifted into one "higher" and "larger" experiential field after another. With each transition I entered a deeper level of quiet and bliss-filled peace. It was as though an amnesia lasting billions of years was being lifted from me layer by layer. The more I remembered, the larger I became. Wave after wave of awakening was pushing back the edges of my being. To remember more was to become more.

Finally, I was lifted into a particularly spacious and peaceful dimension. As I remembered this dimension I was overcome by an overwhelming sense of homecoming and felt fully the tragedy of having forgotten this dimension for so long. I cannot describe how poignant this was. Being fully restored to this dimension would be worth any cost. I asked what had happened, and It explained that we had left time. Then It said, "We never intended so many to get caught in time." It felt like time was simply one of the many creative experiments of the multi-dimensional universe I was being shown.

Though these experiences were extraordinary in their own right, the most poignant aspect of today's session was not the dimensions of the universe I was discovering but what my seeing and understanding them meant to the Consciousness I was with. It seemed to be pleased to have someone to show Its work to. I felt that It had been waiting for billions of years for embodied consciousness to evolve to the point where we could at last begin to see, to understand and appreciate what had been accomplished.

I felt the loneliness of this Intelligence having created such a masterpiece and having no one to appreciate Its work, and I wept. I wept for its isolation and in awe of the profound love that had accepted this isolation as part of a larger plan. Behind creation lies a love of extraordinary proportions, and all of existence is an expression of this love. The intelligence of the universe's design is matched by the depth of love that inspired it.

References

Bache, C. (2019). *LSD and the mind of the universe*. Park Street Press.

Grof, S. (1980). *LSD psychotherapy*. Hunter House.

Chapter Forty-Two

My Story

Kenneth Ring, PhD

*Kenneth Ring, PhD, is Professor Emeritus of Psychology at the University of Connecticut (though he currently resides in northern California). He is the co-founder and past President of The International Association of Near-Death Studies (IANDS), founder and original editor of **The Journal of Near-Death Studies**, and the author of five books on the subject of near-death experiences, including "**Heading Toward Omega**", "**Mindsight: Near-Death and Out-of-Body Experiences in the Blind**" and "**Lessons from the Light**". For many years, he lectured internationally on his NDE research and related topics and has appeared on many radio and television programs in connection with his work. He has also had a long-standing interest in psychedelic experiences and research.*

It all began with two little purple pills. But they weren't Nexium.

They were two **LSD** capsules, but I didn't know that then.

I had better back up and explain.

In the early 1970s, just after I had turned 35, I was a newly minted full professor of psychology with tenure at the University of Connecticut. And I was discontented. Not with my personal life, but with the field of social psychology in which I had been trained and hired to teach. I had recently published a critique of experimental social psychology, castigating it for the pursuit of merely clever and flashy research of the "can you top this" variety, which did not make me many friends. In any event, I was suffering from a sort of early career crisis, having become disenchanted with this domain of psychology.

In March of 1971, when my wife and I went off to the Berkshires to celebrate our anniversary, I happened to pick up a book that my wife was then reading – Carlos Castañeda's first book, *The Teachings of Don Juan*. It looked intriguing and after she had finished it, I read it.

I was then a typical Jewish professor - wedded to rational thought, committed to science and atheistic in my worldview. I had no interest in religion and very little knowledge of mysticism. But I was open to new experiences, and what had particularly excited me about Castaneda's book was his discussion of what he called "seeing the crack between the worlds," which he had apparently effected through the use of mescaline.

At the time, I had never considered using psychedelic drugs and my only familiarity with anything close was having smoked marijuana a few times. But since I had never been a smoker, even that was difficult for me, and my experiences with it, though of the usual kind, did not have any particular impact on my life.

Nevertheless, since there was a colleague in my department at the time who I knew was familiar with psychedelics, I approached him to tell him about my interest to take mescaline and why. He had read Castañeda's book and knew what I was after.

I came to the point. Could he provide me with some mescaline? He could.

By then it was early May. The semester was just about over. He told me not to read anything further on the subject and just come to his apartment on the following Saturday.

That day turned out to be a rare beautiful sun-splashed day with everything beginning to bloom. My colleague lived at the edge of a forest. He suggested that I take the mescaline in his apartment, wait just a bit and listen to music and then go outside and into the nearby woods.

And then he gave me two purple pills to ingest.

I did not know my colleague well, and as I was soon to find out, he was not only impish, but embodied the trickster archetype. While he gave me to believe I was taking mescaline, he had actually given me 300 micrograms of **LSD**.

I will not bore you with an account of the next twelve hours. Suffice it to say that all the pillars of my previous ontological categories soon began to crumble into dust. I had the undeniable feeling I was seeing the world with pristine eyes as it really was for the first time. At the time and afterward I realized that this was the most important and most transformative experience of my life - and fifty years later, I still feel the same way. Nothing could ever be the same.

The one portion of the experience I will allude to here   -- because it eventually led me to the study of near-death experiences -- took place when I was sitting on a log near a stream in the woods. I don't know how long I was there, but at some point for a moment outside of time I - except there was no "I" any longer- experienced an inrushing of the most intense and overwhelming rapturous LOVE and knew instantly that this was the real world, that the universe, if I can put this way, was stitched in the fabric of this love, and that I was home. However, again I have to repeat: There was only this energy of love and "I" was an indissoluble part of it, not separate from it.

I spent the next three years trying to come to terms with what had happened to me.

I don't have the space here to continue to provide an account of my "spiritual adventures," so to speak, and related professional pursuits over the next few years that eventually led me to the study of near-death experiences, so let me just fast-forward to the spring of 1976. I was sitting outside my house, just after the spring semester had ended, and was reading a little book that I had come to my attention through a journal review by a new friend of mine. The book had been brought out by a small publisher in Georgia and was entitled *Life After Life*. Written by a psychiatrist named Raymond Moody, Jr., it was an anecdotal account of what Moody dubbed "near-death experiences."

I am holding a copy of the book now and I see all the excited marginal notes, exclamation points and underlinings that I made at the time. What I remember thinking was: "This is it!"

I knew that I wanted to find a way to do research that would help me understand what had happened to me during my LSD trip - and that my own spiritual explorations weren't sufficient for me. I had always enjoyed doing research and needed to find a way to satisfy that need of mine. And from reading Moody's book, I could see, with increasing clarity, that his near-death experiencers had indeed encountered the same realm - and so much more - that had so shattered me. I could learn from them. They would be my teachers.

You see, I was never interested in death per se, much less with the question of life after death. What animated me and drew me to study near-death experiences was my desire to understand the state of consciousness and the transpersonal domains that I had begun to experience when I took LSD. Even then, of course, I could understand that NDEs were a kind of transpersonal experience in their own right since, according to Moody's account of them, they clearly transcended space, time and ego. Thus, researching NDEs, I immediately saw, could marry my spiritual search with my work as a transpersonal psychologist.

This initiated a change in my career as I soon began to focus on this new exciting area of study. Over the next year I sought out 102 near-death survivors to begin my NDE research. My book, *Life At Death: A Scientific Investigation of the Near-Death Experience,* was the outcome of that research and was published in 1980. The next year, with Bruce Greyson and John Audette, I founded The International Association of Near-Death Studies (IANDS), and became its first President. I was also the founding editor of *The Journal of Near-Death Studies.* My colleagues and professional friends who became interested in NDEs now became and have remained my primary peer group.

PART SIX

STEs Triggered by Near-Death Experiences

Near-death Experiences (NDEs) have been described in the written history of many cultures for more than 2000 years. One of the first known NDEs was mentioned in Plato's Republic, as that of a warrior named Er who was left dead on the battlefield, but revived as he was placed on the funeral pyre (van Lommel, 2011; Lorimer, 1984). And the first medical report of such an experience was published in 1740 by Pierre-Jean du Monchaux, a French military physician (Gholipour 2014). In the past thirty to forty years there has been a blossoming of medical research on the nature of NDEs including work by researchers such as Bruce Greyson, Raymond Moody, Peter Fenwick and Kenneth Ring, which indicates the accuracy of the NDE out-of-body experiences that a number of individuals have had during cardiac arrest with flatlined EEGs; these studies show that individuals had clear awareness of the resuscitation events in the hospital room and even elsewhere in the hospital, in addition to mystical experiences. There is also an interesting characteristic that NDEs have in common with deep meditation and psilocybin experiences, in that the brain cortex networks, including the Default-Mode Network responsible for much neural filtering, are essentially inactive during their experiences.

As you read these essays, we invite you to bring your curiosity with you, and notice your own responses to these first-person reports. Do they seem credible to you, and reinforce your own current understanding of the nature of consciousness, that it is fundamental? Or perhaps you may choose to withhold an opinion on their veracity. Or alternatively do you possibly "roll your eyes" at the possibility that these first-person reports are scientifically verifiable? As you watch your inner response, you might ask what it is that convinces you that it is the most suitable, considering the data reported.

Reference

Gholipour, B. (July 24, 2014). Oldest medical report of near-death experience discovered. *Live Science*. Retrieved October 16, 2018.

Chapter Forty-Three

Following the Thread From a Crack on the Head

Joyce Hawkes, PhD

Joyce Hawkes' doctorate in Biophysics opened her to a career at the depths of cellular function. She received a National Honorary Award and was elected as Fellow in the AAAS based on her research. Seven years after an NDE in the late 70s she was 'called' to change careers and became a healing facilitator, teacher, and author. She has published books, taught internationally and has a TEDx talk with over 1 million views. Additional television appearances and interviews are linked on her web site: CellLevelHealing.com. Joyce has followed a deep sense of guidance to combine science and spirit for physical, mental, and emotional healing for nearly 40 years. The efficacy of this approach for the unique needs of each individual has led to abundant results.

News Flash: A 36-year-old dies a sudden and totally unexpected death. That was me!

In 1976 I was employed as a research scientist and head of a cell-biology laboratory for National Marine Fisheries Service in Seattle, Washington. With my team we were very busy examining the effects of parts per billion hydrocarbon pollution on newly hatched salmon. Additional research studies included the effects of nano-second pulsed laser irradiation on pigment cells in fish skin. All of these studies probed deeply to the cellular level utilizing the highly technical tools of both transmission and scanning electron microscopy. I received a National Honorary Award and also election to Fellow in the America Association for the Advancement of Science (AAAS). Not only was I extremely busy, I was ecstatic with my job and my life that included summiting mountains such as Mt. Hood and Mt. Adams and Mt. St. Helens before it erupted. Winter weekends included skiing every steep mogul slope at local ski areas.

I was living alone and had great friends both at work and outside of work. I was not active at any church or spiritual community as I had become an atheist.

This was not because of science but an event that had happened when I was in graduate school at Pennsylvania State University and majoring in Biophysics. My beloved Mother died suddenly of an embolism in Portland, Oregon. The pastor of the fundamentalist church where I had been quite active before moving across the country to grad school called me on the phone and told me that God had punished me by taking my mother since I had chosen to study physics. I was in deep grief over her loss and that message was so cruel that it pushed me into atheism. This happened in the late 1960s and here I was in 1976 with my PhD in Biophysics successfully doing the scientific research that I loved.

One weekend I was at home with a vacuum in hand, actually cleaning house. I was close to completion of the task and in front of a mantel over my fireplace upon which sat a thick glass art piece in and oak frame. I did not bump any part of the fireplace nor mantel but suddenly the heavy piece fell off and onto my head. I remember the painful impact as my body began to fall. There was no sensation of hitting the floor. I had a feeling of floating and could see a long dark tunnel with a beautiful light at the far end. The light began to draw me toward itself and I was no longer floating in one place but flying rapidly. A circular doorway where the light was shining through was closer and closer and I suddenly stopped just before the entrance. I looked to my left and the edge of the tunnel faded into a wall. I looked to my right and was startled to see my Grandmother Ada and my mother standing there looking steadily at me. I moved toward them and became wrapped in my mother's arms with Grandma embracing both of us. I felt their love reach every part of me. Next, without any preface whatsoever, I was through the entrance into a well-lit and wide-open space. The sky was strikingly blue, and there were rolling hills and a trail. As I walked slowly and looked around, there was green grass and colorful flowers but no people or buildings. All of the colors were bright and clear as crystals but in no way harsh. I was neither afraid nor driven by an internal agenda, but just simply wandering.

In a flash without flying, floating or walking I found myself in the middle of a glowing white stair-case with an open door at the top that beckoned me. I walked up the last step, through the doorway and into a large room without windows or any obvious lighting. If I perceived the stairs as glowing, they barely compared to the radiance of the room. Every wall, the floor, the ceiling and a being of light shone brightly. I felt utterly loved by all of it.

The blessing of love was beyond anything I had felt in my life. Not that I had lacked love in my life. My childhood was safe, delightful and I was amiably loved by my parents. The feeling in the radiant room was of being totally known. There was no judgement. I was at one with Source, and the translation of that Oneness into human terms was beyond what any words could fully describe. That I was absorbed in pure love is as close as words can get. LOVE abounded beyond the beyond.

I could have stayed there forever, but another instantaneous and unannounced transfer happened and I was back lying on the floor in my living room. My head hurt at a plus 10 level and it felt strangely heavy on the right side just past the middle and an inch or so from the hairline to the scalp. I slowly got up and went to look in a mirror at the painful spot and saw a six-inch lump of clotted blood mixed in a mass of my hair. I must have been out much longer than a few minutes. Was it an hour or two? How could I be alive after all that?

When I got to a doctor and a CT scan, I had some blood on the brain, but not enough to require surgery. I did have to take six weeks off work and rest. Near the end of the six weeks, I drove to my favorite bookstore. I was headed along a nonfiction aisle when a book popped off the shelf. I grabbed it before it hit the floor and was about to put it back when I noticed the title: 'Life After Life' by Raymond Moody. It was published in 1975 about near-death experiences. I had never heard of the author, the book, nor those NDEs. I opened the cover and read quotes from people who died and came back after journeying down tunnels that led to light. The common elements overwhelmed me. Shortly thereafter, I discovered an International Association of Near-Death Studies (IANDS) group in Seattle and met Kim Clark Sharp who significantly helped me understand and honor my experience. We are still friends today.

For seven years I explored many new dimensions of awareness that the NDE opened. Then one day I met a healer who could bring health to people via energy healing. I was fascinated, took his classes, and ultimately worked beside him. People also responded to my work and astonished me with their health improvements.

One week he took four of us students to Mt. Shasta where we climbed to 9,000 feet and spent several nights camped in the snow. On the journey back to Seattle, we stopped in Portland, Oregon and spent a few hours at the Grotto, a Catholic sacred shrine. While there, I knelt before a huge cave which housed many burning candles and a statue of Mother Mary holding Jesus' body. I was at that location alone when I heard a female voice say "You are called to heal." Overwhelming emotions of love arose and I was touched as deeply as by my NDE. I resigned my position at NMFS the next business day. This was in 1984 and I continue to pursue that calling today. Along the way, I studied with indigenous healers in the Philippines, Bali, India, the UK and the US.

I was guided to engage a path of union of Science and Spirit: Cell Level Healing which has blessed and assisted healing for thousands. I am grateful for every day, breath, and the ability to serve.

Chapter Forty-Four

Illuminating Consciousness Through Extraordinary Experience

Eben Alexander III, MD

Dr Eben Alexander III received his BA in Chemistry from UNC-Chapel Hill in 1976, MD from Duke University in 1980, completed neurosurgical residency at Duke in 1987, and a cerebrovascular fellowship at Newcastle General Hospital in the U.K., before teaching neurosurgery at the Brigham & Women's and Childrens' Hospitals and Harvard Medical School in Boston for 15 years, achieving the rank of Associate Professor. He also held academic positions at UMass Memorial and the University of Virginia, and wrote over 150 peer-reviewed papers and chapters: (https://ebenalexander.com/about/publications/). His clinical expertise and leadership included advances in linear accelerator-based stereotactic radiosurgery for numerous indications, development of the world's first intra-operative MRI system, and advanced management of brain tumors and functional disorders (movement disorders, refractory pain syndromes).

Growing up in a scientific household felt like a blessing. My adoptive father was a globally-renowned neurosurgeon fascinated by science, even outside of his specialty. His own father had been a general surgeon who instilled in him a rich religious faith, honed by regular attendance of a Presbyterian church. My father read from his New Testament pocket Bible all through his 2 ½ year deployment in the Pacific Theater during World War II, and regularly resorted to prayer in his work as a surgeon. For him, there was never any conflict between his belief in a Christian God and his pursuit of science.

My parents instilled Christian values with regular church attendance and daily prayers. Growing up in the 1960s & 70s, I wanted to believe what I was taught in church, but I always understood that science was the actual pathway to truth and devotedly followed the latest advances in *Scientific American.* When I started college in 1972 at the University of North Carolina in Chapel Hill, my heart was set on studying astrophysics. But after spending a summer working as an orderly in the operating room, my passions shifted to medicine, with a devotion to helping people heal.

My advanced training in medicine focused on highly technical aspects of evolving neurosurgical practice, leading me to further question my childhood religious teachings. As a neurosurgeon, I fully adhered to conventional scientific views of reductive materialism and could not comprehend how consciousness, or a soul, could exist independently of the body. Patients, families and nurses would report inexplicable phenomena, but I held to "promissory materialism," believing these occurrences would all someday be explained by a deeper understanding of the brain's complexities.

My world view was entirely turned on its head in November 2008 when I suddenly entered a deep week-long coma due to an aggressive and near-lethal case of gram-negative bacterial meningoencephalitis. During that coma I experienced the richest, most detailed and multi-faceted events of my entire lifetime – a near-death experience (NDE) apparently taking place in a non-physical spiritual realm, all while my neocortex and brainstem were suffering major disruption. One of the most remarkable qualities was the ultra-reality compared with normal consciousness in the material world. This was tightly coupled with the ineffability, or inadequacy of our language to describe such events. If I had to boil this entire message down to one sentence, it would run this way: You are loved.

The trickle of consciousness with which we are most familiar consists of a here and now in the physical realm, and a confined sense of self, is massively constricted compared with the flood of consciousness across time and space and beyond apparent selfhood that I witnessed while I was perceived by family and caregivers as being in deep coma. Modes of acquisition of information consisted of becoming huge swathes of the scenes in a process I call "knowledge through identification."

If the brain were truly responsible for generating conscious experience, my robust memories should have been impossible, and yet it had happened. In the months after recovering, the documented damage to my neocortex and brainstem revealed that my brain was far too incapacitated to have generated any dream or hallucination. Bundled with this profound mystery was the fact of my full recovery, which appeared miraculous from a medical perspective. An objective case report of my medical records by three physicians who were not involved in my care, but were amazed by my extraordinary recovery, confirms the stunning nature of my case.*

This near-death experience had one major feature that is uncommon in other such cases. During my entire coma experience, I had absolutely no memories of my life on earth: no language, knowledge of earth or this universe – essentially, a tabula rasa, or empty slate, on which to have the experience. Early on, as I was learning of the damage to my neocortex (and while many of my memories, including semantic knowledge, had not yet returned), I crudely assumed the memory loss was due to neocortical damage, defaulting to my prior views of memory being stored in the neocortex, but this was soon disproven as my memories fully returned.

This challenge, and the miraculous nature of my recovery, energized my search for a deeper understanding of the whole experience. As I read more of the NDE literature (to which I had paid no attention until my coma), I came to realize that the spiritual guide one encounters is often of central importance in one's life. I would have expected to see front and center my adoptive father, who had passed over four years before my coma, and yet he was nowhere to be found. Instead, my comforting spiritual guide was a beautiful young woman who accompanied me through the Gateway Valley, an intersection of earth-like and spiritual realms. Her message came directly into my spiritual awareness with a profound sense of personal connection, and yet, in spite of that deep familiarity, when I returned to this world, I had no idea who she was. When I received a photo of my birth sister Betsy, received four months after I awakened from coma, in the setting of reading a similar story in a book by Elisabeth Kübler-Ross, I was utterly shocked to recognize my spiritual companion to be my birth sister who had passed from this world in 1998, two years before I even learned of her existence.

My journey in the 13 years since that revelation has been one of reconciling my scientific world view with my personal spiritual experience. I was forced into realizing that the basic tenet of materialism (consciousness arises from the brain) was fundamentally incorrect, and this caused me to recast the entire foundation of my belief system. The memories of my NDE remain as fresh as if it all happened yesterday, providing a reference point that I have used in daily meditations to unify a more complete understanding of the nature of reality, one that is leading towards the concept that the brain and the entire physical world arise from primordial consciousness. My scientific journey has focused on the study of evidence supporting the primacy of consciousness in the universe as a layer of information assimilation/integration that guides the emerging will of the universe.

*https://med.virginia.edu/perceptual-studies/wp-content/uploads/sites/360/2018/09/Greyson_-Alexander-JNMD-2018.pdf

Chapter Forty-Five

Spiritual Awakening is a Life-Long Process

Yvonne Kason, MD

Dr. Yvonne Kason, MD, MEd, CCFP, FCFP is a retired family physician and transpersonal psychotherapist, previously on faculty at the University of Toronto, Faculty of Medicine, an internationally renowned expert on Near-Death Experiences, Kundalini Awakening, and other Spiritually Transformative Experiences™. She is the person who first coined the phrase "Spiritually Transformative Experiences™ in 1994 who has had many STEs herself. She is the Co-Founder and President of Spiritual Awakenings International, www.spiritualawakeningsinternational.org, the Co-Founder of Toronto Awakenings Sharing Group, www.torontoawakenings.org, and the Past-President of IANDS (2019-2020). She also co-founded the Spirituality in Health Care Network in 2000, and the Kundalini Research Network (KRN) in 1990. The results of the KRN Questionnaire research project Dr. Kason chaired was published in Explore in 2020.

My life and the course of my medical career have been profoundly impacted by the Spiritually Transformative Experiences™ (STEs) and resulting spiritual awakening that I have experienced in my lifetime. My spiritual awakening process has not been one isolated powerful experience that impacted me, but rather a series of many STEs which together transformed my life in a progressively more spiritual direction.

By some twist of fate, I have had five Near-Death Experiences (NDEs) over the course of my lifetime, as well as a Kundalini Awakening, multiple mystical experiences, and many psychic/intuitive experiences including past-life recall.

Although I had two NDEs as a child, and a Kundalini Awakening with mystical experience in 1976, it was my first adult Near-Death Experience in 1979 that launched me on my quest to understand STEs. On March 27, 1979, I was assigned as a young medical doctor on a medevac on an airplane that flew into a winter storm, developed engine problems, and crashed onto the surface of a semi-frozen lake and sank. I managed to get myself out of the sinking plane and then had to swim about 200 yards to the closest shore.

I struggled intensely to swim to shore, with my water-logged winter coat and boots pulling me down into the water like dead weights. I went under several times, desperately struggling to surface again. Part way to shore, I suddenly heard a loud low-pitched whooshing noise and I felt my consciousness abruptly rise up, out of my body. Most of my point of perception was now 20 or 30 feet above my physical body, with a small part of my consciousness remaining in my struggling body, as if my consciousness was in two places at the same time.

Most of my awareness then rose higher, into a space filled with warm welcoming light and a powerful feeling of unconditional love. I instantly knew in my soul that this intense love was the universal Higher Power, what I had been raised to call "God". This was the most profoundly beautiful experience I had ever had in my life. I felt like I was "HOME".

From above, I watched with peaceful detachment as my physical body struggled to swim to shore. Miraculously, my physical body was able to make it to shore. The bulk of my consciousness remained floating high above my profoundly hypothermic body.

Through a series of "coincidences" and remarkable heroism, I was rescued later that day by helicopter and flown to the closest hospital. When my near-frozen body was reheated in a hot whirlpool bath, I finally felt my consciousness re-enter my body. I heard a loud whooshing noise and suddenly felt as if I was being sucked down, abruptly shrinking from an expanded space above, and pulled down through the top of my head back into the small confines of my body. Suddenly my point of awareness/consciousness was fully back in my body again. I then knew I was going to live.

This NDE changed the course of my life. The spiritual impact was immediate. I lost my fear of death. I was convinced of the reality of our Higher Power, God. I felt filled with love, and was able to rapidly forgive.

Soon after this plane crash experience, I talked with many "experts" around me, to try to figure out what on earth had happened to me. "Has anyone heard of such an experience?" I asked. I had no name or label to call my profound experience. The responses I received were not helpful. My medical doctor colleagues postulated various medical explanations –dismissing my experience as a hallucination, brought on by an electrolyte imbalance, low blood sugar, or hypothermia of the brain. None of these explanations rang true for me. Additionally, a self-professed expert on Near-Death Experiences who I consulted in 1979 adamantly insisted that my experience was not an NDE, because I had never been dead during the experience and because I had not gone through a dark tunnel. I struggled for years with not having an accurate label to help me understand what had happened to me.

Fortunately, I did eventually find an explanation which rang true for me... for the time being. A devout Christian friend suggested, "Yvonne, I think you had a mystical experience." Yes! That label finally resonated with my soul. For almost 10 years I called my 1979 NDE a "mystical experience". Now, after years of STE research, I know that my plane crash mystical experience was in fact a type of Near-Death Experience.

To my great astonishment, the Divine hand touched me again in 1995, and blessed me with another powerful Near-Death Experience. Remarkably, this NDE left me in a profound state of ongoing unitive consciousness for two months afterwards. Then, on November 8, 2003, I had yet another powerful Near-Death Experience when I sustained a Traumatic Brain injury and died for several minutes. [I describe all my NDEs in greater detail my book *Touched by the Light* (Kason, 2019)].

Thankfully, on February 24, 2016 I experienced yet another type of STE – a spontaneous brain healing experience with an eruption of liquid light in the center of my brain, possibly related to Kundalini, and certainly related to the Grace of God!

Having had five NDEs and multiple STEs over the course of my life impacted me profoundly. My 1976 Kundalini Awakening and 1979 NDE prompted me in 1990 to shift my medical specialty into pioneering STE research and counselling in Canada. In 1990 I also co-founded the Kundalini Research Network (KRN) and became the Chair of the KRN Questionnaire Research Project (Woollacott et al., 2020). My personal struggle for understanding convinced me of the need to spread awareness of STEs both to the public and to the medical community, and to affirm that STEs are not hallucinations or signs of mental illness. My medical practice became flooded with patients wanting to speak with me about their STEs: mystical experiences, kundalini awakenings, Near-Death Experiences, past-life recall, and more.

In 1994, my clinical experience and research led me to coin the phrase "Spiritually Transformative Experiences" ™ (Kason, 1994 a,b) as an umbrella term. I defined STEs into 6 broad categories, each with many subtypes: Mystical Experiences; Spiritual energy/Kundalini awakenings; Psychic Episodes; Near-Death Experiences; Other Death-Related STEs; and, Inspired Creativity and Genius. Over the years, I have counselled over 1,000 persons who had diverse types of STEs.

My NDEs also impacted me profoundly personally, as a spiritual seeker. Each NDE or STE added to my spiritual understanding in a progressive manner. My multiple experiences on "the other side" taught me many spiritual truths.

The most powerful lessons I learned were:

1. I realized beyond a shadow of doubt that a Higher Power exists and underlies all creation. I experienced this Higher Power to be infinitely vast/omnipresent, infinitely intelligent/omniscient, unconditionally loving, and encompassing everything in past, present, and future.

2. I lost my fear of death. I directly experienced that we are immortal souls, temporarily encased in physical bodies, and we live on in another realm after death of the physical body

3. I know that reincarnation is real, because in my 2003 NDE I recalled all my past lives.

4. I know that it is possible to speed our soul evolution in our present lifetime. This can be done [as taught in Yoga] by: balanced spiritual living – according to the universal spiritual/moral principles; doing our psycho-spiritual housecleaning; and most importantly, meditating daily - to calm and expand our consciousness.

In conclusion, my spiritual awakening was a life-long process, propelled forward and deepened by multiple STEs I had over my lifetime.

References

Kason, Y. (2019). *Touched by the light: Exploring spiritually transformative experiences.* Dundurn Press.

Woollacott, M., Kason, Y., Park, R. (2020). Investigation of the phenomenology, physiology and impact of spiritually transformative experiences – kundalini awakening. *Explore,* electronic publication. https://doi.org/10.1016/j.explore.2020.07.005.

Kason, Y. (1994a). Near death experiences and kundalini awakening: Exploring the links, *Journal of Near Death Studies*, 12(3), 143-157.

Kason, Y. (1994b). *A farther shore: How near-death and other extra-ordinary experiences can change ordinary lives.* HarperCollins Canada.

Chapter Forty-Six

A Being of Light
Radiating Immense and Unconditional Love

Mario Beauregard, PhD

Mario Beauregard, PhD, is a neuroscientist currently affiliated with the Department of Psychology, University of Arizona. He is author of more than 100 publications in neuroscience, psychology, and psychiatry. Because of his research into the neuroscience of consciousness, he was selected (2000) by the World Media Net to be one of the "One Hundred Pioneers of the 21st Century." In addition, his ground-breaking research on the neurobiology of spiritual experiences has received international media coverage. As an author, Dr. Beauregard has published **The Spiritual Brain, Brain Wars**, *and* **Expanding Reality**. *He actively contributes to the articulation of the postmaterialist paradigm. In addition, he is one of the founders of the* Academy for the Advancement of Postmaterialist Sciences *(AAPS).*

As a scientist, empirical evidence related to my research has been crucial in the key thematic areas addressing specific sectors of my research program. However, to be honest, my work as a researcher has been primarily influenced by a few life-altering spiritual experiences.

The first one occurred when I was only 8 years old. My parents' farm was situated near a vibrant and mysterious forest, which I explored every now and then. One beautiful summer day back in 1970, I ventured into the entrancing woods. It was hot, and after walking for some time, I realized I was exhausted. I sat down on a large grey rock and gazed at the magnificent trees around me. After a few minutes, I started to feel a strong connection with the trees and the rock— I could sense that they were imbued with life. It felt like the rock, the trees and I were part of a much larger whole, much bigger than my "small self." My life's goal became very clear following this powerful experience— I would become a scientist who would help demonstrate that the human essence is not created by the brain.

Some 12 years later, a new life cycle began for me. This new cycle was also marked by various determining spiritual experiences. It was new, as until then I had been blessed with perfect health. Not anymore.

One January morning in 1982, I woke up to find that my body was not functioning like it did the day before, and that my visual perception was dramatically altered. I felt completely drained of energy and my stomach, back, and multiple joints were hurting. I also felt dizzy and nauseated, and my breathing was laboured. I was experiencing a kind of mental fog and my visual perception of the outside world was not the one I was used to. In fact, all the objects in my line of vision seemed to be continuously whirling.

I felt way too sick and weird to attend my classes at university. I did not understand what was happening, but I was convinced that it was something serious. The next evening, I called my parents to tell them about my predicament. They asked me to return home as quickly as possible— which I managed to do the very next day, after gathering all my willpower, but not without difficulty and misery.

I stayed in bed for almost a year. Weak and barely feeding myself, I had no other choice than to temporarily drop out of university. My parents were desperate and utterly helpless. We agreed that we had to find the underlying source of my condition, which might be the solution to my problem.

My mother took me to see several medical specialists, including a neurologist, a psychiatrist, an ophthalmologist, a gastroenterologist and an internist. Some of these doctors decided not to further the investigation, dismissing me as a hypochondriac. One doctor, claiming I was showing signs of schizophrenia, prescribed an antipsychotic which I threw out right away. The other medical specialists, puzzled by the mysterious accumulation of my symptoms, subjected me to a battery of tests— all negative.

I could feel myself slowly withering away and I could not reconcile what I was going through with the experience that had left such a mark on my childhood. It did not seem to make any sense and it filled me with bitterness—I would never be able to accomplish my life's mission in such a deplorable state. I found myself in a very dark place and suicidal thoughts started to creep into my consciousness—I could not live like this anymore.

One evening, I was so desperate that I mentally implored God's help. Apparently, my supplication did not fall on deaf ears as a few days later, in the middle of the night, I underwent a near-death experience (NDE). It began suddenly when I felt that I was leaving my physical body through my heart. I then sensed a Being of Light, radiating immense and unconditional love. The Being of Light reassured me telepathically that what I was experiencing was no disease, but rather a process of transmutation of my consciousness that played a crucial role in my life plan. He also told me that I was not alone and that I had to hang in there. Moreover, to restore my confidence, this Being of Light told me about events that would take place shortly, and he also mentioned that the severity of my symptoms would gradually decrease over the following months. All the Being of Light's predictions came true. Many other things happened during this life-defining episode, but I will not mention them due to space limitations.

After that, I mustered enough strength to resume my studies, and my symptoms faded slowly but surely, just like the Being of Light had predicted. Still, getting back on my feet was no easy task.

Seven years after my health problems first started, a friend introduced me to a famous doctor and microbiologist at the Hôtel-Dieu Hospital in Montreal. The latter performed a thorough battery of medical tests. He detected the presence of viral agents in my body— the Epstein-Barr virus, cytomegalovirus and Coxsackie virus. Together, these viruses could explain most of my symptoms. I also learned that I had cerebral vasculitis, an inflammation of the blood vessels of the brain. The severity of the viral infections left the microbiologist bemused as to how I had managed to remain on my feet and continue with my studies.

It took me 12 long years to get back in perfect health. During this life cycle, my psychic faculties developed remarkably, and I have remained in close contact with the spiritual world since this lengthy episode. I saw the microbiologist again one last time when everything was over. He told me that there was no explanation for my remission, which was simply "miraculous," from a medical point of view.

These two experiences — the one when I was 8 years old, and the other one in my early twenties — have had a profound impact on my personal life and my professional career. During the first experience I received important information related to my life plan. The information concerned mainly my future career as a neuroscientist and the type of research I would conduct. It is this experience that led me, years later, to become a neuroscientist. I received my Ph.D. from the University of Montreal and as a research scientist, I first worked at the University of Texas Health Science Center at Houston for a few years. Then I worked at the University of Montreal for almost 20 years. I am now affiliated with the University of Arizona.

The NDE that I experienced when I was 20 years old, gave me joy, strength, and sacred knowledge. During this experience, I became united with the Cosmic Ground of Being. In that spaceless and timeless state, I realized that I was united with the source of the Universe and all life on our planet. I also realized that All is One. My NDE led me to the elaboration of my future research program on expanded states of consciousness and spiritual experiences. Decades later, it is this mystical aspect of my experience that impelled me to create Holosynthesis, a transpersonal approach to self-realization through the harmonization and integration of the different human dimensions.

Chapter Forty-Seven

"I'm Not Ready Yet"

Natasha Tassell-Matamua, PhD

Natasha Tassell-Matamua, PhD, is an Associate Professor at the Centre for Indigenous Psychologies, School of Psychology, Massey University in Palmerston North, Aotearoa New Zealand. She has been researching near-death experiences and other extraordinary experiences for 12 years, and is particularly interested in cultural influences of NDEs, as well as the potential beneficial implications of NDEs across a range of disciplines and life domains. Natasha teaches courses in Indigenous Psychologies and established and is currently Director of the Centre for Indigenous Psychologies. She has been a practitioner of Buddhist philosophy for more than two decades. Natasha shares three children with her husband Nathan, and feels blessed by the obligations and responsibilities of motherhood.

"I'm not ready yet". Why did I say that? What just happened to me?

I was in my second year of university studying zoology. I hadn't done very well in the first year. Actually, I had done terribly! I'd failed most of my courses and needed to re-sit them to progress any further in my Bachelor's degree. Still, university was enjoyable and I was lavishing the liberty of having moved out of home, despite still being in my late-teens. Given my very nonchalant existence, the experience I had seemed to occur out of nowhere and made absolutely no sense to me at all at the time. What had happened to me? "I'm not ready yet"? Not ready for what? Why did I say that? I had no idea why, other than it felt like the experience I had was pre-planned in some way, although I have no conscious memory of ever planning it.

So, what happened? I was home alone one afternoon, feeling unwell enough to lie down on my bed, which was (and still is) quite unusual for me as 'being unwell' wasn't something I excelled at! I assume at some point I lost consciousness; although perhaps it is more apt to say I lost awareness of my physical body, as another part of me was very conscious throughout the experience. I recall being suddenly propelled through a tunnel at very high speeds – unlike any speed I had felt before or since. I could see a light at the end of the tunnel and there was a silhouette of a 'being' in the light. I was slightly confused and a little fearful of the speed. I was not sure what was happening to me, but I do remember it felt very real. I need only close my eyes now, more than two decades later, and I am right back in that tunnel, feeling the same sensations once more. I was moving closer and closer toward the being at the end of the tunnel, wondering who it was. However, I suddenly had the thought that I wasn't ready for whatever it was that might be about to happen, and so I communicated telepathically to the being, telling him/her that "I'm not ready yet". As soon as that was communicated, I was propelled back through the tunnel, away from the light. I returned to my body and physically 'woke up' (although of course my consciousness had been awake the entire time). I had a high fever and was covered in perspiration.

At the time, I had no idea what had happened, as I had never heard of any experience like that before. Being the only unusual framework I had to explain the experience, I did initially wonder whether it was some sort of alien encounter! But, not wanting anyone to think of me as crazy, I told no one about the experience, instead bottling it up inside for the next 10 years.

Although I wasn't sure why at the time, the experience did catalyze some immediate changes in me. I felt an insatiable longing for knowledge; one that I knew the university environment could not provide. It now seemed far too constrained to me. I felt I needed to travel and experience 'something', yet I did not know what that something was. I just wanted to live life... fully. So, I found myself booking a one-way plane ticket to the UK one Saturday afternoon. I then sold all my possessions, left university, and spent the next 18 months working intermittently and travelling around Europe from the UK, on a search for that elusive 'something' I felt an internal longing for.

My family could not understand why I had left 'everything' to travel to foreign lands. They struggled with this 'new' me and, perhaps partly on account of my age at the time and also the fact I had not told anyone about the experience I had, I could not fully articulate why I needed the changes either. This left them feeling confused and unaccepting. This lack of approval for who I was becoming led to a period of disconnection from my family, which was incredibly hard because my mother had passed away when I was 6 years old and so the separation from them initially led to the re-surfacing of some deeply repressed attachment issues. But, I just knew the life I had been living was no longer the life I wanted or needed, and so there was no other option for me but to do what I felt I needed to do.

Interestingly, immediately after my experience and without rational explanation, I was intensely drawn to Buddhism – a way of being I had never heard of or had exposure to up until that point in my life. The first book I read was the Tibetan Book of Living and Dying, where I came across descriptions of NDEs for the very first time and felt like I had finally found an explanation for my experience. I still have that book and have been following a Buddhist philosophy of living ever since. It helped me to overcome the sadness of the broken familial relationships, to better understand my experience and what it meant (and still means) for me and others, as well as continuing to have an enormous influence on the way I navigate life.

When I finally decided to return home to New Zealand, I felt a strong desire to study psychology (rather than zoology). I completed a Bachelor's degree, and while I spent the next decade in a cycle of periodically travelling the world and then returning to New Zealand only to travel again months later, during this time I was also able to complete a Master's degree and then eventually a PhD in psychology. I obtained a lectureship at a university in New Zealand during the final year of completing my PhD and am still at that university now! I have progressed to an Associate Professor in Psychology, and spent the past 11 years professionally researching NDEs, including their incidence, after-effects and implications. Although it is difficult to fully capture the enormity of its impact, I can say with certainty that the experience I had more than two decades ago changed the entire trajectory of my life. I continue to learn about myself and about NDEs, and I could not be more grateful for the persistent fulfilment that experience and its after-effects bring.

PART SEVEN

STEs Triggered by Psychic Experiences

Psychic experiences also play a significant role in triggering spiritual awakenings or STEs. It is interesting that in the US and Europe psychic phenomena have been experienced by a substantial portion of the population, ranging from 21-34% in Europe and 25-50% in the US for such phenomena as telepathy, clairvoyance and contact with the dead (Wahbeh et al., 2020). Yet many people in our culture consider these to be simple random occurrences that we incorrectly interpret as having spiritual significance.

The STEs in this section ranged from a young woman having a shared experience of seeing her deceased grandfather bring her mother onto shore after she was in a swimming incident, to communication from a friend who had recently and unexpectedly died when struck by a car, and an apparently miraculous self-healing through an energy healing practice.

Were these triggered by a quieting of mental activity? It is not clear from the essays; however, it may be that a quiet mind allows a clearer perception of these phenomena when they occur. As you read these essays, we invite you to look back on your own experiences to see if these readings trigger any memories for you of events that may have originally been interpreted as mere coincidences, but may have been more than this, and possibly true psi phenomena.

Reference

Wahbeh, H., Yount, G., Vieten, C., Radin, D., Delorme A. (2020). Measuring extraordinary experiences and beliefs: A validation and reliability study [version 3; peer review: 3 approved]. *F1000Research*, 8:1741. https://doi.org/10.12688/f1000research.20409.3

Chapter Forty-Eight

From Depression to Transcendent Non-Duality

Helané Wahbeh, ND, MCR

Helané Wahbeh is the Director of Research at the Institute of Noetic Sciences, an adjunct assistant professor in the Department of Neurology at Oregon Health & Science University, and President of the Parapsychological Association. Dr. Wahbeh is clinically trained as a naturopathic physician and research trained with a Master of Clinical Research and two post-doctoral research fellowships. She has published on and spoken internationally about her studies on complementary and alternative medicine, mind-body medicine, extended human capacities, stress, post-traumatic stress disorder, and their relationships to physiology, health, and healing. Dr. Wahbeh is especially known for her research around — and noetic approach to — channeling.

My spiritual awakening evolved as a series of leaps of deepening knowingness. It continues to unfold to this day, and I imagine that it will never stop. The first spiritual leap I can remember was when my uncle died suddenly from a heart attack during a running race. Faced with mortality, I pondered what it meant to die. I had an intuition or noetic experience that my true essence was not limited to my physical body.

Around the same time, my mother initiated me into the esoteric world of trance channeling. We attended weekly meetings at my grandparent's house, where 30-40 people watched my uncle and sometimes my grandmother trance channel. I found it fascinating and frightening: the strangeness of it all. Sometimes the "being" directly communicated specific messages for me. Observing my relatives channel various "beings" and bring forth incredible information neither of them knew from their personal selves was world-changing.

My worldview was forever changed. I had little doubt that my relatives were channeling something other than their personal selves. I cannot say whether the source was their higher selves, collective consciousness, or non-physical beings.

I can say that my uncle could not fake the different voices, the mannerisms, the accents, and especially the knowledge he brought forth during channeling. He was only a high school graduate at the time, and some of the knowledge he shared during his trance states was far beyond his education. I was imprinted at a young age that there were invisible realms my five senses could not perceive, things not taught in school, church, or anywhere else.

These two leaps expanded my awareness of non-physical aspects of reality, supporting the manifestation of my career in alternative medicine. I chose naturopathic medicine rather than allopathic medicine because of its more holistic approach to health and healing. The physicalist model to health and healing focusing on symptoms and the physical did not resonate with me, nor did I think it represented the complete picture of our bodies and its interaction with the mental, emotional, energetic, and spiritual aspects.

Like many other spiritual seekers, my next big leap in spiritual awakening began with a dark night of the soul. I was married and had an eleven months-old child when my marriage fell apart. The breakup sent me into a whirlwind of emotions: sadness, grief, anger, and then into a deep, deep depression. I went into the downward spiral of despair and did not see a way out.

Synchronistically, I went to a darshan with Leslie Thurston of Corelight. I felt a deep resonance and connection to her and the organization's work. I began extensive processing work using tools I learned that focused on balancing the dual nature of our physical world. I finally understood and cleared many patterns of my ego, a conglomeration of ancestral, familial, archetypal, and personal patterns. I processed the main human archetypes of victim, tyrant, rebel, savior, and martyr. I strengthened my witness. The witness is the meta-cognitive awareness usually associated with our higher selves or awake-self that can observe and notice the ego-self having thoughts, experiencing emotions, and acting out particular behaviors. By acknowledging and witnessing duality (e.g., good/bad, worthy/worthless, victim/tyrant) and the intention to unify that duality, I achieved greater alignment with non-dual balanced states such as unconditional love, equanimity, and compassion.

Simultaneously, I learned how to meditate and began a regular meditation practice. The more I cleared my patterns, the more easeful my meditation practice was. I quickly experienced a transcendent oneness state during meditation that solidified an understanding that I was so much more than my physical body. My consciousness expanded beyond my personal self. The "I" associated with Helané dissolved. I was aware and a part of everything around me. The state was timeless and blissful, and ineffable. My continued ability to go into transcendent states during meditation only reinforces my inner knowing that I am more than my body and that my consciousness is not limited to it.

My clinical practice benefited from having this intrinsic knowledge as I could incorporate multiple levels for healing. It also led me through a beautiful series of synchronistic events to be working at the Institute of Noetic Sciences (IONS). I can now freely research the various aspects of non-local consciousness and support others to study and nurture these capacities within themselves.

At IONS, we speak of the noetic handshake, a synergy between science and direct experience. I can talk until I am blue in the face about the many studies that demonstrate our consciousness extends beyond the physical. However, suppose the person I'm talking to has not had a direct experience themselves. In that case, accepting those findings is difficult for them. I find that direct experience or what this book might call "the spiritual awakening" is the quickest and most reliable way for someone to understand the expanded nature of consciousness. What I find most challenging about spiritual awakening experiences is that they are so profound and life-changing but cannot be adequately described with words. They are ineffable. We want to share our transformative experiences with others, yet words so inadequately impart the enormity of the experience - we feel at a loss.

I am deeply grateful that my career path allows me to delve into our capacity to describe, study, and nurture spiritual awakening experiences in myself and others. I look forward to where my personal and professional awakening journey will take me.

Chapter Forty-Nine

Why?

Jude Currivan, PhD

Jude Currivan has a master's degree in physics from Oxford University and a doctorate in archaeology from the University of Reading. She is a cosmologist, planetary healer, futurist, author who was previously one of the most senior business women in the UK and in 2017 she co-founded WholeWorld-View (www.wholeworld-view.org). Integrating leading edge science, research into consciousness, and universal wisdom teachings into a wholistic world-view underpins her work serving conscious evolution and empowering transformational and emergent resolutions to collective human and planetary issues. For over two decades she has also travelled around the world in service to planetary healing. A member of the Evolutionary Leaders Circle (www.evolutionaryleaders.net) she is also the international and award-winning author of six books to date, latterly **The Cosmic Hologram: In-formation at the Center of Creation**. *Her next book,* **Gaia: Her-Story** *will be published in 2022.*

From when I was a young child, as my very patient Mum would testify, my favourite word was why? To my darling Mum's great credit, she always tried to answer my numerous questions and when she couldn't, did her best to point me in the hopeful direction of answers.

Whilst many of my questions were mundane, my most deeply felt yearning was to understand the nature of reality itself and my personal and our collective human place in the Cosmos. The primary reason for my queries was that from that early age I began to have so-called nonlocal experiences, beyond the limitations of our five physical senses and what researchers sometimes call supernormal phenomena. For me, these have included telepathic connections, precognitive and remote cognition and an ability to enter altered states of awareness where I've also been able to access meaningful and often verifiable information and communicate with discarnate, multidimensional and archetypal intelligences and sentience.

Whilst such experiences have continued throughout my life, for many years I didn't share them with any of my family, friends, teachers or indeed anyone else in my communities and workplaces. Rather than being concerned that they might have been dismissed in a prevailing societal paradigm of materialistic separation, it just didn't occur to me to do so until well into my adulthood.

Rather than a 'spiritual' awakening, they revealed to me what the Vedic sages of ancient India referred to as an Indra's Net of a cosmic web of reality. A Cosmos where everything is interconnected with everything else and all are ultimately relational parts of a greater whole of all that is. Their perception, as perhaps most clearly expressed in the *Ishavasya Upanishad*, describing the understanding of the fundamental nature of reality as being mind and consciousness, reflected my own experiences. It is also, as I was to learn, the same perspective as scientific pioneers such as Albert Einstein, Max Planck, Sir James Jeans and David Bohm espoused.

My dear friend and evolutionary biologist, Elisabet Sahtouris offers what I feel is an excellent analogy of this worldview. Instead of perceiving implied divisions between the physical, emotional, mental and spiritual aspects of our consciousness, Elisabet invites us to consider them all as notes along a vibrational musical keyboard, where the physical realm is essentially the lowest octave and discarnate realms the higher notes of individuated and ensouled sentience.

My life-long curiosity has been continually answered in many ways that have challenged, inspired and empowered me to continue my journey of inner and outer discovery. My quest to understand the deeper whys of the world, has elicited the response of a Universe that exists to evolve as a nonlocally unified entity, from simplicity to complexity and ever greater self-awareness. Where we are micro-cosmic co-creators of its innately and meaningfully in-formed and holographically manifested appearance - where reality is real but separation is an illusion. And this is above all an essentially benign Universe, where everything in existence has inherent meaning and purpose.

My ongoing quest for understanding also naturally extended to include a more prosaic exploration of how the wonder-full nature of the realities I was experiencing and the Universe came to be. This involved my studying for a

Master's Degree in physics at Oxford University specializing in cosmology and quantum physics, and then after a twenty-five-year international corporate career, returning to an academic environment, this time at the Department of Archaeology at the University of Reading in the UK to research ancient cosmologies for a PhD.

In the last fifteen years since completing my PhD I've continued and increasingly focused my research for answers as to how the manifest appearance of the energy-matter and space-time of our Universe comes about. During this time, leading-edge science at all scales of existence and across many fields of study has progressively converged with universal wisdom teachings and my own experiences, supporting the perspective that its semblance is emergent from deeper nonphysical realms of causation.

My own work considers that cosmic mind and its sentience, expresses itself through information based on a universal alphabet of just two digitised 'letters' of 1s and 0s, and then articulating these as meaningful in-formation, literally and dynamically in-forms the reality of our Universe. The so-named holographic principle which models our entire Universe as a holographic projection from the boundary of what we perceive as space enables the insight that it does so in complementary ways based on the three laws of thermodynamics. I have restated and expanded these as a new IN-SCIght of IN-formational SCIence into three laws of infodynamics. This leads to in-formation expressed in complementary ways as quantized energy-matter and to restating entropy from the energetic microstates of a system to in-tropy as its meaningful in-formational content applied to the space-time of our entire Universe. Then as space expands and universal time flows, ever more in-formational content is embodied and experienced within our Universe, enabling its innate evolutionary impulse to be realized.

Writing *The Cosmic Hologram* published in 2017 to describe and share the extensive and growing evidence for this cosmology of consciousness, I realized that its message could serve the healing of our collective fragmented world view and help us transcend the illusion of separation and so co-founded WholeWorld-View as a unifying framework to share the understanding and serve the experiencing and embodying of its unitive and evolutionary perspective.

Its science of love naturally encompasses multidimensional experiences that are variously described as numinous, mystical and spiritual. It naturalizes supernormal phenomena, supports the power of conscious intention and empowers our innate superpower of intuition.

Having just completed the manuscript of my next book *The Story* of *GAIA* for publication in 2022, my life-long wonder and awe of our Universe and my love for our planetary home Gaia continue to inspire and instil me with a profound sense of belonging. In these pivotal times, Gaia herself, it seems to me, is calling on us to consciously wake up and grow up, to re-member why we're here, who we really are and to become her co-evolutionary partners, as Gaians.

Chapter Fifty

An Experience in Psychometry

Laurel Waterman

Laurel Waterman, currently a doctoral student in Curriculum and Pedagogy at the Ontario Institute for Studies in Education, University of Toronto, has been teaching creative non-fiction writing at the University of Toronto since 2009. She published About Local Food: four conversations with Toronto food activists, a book based on her MA research in Adult Education and Community Development. Waterman has been a writer, researcher, and editor for several books, essays, research projects, and conference presentations throughout her academic career, mostly in the areas of non-fiction writing, education, food systems, and environmental sustainability. In 2021, she was awarded a grant from the Ontario Graduate Scholarship fund for her doctoral research in consciousness studies education. She is a student member of the Academy for the Advancement of Post-materialist Sciences (AAPS), and co-moderator of their Facebook page.

The experience that transformed my understanding of consciousness happened on July 6, 2019, at "Miracles Happen," a past life regression hypnosis workshop with Dr. Brian Weiss at the Omega Center in Rhinebeck, New York. It was almost a year since my husband died unexpectedly at 41 years old, leaving me a 36-year-old widow raising two young children on my own. The grief was psychologically crippling. I found no solace in the idea that individual consciousness could continue after bodily death. I knew it wasn't true. The brain creates consciousness, so when the brain dies, the person is extinguished. That's what science says. But I let myself read books that entertained the possibility of life after death because they helped me to feel better. I found Dr. Weiss's books on past life regression hypnosis and felt inspired to attend a workshop with him.

I'd recently started hypnotherapy sessions in Toronto with Dr. Adam

Crabtree (a co-author of one of the foundational books in consciousness studies, *Irreducible Mind*, but I didn't know that at the time). Dr. Crabtree had led me into a few past life regressions in his office, and I saw some vivid scenes in my mind. I wanted to believe these were memories from past lives that prove reincarnation, but how could I know that they were not just my imagination?

On the Saturday morning at the workshop, Dr. Weiss instructed us to partner with someone whom we did not know. I paired up with a woman one seat over named Beco. I knew only three things about Beco: she lived in Seattle; she looked ethnically Chinese and spoke with an accent; and she wasn't having any past-life regression experiences. After each exercise, she'd sit up and say, "I can't believe I fell asleep again!"

Dr. Weiss asked us to exchange objects with our partners, something we had owned for more than a month. I unclasped my earrings and placed them in her palm. She searched her bare wrists and empty pockets for an object before handing me her phone. I cradled it in my hands. Then Dr. Weiss led us into a relaxation and said, "Let any information that would be helpful for the owner of the object in your hands to come to your mind."

A scene took form. I saw Beco diving into an Olympic-sized swimming pool. I saw Beco boarding a large passenger ship. Then I saw an elderly Chinese man in a wheelchair. A scene of a small, clean apartment formed around him. A sliding balcony door overlooked an ocean, and a young Chinese girl in a red party dress held a red balloon. I interpreted this as a small birthday party for the elderly man. Then I saw Beco crouched beside the man in the wheelchair, holding his wrinkled hand. An overwhelming emotion of gratitude flowed from him to her. The man said something in Mandarin or Cantonese. Then I saw Beco sitting on a balcony overlooking the ocean, cupping a mug of tea.

"Slowly return to the room," Dr. Weiss instructed. "Share with your partner anything that you experienced."

Beco didn't have much to share with me. I shrugged, took a deep breath, and said, "Well, I saw some pretty specific scenes. I don't know if any of this will make sense to you, but here we go. First, I saw you diving into a large swimming pool. Do you swim?"

"Sometimes," Beco said.

"Okay." I tried not to feel discouraged. "Then I saw you boarding a ship."

Beco inhaled sharply. "A cruise ship?"

"Yes, a cruise ship. A big one."

"Oh my god," she said and clasped a hand to her mouth. "Go on, go on."

"Then I saw an elderly Chinese man in a wheelchair."

She gasped and clasped her hands to her mouth. "My father!"

"Your father is in a wheelchair?"

She nodded and teared up. I told her the rest of it: the birthday scene, her holding the man's hand, the feeling of gratitude he felt toward her, the balcony overlooking the ocean. "And he said something," I continued, "but in a language I don't know. Does he speak English?" By this point, Beco was sobbing uncontrollably.

"No, he doesn't know English," Beco managed to say. She fanned at her eyes, took a deep breath, and said, "You are not going to believe this. Two months ago, I had a cruise booked for my family to celebrate my father's 89th birthday. Two weeks before the cruise, my father, who was perfectly healthy, had a massive stroke. He was paralyzed, couldn't speak, and the doctors said he would likely die. I flew home to China, sat by his hospital bed, and held his hand. I said to him, 'Dad, I want to help you get better, but I need to know that you want to live.' He nodded to me with his eyes. I contacted a Reiki master. He came and met my dad once and continued remote healing on him. In one month, against everything the doctors said, my father recovered to the point where he can speak, sit in a wheelchair, and move one arm. And it is my greatest dream that he will be well enough so that I can take him on the cruise for his 90th birthday." Beco believed my "visions" were confirmation that this would happen.

Now, I do not know if Beco's dream and my "visions" came true or not. I was preoccupied with the significance of the experience. Where did these scenes come to me from? How could I imagine a series of scenes that were so specific to emotionally charged recent events in Beco's life? The cruise ship, the elderly man, the stroke, the gratitude for her helping with his recovery, the wheelchair. This was beyond coincidence. This was validation.

I know that I knew nothing about Beco. I know that I had my eyes closed and these scenes came to me from somewhere. And because of their relevance to her, and the intensity of her reaction, I know that it couldn't have been just my imagination. I experienced a "download" from some information source outside of myself or that was somehow transmitted between us. This experience doesn't prove life after death, and it doesn't prove psychic accuracy; but it convinced me that my consciousness is connected to something beyond myself.

Following this experience, I tumbled down the rabbit hole of consciousness studies research. The recent illuminating academic and scientific work in consciousness, combined with my experience in psychometry, inspired me to change the focus of my work in education. After thirteen years as a lecturer of narrative non-fiction writing at the University of Toronto, I decided to return to research and pursue a PhD in Curriculum and Pedagogy at the Ontario Institute for Studies in Education. My research asks how we can integrate consciousness studies into education? The education system seems so deeply entrenched in the scientific materialist paradigm that the concept of consciousness is not included in curriculum, or even part of the academic discourse in education. I think that young people should learn the truth about consciousness as we currently understand it, not some censored version with the most up-to-date, curious, wonderful, inexplicable, and hopeful parts cut out. I want to help shift the paradigm for consciousness in the education system. Imagine how that might change our world.

Chapter Fifty-One

If You're Around Can You Give Me a Sign?

Bradley Heinz

Bradley Heinz is a medical student at the University of California, San Francisco. He hopes to contribute to shifting our scientific and medical frame from one that regards life as nothing more but lifeless atoms bumping into each other according to physical laws in a dog-eat-dog arena to one that embraces our interdependence within a living universe with consciousness as an irreducible core component.

I always had the will to believe, but growing up, nothing quite fit. I felt disenchanted with the Catholicism of my upbringing, which felt to be a showy display lacking spiritual substance. The religion of my family's heritage didn't offer me satisfactory answers to the existential questions of the curious child, but neither did the atheist frameworks put forth in my public schooling. I felt a need to figure it out, so I kept my eyes peeled for some incontrovertible proof that the world was more than it seemed in my day-to-day. In the quiet of the night, as "I lay me down to sleep", I'd give thanks for the good in my life and ask for guidance to navigate around the rest.

When my mom retold the story of my great grandmother's passing in our living room, where her delirium cleared and she spoke to us of her husband, dead many decades, waiting for her in the corner of the room, where my mom saw my grandma's cane, now hanging from the mantle of the fireplace, start to swing on its own accord, I wanted nothing more than my own direct experience. The secondhand account, though so close, still felt like sand falling through my fingers. I now know that over 90% of the American public has had an experience that appeared to transcend the everyday boundaries of space and time (Wahbeh et al., 2018), but mine wouldn't come for a few more years.

The prevailing public cultural paradigm has enough power to have individuals question their own experience. When I was having a sacred-seeming moment late one night on a beach as a twelve year-old and I asked, "God, are you there? Is there more to this world than what I just see?" and a fiery shooting star, the first I had ever seen, lit up my entire night sky, it was easy to chalk it up as a coincidence. Same with two more repeated experiments of the same format. A coincidence makes much more sense than the universe somehow responding to me, especially given the stories of the nature of reality my cultural context provided.

But when two of my friends were struck by a car while walking one dark, winter evening, I had an experience I could no longer chalk up to coincidence. My friend Eric survived relatively physically unscathed. Unfortunately, after a few days in a coma, my friend Jake passed away. The night after his passing, I was crying in my kitchen, mourning the loss of my friend, and crumpling under the weight of an existential dread borne of being fourteen and adrift from any religious or spiritual frame: old enough to understand the gravity of the human condition, aware enough to feel there was no life raft to grasp onto. People in my life had died before, but for them, it wasn't unexpected, and didn't feel unfair. Jake's passing had me wondering if anything could matter in a world where innocent children were allowed to die.

I squeezed my eyes shut and wiped the tears from my face with my sweater sleeve. I looked to the ceiling, and asked something along the lines of, "Jake, if you're around, if there's more than I can see, can you give me a sign? I'm struggling here." At that very moment, the electricity in my house started oscillating. The lights got very dim, then back to bright, on repeat for a few seconds. The digital clocks on our appliances reset. The TV turned off. My jaw dropped. I had never experienced a brown-out like this. The power had fully gone out before, but only when thunderstorms downed power lines. This was a calm winter night. My mind reached for some explanation for this curious coincidence.

Half an hour later, when sitting in the car waiting for my mom to drive me to a friend's house where we'd gather to share memories and mourn, I pondered what had just happened to me. I was in disbelief. "This can't be real, can it? Jake, what the heck!" Just then, a song I had been listening to heavily on repeat since the accident, a sort of anthem of anguish and despair, came on the radio. This was not a popular song, and not one I'm sure ever got played on the radio. The DJ even introduced it as being quite an odd choice to play given their usual schtick, one that he may have had to "grab from the archives". Another mind-boggling "coincidence". I couldn't help but chuckle to myself.

In retrospect, these events didn't quite change my life. I later learned of people who had their worldviews and daily lives completely transformed after they had mystical or near-death experiences. I did not acquire an immediate and overwhelming "God consciousness" as countless people throughout history have described. Mine stoked my curiosity, and opened my mind to the idea that perhaps reality wasn't just the cold, materialist world as described by Western science. My own spiritual development has been of the "educational variety", as William James described. The only conclusion I feel confident in is that reality is not well-described with a materialist frame.

As my spiritual quest unfolded, I knew my business career wouldn't fulfil me, and wouldn't help me answer these bigger questions. I now write this as a future physician, nearly done with my degree. My goal is to make medicine a spiritual practice, as well as pay very close attention. Births, deaths, profound ailments and amazing recoveries, stories that challenge materialism often emerge in these out-of-the-ordinary moments, such as the millions of Americans who have awakened in hospitals having returned from clinical brain death, many reporting vivid, conscious awareness independent of their failing bodies and brains (Parnia et al., 2001; Greyson, 1993). I'm going to see what I can learn and what I can share.

References

Greyson, B. (1993). Varieties of near-death experience. *Psychiatry*, 56(4), 390-399.

Parnia, S., Waller, D. G., Yeates, R., & Fenwick, P. (2001). A qualitative and quantitative study of the incidence, features and aetiology of near-death experiences in cardiac arrest survivors, *Resuscitation,* 48, 149-156.

Wahbeh, H., Radin, D., Mossbridge, J., Vieten, C., & Delorme, A. (2018). Exceptional experiences reported by scientists and engineers. *EXPLORE,* 14(5), 329–341. https://doi.org/10.1016/j.explore.2018.05.0022

Chapter Fifty-Two

A Visit From My Great-Grandfather

Kim Penberthy, PhD

Jennifer "Kim" Penberthy, PhD, ABPP is the Chester F. Carlson Professor of Psychiatry and Neurobehavioral Sciences, Division of Perceptual Studies, and the Associate Director for Clinician Wellness at the University of Virginia School of Medicine. Kim is a board-certified clinical psychologist and conducts research, teaches, and provides clinical care. Her research interests focus on the mind-body relationship and exploring human consciousness as well as extraordinary human experiences and the impact of such on human abilities and wellness. Recent work includes exploring the occurrence and impact of after death communications. She is also dedicated to promoting diversity and inclusion and exploring contemplative practices across cultures and marginalized groups. She lectures internationally, and has published extensively on contemplative practices and psychotherapy, including four books, and scores of manuscripts and book chapters.

One summer when I was in my mid-20s I was at the Outer Banks of North Carolina on the beach with my mother. The Outer Banks is a group of barrier islands on the Atlantic Ocean and a popular destination in the mid-Atlantic region of the United States. We were there together, just the two of us. I'm not sure why my father or my other siblings were not there, but it was just me and my mother. We both love the ocean and we spent some time laying on the sand getting warm and drowsy. My mother told me that she was going in to swim and I murmured a soft OK without opening my eyes.

The sun was dazzling bright as I reclined on the sandy towel, so I covered my eyes with a towel. I might have drifted to sleep. I'm not sure. But I woke to a crowd of voices in the distance. It was not an overly loud sound, but noticeably louder than the typical hum of the beach. I rose to my elbows, and the towel slid off my face. I looked out to the ocean, and saw people gathered at the edge. My eyes were narrow trying to protect from the dazzling sun. I could not see very well because it was so bright and I had no sunglasses on. Finally, my eyes adjusted and I saw an older gentleman dressed in baggy khaki pants with an old-fashioned hat on his head and white short-sleeve button up shirt. He was helping my mother out of the water!

He held her by the elbow, and they were walking together as she struggled to get out of the water. She had a lifeguard on the other side of her and I remember feeling curious and interested but not alarmed. I rose to a seated position and waited for her to approach. For some reason I did not get up and run to her. I was still in a bit of a daze and wondering if what I saw was real. I felt simultaneously curious and yet certain about what I was seeing. I was certain that she was OK and a pervasive mental and physical calm came over me. I waited. Something in me, said it's all ok, as it should be, just wait. When she finally walked up to the blanket where I was sitting, I asked if she was all right and she said yes and told me to lay back down. I laid down and she laid down beside me, breathing out slowly as she lowered herself. We both closed our eyes. After a few seconds I said curiously but calmly "who was that man walking with you out of the ocean, the older one with a hat?" Without hesitation, she replied, "That was my grandfather."

I did know that my mother spent a good deal of time with her grandparents growing up, and they essentially raised her due to her own parents' unfortunate circumstances. Mom was an only child and she was especially close to her grandfather. My mother, Marlene, was apparently the apple of his eye, and he would do anything for her. I learned much of this from her nursing school roommate and best friend, Linda, after mom died in 2008. Mom and I never really talked further about this experience. She was not evasive about it, but we both seemed to understand that there was not much more to be said. I assumed then, as I do now, that her beloved grandfather saved her because it was not her time, and it felt profoundly right to me. I knew that I did not hallucinate him because my mother saw him too. Perhaps we had a mutual hallucination, I don't know.

What I do know is that that vision taught me that perhaps there is more going on in this universe than I can begin to comprehend. Significantly, this knowledge was accompanied by a profound sense of calmness and equanimity. It felt "right" and "true." The impact of understanding in one instance that the universe, time, our "selves" are vast, connected, and benevolent was life changing.

In my mind, this experience meant that so much more was possible - the continuity of lives, the power of love and connection – and it turned the materialistic world view of the sciences I had studied on its head. This single experience opened my mind and heart to the certainty of life after life and the power of human relationships.

This experience solidified within me a sense that the universe is profoundly more nuanced than basic sciences or even religions would have us believe. I believe that I ultimately ended up studying altered states of consciousness and the impact of exceptional human experiences, in part, due to this experience on the beach with my mother and great-grandfather. I believe that this experience helps me understand and accept those experiences of my patients who report their spiritual awakenings or insights or experiences while meditating or practicing mindfulness. I believe this experience has profoundly impacted every aspect of my life, including my career choice as a clinical psychologist and Professor in the Department of Psychiatry and Neurobehavioral Sciences, at the University of Virginia School of Medicine. It also impacted my choice in a husband, to having a child when it was not advised by my physicians, but knowing that it would all be ok.

What I gained from that day at the beach is a profound sense that the universe, although mysterious and powerful, is also benevolent, and that we may all be connected in ways beyond our imagination. These notions have further prompted me to imagine a world focused on promoting and celebrating this inter-relatedness. Imagine the positive impact on the world if everyone behaved as if we were connected in a larger way to others or that we would see each other again. What I have ultimately learned is that there may be more to our existence than we can even imagine. Opening our hearts and minds to possibilities is a start.

Chapter Fifty-Three

Steps Toward an Animated Worldview

Michael Grosso, PhD

Prof. Michael Grosso studied classics and received his PhD in philosophy from Columbia University. He has taught philosophy and the humanities at New Jersey City University, CUNY (City University of New York), and Kennedy University, CA. His recent books include **Smile of the Universe: Miracles in an Age of Disbelief; The Man Who Could Fly: St. Joseph of Copertino and the Mystery of Levitation; The final Choice: Death or Transcendence; Experiencing the Next World Now;** *etc. Michael's focus is on the science of extraordinary human experience and the creative implications of altered states of consciousness. See his blog:* consciousnessunbound.blogspot.com. *He is also a painter who works at the interface of art and the paranormal. See his art site:* paintingthepsyche.com.

I have awakened to a worldview beyond the dead materialism of uncritical everyday life. My awakening was gradual, punctuated by experiences that forced me, stepwise, to arrive at a form of animism I like to espouse—a belief in the primacy of consciousness and creative imagination.

My worldview has been shaped by strange experiences. So, in early boyhood I had a knack for projecting myself into my own movie-world. It was like a lucid dream except that I was awake. I remember going off into my inner movie-house while getting a haircut, sitting in a pew at church, or lying in bed before falling asleep. I was a frequent flier to other worlds, but then lost the knack. But I found it again in a different form: now I drew and painted my images—I made what's called art. And I still do it, as my spiritual practice. These were some first steps in my higher education.

I recall my first paranormal dream—a kid on the block I never spoke with is asking me to play ball. Outside after my dream, first off I see that kid, and he asks me, "Wanna play ball?" I still remember that vivid dream, how it stretched my mind. I was six years old.

A more dramatic dream—three of them, in fact—I had of the near assassination of President Ronald Reagan in 1981. My ordinary sense of time began to melt after these precognitive dreams. And so did my sense of space when one day my lover in Hampstead Heath, England, wrote to me that I appeared in bed with her at the exact time I was missing her with a vengeance. More than one incident showed me the link between love and telepathy. An experience that might salve the fear of loneliness, telepathy increased my sense of living in a sociable universe.

What stymied me was the belief that my consciousness, however magical and fascinating its properties, was nonetheless a mere by-product of my mortal brain. Two things got me past that error. First was the 'hard problem,' the insufferable difficulties of trying, conceptually, to reduce consciousness to brain states. Mind and brain interact, but are different kinds of reality. My mental identity is not reducible to my brain identity.

The second was that my telepathic mind can bypass my brain and interact with other minds, directly, unconstrained by space or time. If then our minds are not in physical space or time, why should they be destroyed by brain-death? In fact, there's much evidence to the contrary.

My own experiences were critical; for example, I was invited to spend a night in a haunted house, in which nine people claimed to see or in some way encounter a particularly obnoxious ghost. So, at two in the morning, I was awake on a couch reading, and nothing was happening. Then, a gong attached to the wall in the room where I was sitting rang. He's here, I thought, stood up, grabbed and rang the gong. Same sound. I was jubilant. The ghost just signaled me!

But then, this. Sitting back, I noticed in the corner of the room a rippling, semi-transparent human figure that suddenly came straight at me, and enwrapped me. I tried to scream—"He's here!" but was paralyzed. It lasted one or two intense seconds. Conclusion? Ghosts are really real. It was conscious and willful, the entity that hugged me. And yet, to be hugged and silenced by a known nasty ghost tore open my mind a bit more.

Time, space, matter, bodily death may not be the impregnable barriers I once thought they were. Slowly, I learned in a tale of many steps that a new story and world-picture was possible, and that the field of possible action and experience was much wider than I supposed.

How shall I put it? Certain experiences opened me to a more animated sense of reality. A UAP (unidentified aerial phenomenon) encounter five days before getting my PhD in philosophy from Columbia University introduced a cosmic element to the mystery play of my existence. A light entity appeared out of nowhere and danced outside my window in the sky in tune with the music of John Coltrane--music that Jane and I were listening to. In fact, a third person on the roof observed the same light-dance. The unknown visitor that night ignited my need to explore the outer limits of the possible.

In the light of these and other anomalies, it was goodbye to the reductive mainstream worldview. Moreover, politics, economics, and scientific technology have devised weaponry that threaten global annihilation. Worse still, they have created a vector of eco-technical force driving us toward climate apocalypse. The 2021 UN Panel on Climate Change concluded: we must change the way we live on Earth or endure unmitigated disaster. Change the way we live on Earth? In short, a philosophical revolution.

Animism is primal humanity's perception of nature. As far as I can see, a more complete animation of human consciousness is the only way to get out of the habit of killing each other and destroying our mother Earth. All the latent magical, mystical, and empathic powers sleeping fitfully within, need to be awakened and called to action.

The extraordinary phenomena point to new ways of being in greater harmony with each other and with our life-giving ecology. But how to pursue this exploration? I found that my brain was the dial and filter of my consciousness, not its producer. I was free to invent methods of widening or contracting the mesh of my mental filters.

This I believe is true for us all. We can, if we dare, learn to unlock the gates of our conscious life. We must, if we hope to evolve as a species, reanimate ourselves and our relationship to everything around us. All the skills and powers to perform this necessary miracle lie within us. Our extraordinary potential is real, wants, and needs to be awakened and activated—and set loose upon the world.

Chapter Fifty-Four

A Surge of Electric Energy Flowing Through Me

Lorne Schussel, PhD

Lorne Schussel, MS, PhD is a Clinical Psychologist, Postdoctoral Fellow and Research Director of the Contemplative Science and Post Materialism Lab at Columbia University, Teachers College. He is visiting faculty at the Spirituality Mind Body Institute and formerly Project Director of the Contemplative Neuroscience and Connectivity Project. His research focuses on the utilization of novel mind-body practices, human connectivity, contemplative neuroscience, and integrating clinical biomarkers (epigenetic, HR, EEG) into clinical research. Dr. Schussel developed a psychological healing practice known as "The Best Self Visualization Method" which has been cited in the New York Times, ABC-online, and the Huffington Post. Lorne has recently taught the technique to appointed state judges as visiting faculty at the California State Judicial College for a course on mental health and employee burnout.

Eighteen years ago, I was living in Tucson, Arizona and I had been afflicted with a cyst the size of a golf ball that was growing on my back. Due to its size, a physician had informed me that it would need to be removed. At this same time in my life, I had just returned from India and during my travels a friend had given me a book on a healing practice known as 'pranic healing'. He had convinced me of the efficacy of the practice due to the success he had with helping his mother through a debilitating back injury. I thought that I could apply the unusual remedy to my own problem.

After following the parameters of the healing practice involving intentional breathing, and hand movements centered on manipulating 'pranic energy' I started to feel a surge of electricity flowing through my body. There was an unusual visceral feeling as well as abnormal surface stimulation to my skin. Was this electricity? Prana? Energy? I couldn't quite put a label to the experience.

Within one day the cyst which was noticeably present before and physically obtrusive had completely vanished. I was in awe and shocked. How could this be possible? What exactly was this invisible and subtle energy that had a causal effect on my own biology?

The miraculous nature of the experience was an impetus for me to start a deeper scientific inquiry to understand it. Through a recommendation from the Psychology Department at the University of Arizona I reached out to Dr. Gary Schwartz and Dr. Melinda Connor who helped me investigate some of the aforementioned questions and broach exploration of the ontological underpinnings of vitalism and pranic energy within the context of psychology, biology and medicine. With Gary and Melinda's much needed support I explored research on "energy healing" and its scientific basis. Through my deeper inquiry I learned about the hundreds of scientific studies that had already been conducted examining 'healing energy' and its application with results that posited a bio-physical effect beyond the explanation of placebo. Many of these studies have a wide range of effects including notably increases in intracellular free calcium concentration, osteoblast & bone cell proliferation, inhibition of liver carcinoma cells, reduced expression of mRNA for tumor simulator genes, enhanced neutrophil function, and other changes (Kiang et al., 2005; Lee et al., 2005; Schussel & Spencer, 2021; Ohnishi et al., 2007).

With a more comprehensive understanding of the power of healing I started to learn how to heal other people and realized I could heal minor ailments such as severe migraines and stomach problems. The experience of projecting healing energy had also given me a sense of euphoria and led me to the exploration of other contemplative and spiritual practices as well as sparking a deeper investigation the power of psi phenomenology, namely the ability of the mind to see beyond the physical reality.

Although I had not directly observed an aura I had sensed the energy "shell" of those I had been working with. For example, when I had applied the healing practice to a friend my hand was pulsating with a stinging sensation when it was placed near their left jaw. After pointing out my observation, they revealed they had severe jaw issues since childhood. I knew such subtle energy existed, although I could not presently see it.

It was late in the night and I was at my computer in Tucson. On this particular evening I was investigating the anomalous nature of kundalini awakening experiences. While many of the experiences were emotionally positive and self-transcendent there were many negative experiences as well. These experiences were quite frightening with individuals being hospitalized for schizophrenia (a common report was people speaking to spirits) and others with severe spinal-cerebral problems.

While reading about these kundalini awakening experiences I started to feel a burning sensation in my spine. Within seconds I experienced a vision of being immersed in flames. My body was surrounded 2 ft on all sides by an intense red-orange flame. I stood up with an agonizing fear and walked to the bathroom to look into the mirror to see the completely abnormal perception. I looked at my hand and it was radiating in a deep red-orange auric fire. The experience was about 45 seconds but had a lasting impact. Later I learned from a deeper understanding of Vedic philosophy the experience was defined in sutra 41 in Vibhuti Pada of the *Yoga sutras of Patanjali* as "samana-jayaj-jvalanam"; "One shines like fire" or "by mastery over pranic energy one experience effulgence or blazing" (Ohnishi et al., 2005).

The continued experiences became the fabric of my life and led me to graduate studies at Columbia University working with my mentor Dr. Lisa Miller, the revolutionary clinical psychologist. I had been inspired by her to integrate the 'energy healing' work into the field of clinical psychology and to continue a deeper investigation of spirituality, consciousness and its application with clinical populations. In the first year of my doctorate working with Lisa Miller we created a program for homeless youth that integrated my understanding of healing and the transpersonal.

The work was featured in the New York Times and was very powerful due to a series of salient individual transformations that individuals had experienced. At around the same time of this deep clinical work I had helped Dr. Miller organize the first conference for Post-Materialist science based on her production of *The Oxford Handbook for Psychology and Spirituality* which I had the helped her with editing. The initial conference held in 2011 had a round table of senior scientists in areas of healing, spirituality, engineering, physics, and medicine with notable scientists such as Robert Jahn, Brenda Dunne, Larry Dossey, Amit Goswami, Wayne Jonas, and Gary Schwartz. After completing my doctorate and given the position of Core Faculty and Adjunct Assistant Professor at Columbia University, I mentored and led doctoral and master's students with an interest in postmaterialist science, and most recently I presented at the Galileo Summit II my chapter from *'Expanding Science'* (the second volume of the Academy for the Advancement of Postmaterialist Sciences) (Schussel & Spencer, 2021). The premise of the chapter and lecture was the power of dreams and visions in the expansion of scientific inquiry and how these experiences are transmitted through an 'entangled' global field via the Schumann resonance. The resonance is a standing wave of electricity that exists between the earth's crust and the ionosphere and is what I believed I tuned into during my own healing experiences.

As I continue along my life journey and connect to a global field, hopefully more experiences will come to inspire a deeper understanding of my mystical nature and shed further light on the fabric of reality.

References

Kiang, J. G., Ives, J. A., & Jonas, W. B. (2005). External bioenergy-induced increases in intracellular free calcium concentrations are mediated by Na+/Ca2+ exchanger and L-type calcium channel. *Molecular and cellular biochemistry*, 271(1-2), 51-59.

Lee, M. S., Kim, M. K., & Ryu, H. (2005). Qi-training (qigong) enhanced immune functions: what is the underlying mechanism? *International journal of neuroscience*, 115(8), 1099-1104.

Prajnananda, P. (2011). *The Yoga Sutra of Patanjali*. Pranja Publication.

Ohnishi, S. T., Ohnishi, T., Nishino, K., Tsurusaki, Y., & Yamaguchi, M. (2005). Growth inhibition of cultured human liver carcinoma cells by Ki-energy (life-energy): scientific evidence for Ki-effects on cancer cells. *Evidence-Based Complementary and Alternative Medicine*, 2(3), 387-393.

Schussel, L. Spencer, J. (2021). Cosmic connections: Towards a post materialist science of self. In G. Schwartz, M. Beauregard, N. Dyer, & M. Woollacott (Eds.), *Expanding science: Visions of a post-materialist paradigm*. AAPS Press.

Ohnishi, S. T., Nishino, K., Uchiyama, S., Ohnishi, T., & Yamaguchi, M. (2007). Ki-energy (life-energy) stimulates osteoblastic cells and inhibits the formation of osteoclast-like cells in bone cell culture models. *Evidence-Based Complementary and Alternative Medicine*, 4(2), 225-232.

Chapter Fifty-Five

My Awakening

Stephan A. Schwartz

*Stephan A. Schwartz is a Distinguished Consulting Faculty of Saybrook University, a BIAL Foundation Fellow, columnist for the journal **Explore,** and editor of the daily web publication Schwartzreport.net. He is one of the founders of **Remote Viewing research**, and the author of nearly two hundred papers in peer-reviewed journals covering a spectrum of disciplines, two dozen book chapters, and an award-winning author of four non-fiction books, and three novels. He is the recipient of the Parapsychological Association Outstanding Contribution Award, OOOM Magazine (Germany) 100 Most Inspiring People in the World award, and the 2018 Albert Nelson Marquis Award for Outstanding Contributions. He is listed in: Who's Who in the World, Who's Who in America, Who's Who in the West, Who's Who in Healthcare and Medicine.*

In 1965 I went to a party on Fire Island given by Truman Capote. I was reasonably successful as a script writer, with the accouterments that came with that. I had a Mercedes, lived on the Eastside of New York, and dated some lovely women. I left the party to go down the hall to the bathroom, and on the way back I stopped next to an antique Italian mirror and looked down the hall. Framed in the doorway I saw the room filled with notable people. I looked into the mirror and spontaneously, with no plan or thought to say it, and said, "You are becoming a very unattractive person. Your values are all screwed up."

I left the party, sat up all night on the beach, took the ferry back, got in my car, and drove to my family's Tidewater Virginia farm. It is the only time in my life I have ever really been depressed. I just didn't know what to do. Yet I knew I was doing something wrong; I just couldn't figure out what it was. I had been at the farm for several weeks, when one afternoon I was sitting on the porch of the house that looked out over the bay. I looked up and there was a couple walking down a crepe myrtle alley. My family's property was at the end of a 7-mile school bus road, only partially paved at the time, and our lane was a nearly a mile long, so it was not a place you got to casually. I certainly didn't expect to see middle-aged strangers walking in the gardens, particularly strangers dressed as if they were on Fifth Avenue in Manhattan. The man wore a double-breasted grey suit and the woman was in a very smart linen dress.

When they saw me looking at them, they came over, walked up the steps to the porch, and I opened the screen door. The woman stepped in, but instead of introducing herself, she asked, "Do you believe in reincarnation?" It was so unexpected, I just responded, "I've never thought about it. I really don't know very much about it, but I think I probably do. It seems very symmetrical." I looked over to where cars parked, and there was no car. I asked, "How did you get here? Why are you here?" And she said, "I had a dream that told me to come up and invite you to the Edgar Cayce Foundation. Do you know who Edgar Cayce is?" When I said I didn't, she asked if I knew what clairvoyance was. I told her, 'No.' She said Cayce was a psychic who went into a trance and could get information on anything. I had never heard of such a thing. The whole conversation struck me as deeply weird; I still didn't know their names. I introduced myself, and they introduced themselves as Ed and Paula Fitzgerald. I asked them to sit down and if they wanted some lemonade. When we were seated, I asked her again how they had gotten here.

"In the dream," she answered quite seriously, "I could see where to turn to get here and I wrote it down when I woke up and we drove it. I came here to ask you, Would you like to meet Thomas Jefferson?' I had gone to the University of Virginia, founded by Mr. Jefferson, as he was called. I could not think how she could know this. There were no computers, no internet in those days, and that question left me dumbfounded. All I could think to say, "Is he back?" She said, "Yes,' and explained Cayce affirmed reincarnation was real, and that he had given a reading for a boy saying he had been Thomas Jefferson. The whole experience was surreal, so out of the norm of my life. But there was something familiar about her husband. I remembered he had been pointed out to me at a movie festival when I was in New York. I asked him if he was the Ed Fitzgerald who had been the production designer on Magnificent Seven, a very popular high budget movie starring Yul Brenner. He said yes, and it gave them a kind of gravitas. I thought, they can't be as crazy as they sound.

As she was telling me this, a car came down the lane with a young couple. The Fitzgeralds got up. She asked me for my telephone number, which I gave her. I stared at the car as it went back down the lane and thought, "What just happened?" What I did not realize was that I was on a new course.

About a week later I got a call, and a male voice said, "This is Thomas Jefferson Davis, and I'd like to invite you down for a weekend in Virginia Beach." I was tired of being depressed and was up for anything, so I answered, "Yes," and he gave me an address where I was met by a woman about my age who directed me to A.R.E. headquarters, what had once been the Cayce Hospital. As we walked into the library, I saw that shelves along one of the walls were filled with green three ring loose-leaf notebooks. I asked what they were, and she told me they were the transcriptions of what Cayce called readings which, today, I would call remote viewing or nonlocal perception sessions. As I walked down the wall at random, I pulled one of the notebooks off the shelf.

It was a reading given in 1936 for a woman; her name had been deleted and replaced with a number to preserve her anonymity. Cayce told her that in a previous incarnation she had been a member of the Essene community. From his description I recognized the location as Khirbet Qumran, and he told her she had been a teacher of astrology. You know when they say your hair stands on end? It was so weird. The last thing that I had done when I had worked for National Geographic, before being drafted into the Army, was research for an article on the Dead Sea Scrolls. I knew that in 1936 nobody knew they existed and nobody knew that Khirbet Qumran was an Essene community. 1936 was 11 years before the scrolls were discovered in 1947. A young Bedouin shepherd boy following his flock walked by a cave and chucked a rock in. He heard it go clunk, went into the cave to see why, and found the urns containing the scrolls. As I read the mimeographed pages in the notebook, I knew that everything Cayce said was correct but unknown at the time he said it. My question was: how could Cayce possibly have known things 11 years before the scrolls were found, the site excavated, before archaeology discovered there was an Essene community at Khirbet Qumran? And in that moment, I woke up and changed the course of my life. I was 24 years old, and in that moment the study of consciousness became the sovereign interest of my life.

I turned down a lucrative script writing contract moved to Virginia Beach, and with the help of Gladys Davis Turner, Edgar Cayce's lifelong secretary and archivist, began what became a five-year program to read, in chronological order, the 14,306 Cayce readings and associated documentation that ARE had in its archives. Two years into this process I decided I needed to know what science had so say about phenomena like Cayce's readings, and systematically began to read every parapsychology journal starting with the first issue of the *Journal of Parapsychology,* as well as the works of Gurdjieff, Ouspensky, Blavatsky, Jung, Bailey, Steiner and other leaders in the late 19th early 20th century consciousness movement.

In 1968, I decided that I would spend the rest of my life as an experimentalist doing research on consciousness and that is what I have done even when I held positions such as Special Assistant to the Chief of Naval Operations. I accepted this appointment because in 1970, I realized that if all consciousness was interconnected and interdependent, as I had become convinced it was, I needed to expand my consciousness research from the individual experience to include the social effects, and that if, as Max Planck said in 1931, "Consciousness is causal and fundamental," understanding both the individual experience and the reality of culture were two facets of a unity. And that has been my life's work ever since.

Chapter Fifty-Six

Spiritual Activism Informed by Psychic Experience

Natalie Tobert, PhD

Medical Anthropologist Dr. Natalie Tobert is an itinerant scholar who teaches in medical schools, hospitals, and universities. Her course modules support integrated health and explore multiple narratives and plural ways of understanding consciousness. As Education Director of Aethos Training, Natalie designed 8 - 10 weekly courses covering "Cultural Diversity, Mental Wellbeing, and Spirituality". She developed a Training Manual on Cultural Equalities for Frontline Health Service Providers, and has facilitated workshop seminars in UK, Ireland, Poland, Spain, Sweden, Switzerland and USA (CIIS - California Institute of Integral Studies). Dr Tobert conducted three ethnographic fieldwork projects: one in Sudan for her doctorate, and two in India. She also undertook research on the relationship between mystical, spiritual, and religious experiences and mental health (Alister Hardy Archive).

Spiritual awakening?

Throughout my young life, I'd heard about Nazis and concentration camps but I never read, listened to or watched anything. My mother always said: "there is no such thing as god, as he wouldn't have allowed Nazis". Both my parents were Jewish (my great grandparents were from Poland / Russia). We were brought up English, and I've never been touched by faith.

I recently returned from a trip to Poland, where I facilitated a retreat on ancestral memories: participants explored the effects of unspoken histories around memories, and beliefs on death, dying and beyond. We discussed cultural knowledge around survival beyond death and its influence on spirituality, mental health, and extreme inner experiences.

May I explain why this journey to Poland was so important to me and of what relevance it was to mental health and expanded consciousness in general?

When I was in my 20's, I myself appeared to tune into someone's life who was held in a concentration camp in Dachau Bavaria, during the Nazi Holocaust. I had spontaneous visions of life and death there, being experimented on, tortured, and raped, in 'hospital'. Different visions would arrive spontaneously, when I was sitting on a bus or train, but I knew where they fitted into the whole scenario, of that person then, before they were murdered in a gas chamber, before Natalie was born. I know who I am, and I can witness the identity of that person then. I am not aware of any ancestral relatives in the Nazi holocaust. Was I having a spiritual awakening, or did I have an ability to access normal clairvoyant faculties available to humans?

In the 1980's I worked as a museum curator responsible for Indigenous American Collections (North and South). During those years, I undertook shamanic practice workshops with Leo Rutherford and Howard Charing. I learnt shamanic journeying techniques. Later I discovered I was able to shift dimensions of consciousness at will, shifting between mundane and spiritual reality, by intention alone: no ritual, no drumming, no performance, and not consuming any substances.

Transformation of World View. I attended a university conference in 1998, where I chaired sessions and presented a paper. There I listened to one speaker on the platform of a huge hall, who presented on ayahuasca, which I have never taken. While he was speaking, I saw the tall plant deva of an ayahuasca vine (banisteriopsis): she was standing beside me, looking down, smiling. Half an hour later I realised my consciousness was expanding, and I had expanded hearing. I had undertaken shamanic practice for many years and knew what was happening. And so I took myself back to my university residence room, and lay under the duvet for hours, watching screen-loads of artefacts and rituals from all over the world. This was the first and only time in my life I acknowledged to myself that I was having hallucinations. I could witness what was happening, but couldn't stop it. I knew I had to stay under the duvet.

Once the visions stopped, three or four hours later, I got up. I left my university accommodation, chatted to one conference participant, who suggested I tell the speaker, who didn't believe anyone could have visions, without ingesting substances. It felt like I'd been gifted the visions without any side effects of consumption.

During these visions, the plant deva told me I was forbidden to engage in any kind of psychic or shamanic activity again. I obeyed: I stopped attending workshops, held the intention to ban visions, and today I can only see mundane reality. I was ordered to register for a degree in Medical Anthropology, to give me the language to question psychiatry, and to support people who found themselves diagnosed and labeled within the mental health system.

Changes in Career. I already had a doctorate in ethno-archaeology, based on observational fieldwork research in Sudan, and was accepted at a university to study Medical Anthropology. The weeks were strange: some days I was a university lecturer, teaching course modules on anthropology and spirituality. On other days, I was a student, learning about medical anthropology and multiple narratives around health.

As Education Director of Aethos Training and Consultancy, I developed a ten-week course module on medical anthropology, which I have been teaching since 2007, and still teach in medical schools to this day (Tobert, 2016). The aim of the course is to raise awareness with medical students that there are multiple ways of understanding health, particularly mental health. I produced a Training Resource Pack (unpublished) to support others who wanted to teach this, which was funded by the Scientific and Medical Network.

Former Career. Years ago, when I studied at the School of Oriental and African Studies, a colleague told me: "as a scholar, you have to publish or die". I followed her advice, and my good publication record meant I could slip easily into freelance contract jobs at universities, as a researcher or lecturer. I was not based at any particular university; rather I was a freelance consultant, wherever work was offered. I was an itinerant scholar.

When I undertook fieldwork in Sudan for my doctorate, I only knew about mundane things, which I and others could observe. However, I was aware of altered states of consciousness by the time I did fieldwork in India. In addition, psychiatrists I met there at Sri Aurobindo's Ashram were knowledgeable about aspects of consciousness, which were invisible to others (Basu & Miovic 2022). In India I explored the way psychiatrists worked, and how their practices might be transferable to western populations. This research is published in the book "*Spiritual Psychiatries*" (Tobert, 2014).

What Now? When I set the intention to ban visions, they stopped in 2002. However, I retain a sense of knowing, and personal sovereignty to this day, so that on rare occasions I can feel spirits of the dead, if I choose, and invite them to leave. But I practice mundane spiritual activism: I hold a skill as a trainer of medical students and health care staff, knowing which of the many cultural versions of reality to present, to whom, at which time, and which aspects of consciousness to remain silent about.

I assumed then, as I assume now, that the beings and entities I saw earlier were veridical. This meant a radical rethink had to happen around the way societies treated human experiences labeled as 'mental illness.'

What Next? I am aware of plural cultural versions of reality, and how people are treated within the mental health system, if they cannot manage their experiences, and the people around them (lay and professional) cannot manage (Tobert, 2018). Today I am in dialogue with colleague Joe Bartholomew discussing the establishment of a global indigenous and transpersonal therapies alliance (ITTA), to address issues regarding multiple narratives for spirituality and mental health. We believe that spirituality must consider going beyond individual experience, exploring broader perspectives for the community and the land, and include not just western societies, but other global societies.

References

Tobert, N. (2018). Cultural U-turns in mental well-being: Acknowledging the dilemma. *Journal of Humanistic Psychology, Special Edition on "Humanistic Perspectives on Understanding and Responding to Extreme States"* M. Cornwall, (Ed.). Sage Publishers:
http://journals.sagepub.com/eprint/pMSttwczHB8jdEqvgBjD/full

Tobert, N. (2016). *Cultural perspectives on mental wellbeing: Spiritual interpretations of symptoms in medical practice.* Jessica Kingsley Publishers.

Tobert, N. (2014). *Spiritual psychiatries: mental health practices in India and UK.* CreateSpace.

Tobert, N. (completed 2013 - Unpublished), *Cultural equalities: Training resource pack for front line service providers (medical, health and social care). A vision for social inclusion.*

Basu, S. & Miovic, M. (2021 - 2022). *Consciousness-based psychology: Integral yoga and transpersonal growth in Sri Aurobindo's worldview.* Springer Publishers.

Chapter Fifty-Seven

Walking in Two Worlds

Isabelle Goulet, PhD

*Dr. Isabelle Goulet is both a cellular and molecular biologist specializing in epigenetics and a healing facilitator trained in shamanic practices. In 2014, she founded **Scientive** to bridge two worlds: the physical and the non-physical, science and spirituality. She is presently working on her first book, in which she speaks openly about her personal healing and mystical experiences and explores a possible model of the nature of consciousness and the powerful interactions between body, mind, heart, and soul. Through the publication of this model, she wishes to help scientists define better rounded questions to explore and propose new approaches to include the influence of non-physical forces in the study of our human nature and its biology.*

"What are you doing here? What were you thinking?" were the first thoughts that crossed my mind as I sat down with a bunch of eccentric-looking people to receive my first teachings on the way of life and shamanic practices from the Algonquin medicine man Pete Bernard *(The 8ᵗʰ Fire,* 2021).

It is true that I wanted to learn how to work with systems in the way Indigenous people of Turtle Island—and Indigenous populations all around the world—so intuitively do, but was this rite of passage really necessary? Yes, I wanted to gain a different perspective on our body's healing processes, but perhaps I had gone too far out to get it?

I reluctantly decided to stick with it—for that moment anyway—and see where it would lead me. This single decision turned out to be the best I have ever made.

At the end of two days of teachings and healing practice, I had to sit down for a minute because of what felt like hundreds of spiraling fireworks going off in my spine. In that moment, I finally let go of any resistance to the peers and their explorations I had previously considered eccentric. I was in awe. How could I feel something so unusual in my body without anyone else having actually touched it?

As I sat, curiosity overtook any fear I might have had of stepping outside of my comfort zone. A whole new world had just opened for me, and I couldn't wait to find out what it could teach me about human biology. It was in that moment that I vowed to dedicate my scientific career to the study of non-conventional healing practices—even if this meant straying away from academia and mainstream science.

Of course, I had always had a strong feeling that something was missing. This feeling persisted well into my graduate studies. At the time, I was studying epigenetic factors influencing the onset and progression of breast cancer. As I spent countless hours observing cells under the microscope, tracking the behavior of only a few cellular proteins at a time, I came to compare my work to trying to look at the entire universe through a telescope. From this single point of view, there is a lot of information missing. Yes, my focus was on those specific proteins, but weren't they part of a larger system: the cell? What about everything else that was happening at that moment in the cell? Wasn't the *whole* intracellular context having an effect on the behavior of those proteins? Were we looking at the appropriate organizational level to find a cure for cancer?

It is at the time that I was asking myself these questions and considering a career shift to systems biology that my training and ritual work with Pete Bernard and both North and South American Indigenous Elders began. That was ten years ago. I reached the point of no return not long after that, when events that modern medicine would categorize as "miracles" became the norm.

Through this work, I came back to consciousness. I learned that thoughts, emotions, and beliefs are as critical aspects of our health as physical ones. I got a glimpse of how our past informs our present and future, how this information is stored in our body, and how it is passed down from generation to generation, from a previous version of ourselves to the next. I learned how to bend time, to alter reality, and to change matter. In the realm of non-conventional healing practices, this is nothing extraordinary: these abilities exist in everyone's potential. Through my exploration of this new world, I found the missing piece in 95% of the light we cannot see: the non-physical aspects of our reality.

This 180-degree turn has had I profound impact on my life, both personally and professionally. It has provided me with both a new 'inlook' and a new outlook on myself and others, our consciousness, and our body's inner workings. It has given me the opportunity to approach cancer—amongst other things—from a point of view inaccessible to most cellular and molecular biologists. For example, finding a cure for cancer might not be so much dependent on the systems level after all, but rather on the information exchanged between systems (Goulet, 2020).

From my experience, I believe scientists should not be afraid to study the non-physical aspects of our human nature on the premise that such aspects are not consistent with their conception of the world (Sciences). As His Holiness the 14th Dalai Lama so eloquently puts it: "[o]ur ability to perceive physical matter cannot provide the sole basis for our knowledge of the world" (Bstan-Ṭdzin-rgya-mtsho & Vreeland, 2002). The true spirit of scientific inquiry allows us to freely explore any hypothesis, theory, or model, whether it is favored by current thinking or not (Sciences). The ability *to walk in two worlds* is a great advantage since, as Daniel J. Benor pointed out in his book *Spiritual Healing*, "very few healers are trained in scientific observation or in research" (Benor, 2001), and thus only a few can describe biological or other phenomena from such radically different points of view. Who knows what we could discover if we would only dare to venture into new territories?

References

The 8th fire. The 8th Fire - Pete Bernard. (2021, October 2). Retrieved January 30, 2022, from https://the8thfire.com/

Benor, D. J. (2001). *Spiritual Healing: Scientific Validation of a Healing Revolution.* Vision Publications.

Bstan-Ṭdzin-rgya-mtsho, & Vreeland, N. (2002). *An open heart: Practising compassion in everyday life.* Back Bay Books.

Goulet, I. (2020). In *Expanding Science.* Academy for the Advancement of Postmaterialist Sciences.

Sciences, O. (n.d.). *Home.* The Manifesto for a Post-Materialist Science - OpenSciences.org. Retrieved January 30, 2022, from https://opensciences.org/about/manifesto-for-a-post-materialist-science.

EPILOGUE

The essays in this volume are a wonderful and varied collection of personal insights into individual STEs and their resulting transformation of individual lives. In many respects these essays are like having an array of the most delicious chocolates on a platter and having the opportunity to sample and savor each one. As readers, we have the opportunity to explore and study these essays carefully so that we might absorb their insights, create our own understandings, and possibly implement these understandings in our own lives. In this epilogue, we have aimed to do this, and hope that you will add for yourself further moments of recognition of deep truths in your own life.

One first observation is that, although we divided the events triggering the awakenings or spiritually transformative experiences into six groups, this set of groupings somewhat conceals the many beautiful and subtle variations on the awakening theme. For some individuals there were multiple subtle experiences, one cascading on top of another, and it was hard for them to distinguish the relative importance of each in the awakening process and the subsequent transformation of their world view and their lives. The first may have been the experience of a paranormal event, such as a sense of the presence of a deceased friend, and this may have opened a door to their exploration of practices like meditation, which further shifted their world view and accelerated the ongoing transformation in their life. For others, the awakening was like a volcano erupting, sometimes with murmurs or tremors in advance, but with the energetic fireworks that immediately transformed their worldview and their entire life course.

Though we have grouped these essays according to their triggering events, the nuances within each STE described are as varied as the personalities and backgrounds of the authors who experienced them. Yet, despite their variability, each of these transformative experiences leads the individual inexorably toward the awareness of their own connection with a vaster consciousness. Each STE softens and expands the world view (including the egoic narrative used to interpret the boundaries of experience), and as the underlying worldview transforms there is an increased receptivity to a variety of other STEs.

In this epilogue we discuss some of our insights, and at the same time encourage you, the reader, to explore your own insights gained through reading the essays.

Events Prior to the Awakening

It is fascinating to see that many contributors noted that prior to their STE they experienced a period of mental turmoil that seemed to motivate a search for something more meaningful in their lives (Taylor, 2021). This period of turmoil was followed by their awakening or STE, as either a spontaneous event or one that sometimes occurred as part of a deep commitment to spiritual practices. One person noted that he had reached a crisis in his life and decided to take a half-year retreat from the work he had been doing and devote himself wholeheartedly to self-directed study and meditation. It was after this intensive meditation practice that his awakening occurred. He says, "In an instant of grace, the years of accumulated questions and yearnings opened into a joyful, sacred and crystalline space of Knowing."

Another explained, "I started to follow a typical musician's hedonistic lifestyle, smoking and drinking too much, surrounded by other people who did the same. As a result, I lost myself a little. After struggling for so long to connect with the core of my own being, I became disconnected from it again." And then, one night in Germany, the awakening came, and it was the most powerful experience of his life. He says, "I woke up in the middle of the night, for no apparent reason, filled with a marvelous warm sense of well-being. The darkness seemed alive, pervaded with a powerful harmonious force.... It was the essence and the source of all things."

And a third said, "The sense I had of being locked in a hard shell of ego and separation intensified. The simplicity of the environment made all my defenses stand out. I felt a stranger there. More fundamentally, I felt a stranger in life, in the fragile and splendid exuberance of everything.... Then suddenly a radical change happened. One morning...I woke up in a space of pure light. It was as if a veil had fallen from my eyes. The fight with my ego of the previous days had become utterly irrelevant. I was no longer there. All around me glistened as if just created. ...I felt innocent like a newborn. I was not there and yet I was more present than ever."

These experiences suggest that the turmoil and chaos experienced prior to the STE may have created a crack in the individual's current world view, opening them to the experience of the STE. The concept that turmoil can dissolve existing boundaries in an individual's world view, allowing the light of spiritual insight in, is supported by the research of Steve Taylor (one of our contributors). He reports that among his research participants one precursor to awakening was a state of psychological turmoil, including despair and depression. He proposes that periods of intense turmoil may trigger awakenings because the turmoil leads to a dissolving of psychological attachments, including one's self-image and their ideas concerning life and the world. As these contribute to the egoic sense of self, when this narrative begins to dissolve, it is as if the house of cards of their egoic narrative begins to collapse; it allows an opening from their deeper consciousness or a broader nonlocal awareness to come through that shifts them into an expansive state of consciousness (Taylor, 2012; 2021).

As the essays in this volume suggest, the process of awakening is associated with other factors as well, a key factor being a quiescence of the mind, which seem to occur almost simultaneously to the STE itself.

Stilling the Mind – Part of the Awakening Process

One of the themes apparent across the categories of transformative experiences was the pre-requisite or accompaniment of a stilling of the narrative of the mind, consisting of the stories we create about ourselves and how we relate to the world. This stilling of the mind's narrative occurred immediately prior to or during the STE itself. For example, when examining essays in which a spiritual practice triggered the experience, one person shared, "Then, in a sudden and unexpected rush, the seeking of the past six months and the concentration of the past three days finally burned a hole through the 'ego-I.'"

Similarly, the STEs that occurred during the night or upon awakening in the morning were often accompanied for some time by a dissolution of this narrative: One person said, "I was not there and yet I was more present than ever."

This formulation recalls that of the 19th century Victorian poet, Alfred Lord Tennyson:

A kind of walking trance I have frequently had, quite up from boyhood, when I have been all alone. This has often come upon me through repeating my own name to myself silently till, all at once, as it were, out of the intensity of the consciousness of individuality, the individuality itself seemed to dissolve and fade away into boundless being; and this not a confused state, but the clearest of the clearest, the surest of the surest, the weirdest of the weirdest, utterly beyond words, where death was an almost laughable impossibility, the loss of personality (if so it were) seeming no extinction, but the only true life...

Yes, it is true there are moments when the flesh is nothing to me, when I feel and know the flesh to be the vision, God and the spiritual – the only real and true. Depend upon it, the spiritual is the real; it belongs to one more than the hand and the foot. You may tell me that my hand and my foot are only imaginary symbols of my existence. I could believe you, but you never, never can convince me that the I is not an eternal reality, and that the spiritual is not the true and real part of me. (Bucke, 1905)

Tennyson said of his mystical experience (in a letter to the prominent 19th century physicist Professor John Tyndall), "By God Almighty! there is no delusion in the matter! It is no nebulous ecstasy, but a state of transcendent wonder, associated with absolute clearness of mind." (Bucke, 1905)

After recovering from the life-threatening circumstances associate with his NDE another person noted the contrast between "...the flood of consciousness across time and space and beyond apparent selfhood that I witnessed while I was perceived by family and caregivers as being in deep coma." And during her experience with psychedelics, one woman expressed the absence of a verbal narrative in this way, "I had a full ego death, merging and existing as nonconceptual awareness, with no subjective sense of self, no life story, nothing but consciousness. It was eternity and there was no 'I' to reference."

A possible interpretation of these experiences is that the STE resulted in a suspension of the individual's current narrative or world view, allowing its reified nature to become less fixed, more fluid and permeable – thus open to change. It allowed the mind – especially the brain's left hemisphere - to relax its grip on the narrative framework enabling a view of the world through a different lens.

As was discussed in the preface to this volume, the importance of stilling the egoic narrative during the awakening process is supported by neuroscientific research examining the neural correlates of STEs. Research on experiences of individuals in both deep states of meditation and during psilocybin experiences have confirmed that the activity in key parts of the Default Mode Network (DMN) of the brain (medial prefrontal cortex and posterior cingulate cortex), associated with our narrative thinking, is significantly reduced (Barrett & Griffiths, 2018; Brewer et al., 2011). Additionally, research on brain states associated with NDEs during cardiac arrest indicate that, in addition to silencing of the DMN, the entire cerebral cortex is inactive. These studies thus suggest that the self-referential activity that is the core function of the DMN and which sustains the experience of a separate sense of self is significantly reduced during deep meditation, NDEs and the ingestion of psychedelics.

This research supports the first-person accounts presented in these essays, which describe stilling of the mind (the egoic narrative) as an essential aspect of the STE. Perhaps stilling the mind makes the boundaries of the individual's world view more dynamic, less fixed, thus creating an environment receptive and open to anomalous experiences.

Subtleties in the Types of Awakenings/STEs

As we examined the different STEs in this volume, we noted that a substantial number of authors reported an energetic component as a distinct aspect of the STE. For example, one person said, "Actually, I thought I was being electrocuted or having some kind of heart attack. It was that physical.... Then the Conscious Energy imploded into my heart region, and I experienced myself floating to the ceiling, as if drawn 'up' by some kind of invisible metaphysical magnet." Another described this energetic component as feeling a "rush of energy-love emerge from my chest, the like of which I had never felt before and couldn't even imagine possible.... I perceived it as a broad beam of shimmering white light, alive and beatific, gushing from my heart with incredible strength." And yet another, "When I awoke, I felt waves of energy passing through me and experienced the same 'electrical' surges...."

The energetic aspect of spiritual awakenings has been recounted for millennia, and there is a rich literature describing it in India and other Asian cultures. In India the energy is known as the kundalini, in China it is called chi, in Japan it is termed ki), and by the !Kung African tribesmen, the energy is called !Kia. In the Hebrew tradition this vital energy is referred to as the shekinah, while in the Christian tradition it is referred to as the Holy Spirit (Sannella, 1987).

These terms refer to an aspect of the all-encompassing consciousness of the universe that is said to live within each human being, but in dormant form. In Indian philosophy this dormant energy is considered to be awakened through the descent of grace from ultimate consciousness itself. This energetic awakening is seen as one that individuals draw to themselves at the right moment in spiritual evolution. The energy, once awakened, drives spiritual evolution toward nondual awareness of the unity of all things.

There is much that is not known about the role of energy in spiritual awakenings. What is the essential nature of this energetic awakening and its transformative dynamics within an individual's spiritual evolution? Are all awakenings driven by this energy, but simply along a continuum of intensities from very gentle to dramatic? There are different viewpoints in the varying traditions. We will let you draw your own conclusions, based on these essays, your own experience, and historical knowledge of the perennial traditions.

Transformation: Inner and Outer Manifestations

One of the most significant parts of the awakening experience is the subsequent transformation in the individual's world view and how this internal shift manifests outwardly, in their life-work and their relationships with others. William James, the father of modern psychology describes it as a changed attitude toward life, which persists and becomes permanent. He delineates the effects of an awakening in this way: "A feeling of being in a wider life than that of this world's selfish little interests; and a conviction, not merely intellectual, but as it were sensible, of the existence of an Ideal Power." James also observed that these changes in the inner perception of life have practical consequences, including characteristics such as increased patience and fortitude, blissful equanimity, purity, and a sense of greater charity and tenderness toward the other creatures of the world." (Woollacott, 2015, p. 31)

Another scholar (Paloutzian, 2005, p. 334) suggests that "spiritual transformation constitutes a change in the meaning system that a person holds as a basis for self-definition, the interpretation of life, including the overarching purposes, ultimate concerns, values, meanings, and corresponding life directions of an individual." These essays represent many examples of the varied expression of these markers mentioned by James and Paloutzinan of "being in a wider life" and the catalyzing of an inner shift in the individuals' "meaning system" that is their basis for self-definition, as well as an outer shift, that is, the directions they are inspired to follow in their life. We will discuss specific aspects of these shifts below.

Inner Transformation: Shifting Worldviews. In reading the essays, it became clear that there were a number of different contributing factors to the extent and rapidity of the transformation process. The first was the strength of the person's prevailing world view, that is, how much it dominated their conceptual reality. For example, one professor noted that he had a seemingly profound experience early in his career when he woke up one morning at 3 am, thinking about astrophysics, and pondering the stars peeking through the night sky. Completely unexpectedly, his sense of self began gently dissolving into an experience of oneness with everything around him. He felt completely at peace and at home, and he reveled in the experience. But having no background in mysticism, and strongly trained in clinical psychology, he labeled the experience as anomalous, not to be pursued. Only many years later, as he began to explore scientific evidence for psi experiences did he understand that experience and awaken to an awareness of the existence of a greater reality.

Another scientist had an NDE experience when she had a high fever as a student, and lost awareness of her body. As part of the NDE she saw a silhouette of a being of light at the end of a tunnel. Suddenly she had the thought that she wasn't ready for whatever it was that might be about to happen and communicated to the being that she was not ready yet; and the experience ended. She says, "Being the only unusual framework I had to explain the experience, I did initially wonder whether it was some sort of alien encounter! But, not wanting anyone to think of me as crazy, I told no one about the experience, instead bottling it up inside for the next 10 years." Though she didn't understand the experience intellectually, nevertheless, something shifted in her unconscious, as she immediately left the university in order to travel, perhaps as a way to begin to go deeper into these insights and try to understand them.

In the metaphor introduced in the preface, we liken the STE to a seed planted into the soil of our consciousness, which then begins to germinate and grow over time. We might think of the soil as the worldview that we currently hold, forming the lens through which we view the world and interpret experiences. If our worldview dismisses an experience as spurious, trivial or even pathological, the seed of awakening will not germinate, take root, leaf out and blossom. In many of the essays the seed of transformation did not result in an immediate transformation. Rather, it brought the individuals over time to other experiences that eventually caused a shift in world view allowing the transformation process to emerge.

Two other aspects of transformation that grow out of a shift in an individual's world view are the subsequent changes in their actions, including their lifework itself, and also the way they approach every part of their life.

Outer Transformation: Shift in the Trajectory of One's Lifework or Career. Perhaps, not surprisingly, a number of scientists and academics (41%) actually changed their career trajectory after their STE. One scientist and academic noted in his essay, "The impact of that experience on my work and career was not immediate, but it was profound. It opened up a perception of our existence in this vast and mysterious universe that was far from being reducible to rational models. And it brought to my awareness a large gap between the profound mystery we scientists (and especially we astrophysicists!) were trying to capture in our equations and the daily reality of our academic life. The realization of the mystery was confined to the scribbles on our blackboards and completely forgotten in our daily life, where publishing, competition and career were much more relevant concerns. Puerto Angel was the turning point of the inner process that five years later would bring me to leave the academia."

To their colleagues this "abandonment" of academia often seemed incomprehensible, and even crazy. A woman biophysicist said, "When I resigned my position at the laboratory and said goodbye to my colleagues, they just shook their heads and never wanted to see me or talk to me again."

What precipitated this change in career for our essayists? Though there were different outer reasons given by various individuals, one might describe it as a deep sense that they now had a different calling that was more important to them than their previous position in what was often a materialist culture of academia or science. A scientist in astrophysics described it in this way, "But my heart was not in it anymore. I was dreaming a very different dream, a dream involving nature, community, self-sufficiency, inner exploration. Every morning I went to my office and fell asleep with my head on my desk. It was time to give up habit and security and follow the call of my heart."

Though a portion of these academics and scientists shifted their life's work as a result of their awakening, others found that, though the transformations in their world view were radical, they were comfortable shifting their approach to their career, rather than completely altering their life's work. A researcher and clinician said this about her shift in her approach to life after her awakening, "What has changed is the priority I give to my spiritual practice day to day and a better understanding of the underlying intent of that practice. I believe the intent underlying my spiritual practice is to help me remember the truth of who we are and endeavoring to manifest that truth in each moment." A professor in the humanities felt that he didn't need to shift his career after that awakening when he was a graduate student, because his awakening inspired the rest of his career life. He said, "Honestly, if you asked me today what that Night was about, I would say that I think it was all my future books flowing into me, at once, at that moment. I could not understand them, of course, because I had no context for them, but they were all 'there,' all at once, in that Night."

As an accompaniment to our invitation to write essays, we also asked individuals to respond to a short questionnaire about the shifts in their values after their spiritual awakening. In reading the essays and the responses to the questionnaires we have the impression that for many the transformed world view that came from the STE was like a shift in the understanding of the heart. Something was awakened within, and it was now leading the evolution of the spirit. One scientist described it as her heart now rushing forward after this new understanding, while the head, the intellect, was simply running behind, trying to catch up.

Here are some examples of this shift toward a "heart-centered" approach to their career. One person noted, "My teaching changed to incorporate the insights from my transcendent experience; and also all the reading and additional spiritual experiences I had that followed informed my teaching and research." Another noted that she added to her teaching a course for her pre-med students in complementary medicine. And a therapist and clinical psychologist said that this experience proved to him that "many of the strange experiences my patients report are accurate and meaningful." And a scientist said he was "trying to serve the expanding of science's scope and include self-reflection." In addition, an underlying theme for most contributors was that they became less obsessed with work. One said, "I realized that my work focus was a defense mechanism."

When asked about their shifts in their values and approaches to life, it became clear that the spiritual awakening had catalyzed substantial shifts in a sense of connection with others. Eighty-eight percent of our respondents said that they felt an increased desire to be of services to others and 78% had an increased feeling of unity with humanity. One man said that since his awakening, "It is like a veil has been lifted off and love is more deeply revealed. And within that, the notion of unconditional love has deepened and shifted – my understanding is much deeper."

Our respondents also noticed an increase in their creativity (78%) with one individual noting, "I feel like I have deeper access to profound creative potential and that it can manifest spontaneously. Often there are spontaneous eruptions of understandings, knowledge, creative poetic thinking, aesthetic experience; I am overwhelmed with it." Individuals also found that they were more able to cope with stress (84%), had a decrease in their fear of death (84%), and an increase in their belief in immortality (75%). One comment about the subtlety of this change was, "There was a marked awareness of that fear, before awakening. And now I have a very humble recognition of its ever-presence."

When asked about whether their interest in materialist goals had changed, 61% said there was a decrease, and one respondent expressed his thoughts in this way. "I see great value in material things, but not ultimate value; there is less attachment, but deeper appreciation. I can deeply enjoy that materiality in the way it has presented itself in the moment, and not get upset when it changes." He said that it was like becoming a connoisseur of reality.

Concluding Thoughts

Transformation associated with STEs, like the STEs themselves, were varied and nuanced. For the most part they were characterized by both an internal shift in worldview and an outer shift in their lived lives. The comments about transformation in values, beliefs, and approaches toward life described in these essays were very moving, and as we contemplate them, we suggest that the essayists had a deeper connection with their own inner wisdom, and with not only all humanity, but with the planet and the cosmos. It feels like they are speaking with great maturity, from the deep core of their being.

One essayist describes her experience of this higher way of knowing (gnosis, noesis) where we unitively become light and love and arrive at an enlarged context of reality in this way:

What I "saw" -- realized in an indescribable living way, is that the entire world, or rather Being is one, alive, vibrating self-knowing consciousness. That 'experience' was not an experience per se, but rather being beyond experiencing, a seeing that cannot be described in words, as it does not belong within the realm of the mind or knowing, since it is that prior to mind from which mind and understanding emerge and draw their essence. Now I understand why Ancient Greek philosophers had called it 'agnoston' (i.e., beyond intellectual knowledge) and 'allipton' (beyond concepts); hence 'arrheton' (beyond words, ineffable). What for so many years I was reading and - vainly - tried to grasp with the mind, was alive! It was here and now, beyond mind, grasping, understanding or words."

Thus, all STE's, regardless of how they were triggered, resulted in gnosis, a higher way of knowing characterized by a sense of intrinsic oneness and interconnectedness that is beyond intellectual knowledge, and ineffable. It is a seed planted in fertile soil that blossoms into a new world view and leads to a "heart-centered" approach to their life and career.

References

Barrett, F. S., & Griffiths, R. R. (2018). Classic hallucinogens and mystical experiences: Phenomenology and neural correlates. *Current Topics in Behavioral Neuroscience, 36*, 393–430.

Brewer, J. A., Worhunsky, P. D., Gray, J. R., Tang, Y. Y., Weber, J., & Kober, H. (2011). Meditation experience is associated with differences in default mode network activity and connectivity. *Proceedings of the National Academy of Sciences USA,* 108(50), 20254–20259.

Bucke, R. M. (1905). *Cosmic consciousness.* Innes & Sons.

Morales R. L. (Accessed 1 20, 2022) "*Tending the Soil – Lessons for Organizing*" https://www.rlmartstudio.com/wp-content/uploads/RLM-Tending-The-Soil-24pp-Printable.pdf

Paloutzian, R. F., & Park, C. L. (Eds.). (2005). *Handbook of the psychology of religion and spirituality.* The Guilford Press, p. 334.

Sannella, L. (1987). *The kundalini experience. Psychosis or transcendence?* Integral Publishing.

Taylor, S. (2012). Transformation through suffering: a study of individuals who have experienced positive psychological transformation following periods of intense turmoil. *Journal of Humanistic Psychology*, 52, 30-52.

Taylor, S. (2021). *Extraordinary awakenings: When trauma leads to transformation.* New World Library.

Woollacott, M. H. (2015) *Infinite awareness. The awakening of a scientific mind.* Roman & Littlefield, p. 31.

The Scientific and Medical Network
(Founded 1973)

https://www.scientificandmedical.net

Where evidence-based reason meets deep inner knowing

Our Vision

The SMN is working with full awareness and appreciation of scientific method, but exploring and expanding, in a spirit of open and critical enquiry, frontier issues at the interfaces between science, health, consciousness, wellbeing, love and spirituality, to explore how to rediscover a meaningful spirituality to help rebalance our lives.

The Network is part of a worldwide contemporary movement for education, personal development, and compatible "spiritual emergence", networking: scientists, doctors, psychologists, educators, engineers, philosophers, complementary practitioners and other professionals, for mutual and societal benefit.

Raison d'Être

For almost 50 years, the Scientific and Medical Network (SMN), has been a creative force for education, learning, and transformative change, supporting professionals to see that relying solely on scientific method (though excellent and indispensable in its province), cannot fully guide humanity. The results from these misunderstandings and misapplications, are now so startlingly being seen on our environment, health and well-being. This appreciation is not new.

SMN Approach

Heart Brain Coherence

We believe that a better, more intelligent and more heart-led world is possible – a world in which the wisdom of spirituality and the thoughtfulness of philosophy balance the power of science and technology.

Deep Listening, Dialogue and Mutual Trust

It is our view that no single idea or solution has a monopoly on truth. Our events and publications, therefore, create spaces for sharing different ideas and experiences with an ethos of deep listening, dialogue and mutual trust.

Integral Inquiry

We recognise that our world is still plagued by deep problems and enduring conflicts. Many of these are caused by dogmatic, superstitious or ill-informed worldviews. However, we believe that individuals and societies can transform themselves.

The key is learning to integrate evidence-based science, born of rational philosophy, with the love and inner peace cultivated by spiritual practice. The Scientific and Medical Network is a community of professionals dedicated to this task.

Co-creating New Paradigms

We invite you to join us in co-creating new paradigms to bring truth, beauty, health and well-being into harmony, and so help heal our fractured culture.

Galileo Commission

https://www.galileocommission.org

Expanding Science beyond a Materialistic Worldview

The world today is dominated by science and by its underlying assumptions, which are seldom explicitly articulated. The Galileo Commission's remit is to open public discourse and to find ways to expand science so that it can accommodate and explore important human experiences and questions that science, in its present form, is unable to integrate.

Following widespread consultation with 90 advisers representing 30 universities worldwide, we have published the Galileo Commission Report, written by Prof Dr Harald Walach and entitled *Beyond a Materialist Worldview – Towards an Expanded Science*. The report has been widely endorsed as a groundbreaking document and we encourage you to read it for yourself and spread the word among your professional network. Summaries of the argument are available in a number of languages.

A more recent initiative is *A Call for a Renaissance of the Spirit in the Humanities.* This document argues for a return to a spiritual image of the human being capable of direct unitive knowledge or *gnosis* so that we know ourselves more deeply and as essentially identical with the One Universal Mind.

We invite scientists and academics to join our community of over 350 professional affiliates and members of the general public to support us as friends.

Acknowledgments

The editors would like to express their deepest appreciation to our colleague and friend, Anne Shumway-Cook for her collaborative input in writing the ancillary material, including the preface and epilogue, for this volume. We also express our gratitude and appreciation to our AAPS Board member, Stephan Schwartz, as well as Deborah Erickson, for their help in the final preparation of this volume for publication. We had initially hoped to publish this volume with the ICRL Press through our friend Brenda Dunne and regret that this was not possible due to her having an unfortunate accident. Finally, we acknowledge the profound and moving contributions of the authors of the essays in this volume, as they open-heartedly shared their experiences of awakening and transformation with the world at large.

INDEX

Printed in Great Britain
by Amazon

46894791R00169